Ritual Making Women

Gender, Theology and Spirituality

Series Editors
Lisa Isherwood, University of Winchester
Marcella Althaus-Reid, University of Edinburgh

Gender, Theology and Spirituality explores the notion that theology and spirituality are gendered activities. It offers the opportunity for analysis of that situation as well as provides space for alternative readings. In addition it questions the notion of gender itself and in so doing pushes the theological boundaries to more materialist and radical readings. The series opens the theological and spiritual floodgates through an honest engagement with embodied knowing and critical praxis.

Gender, Theology and Spirituality brings together international scholars from a range of theological areas who offer cutting edge insights and open up exciting and challenging possibilities and futures in theology.

Published:

Resurrecting Erotic Transgression: Subjecting Ambiguity in Theology
Anita Monro

Patriarchs, Prophets and Other Villains
Edited by Lisa Isherwood

Women and Reiki: Energetic/Holistic Healing in Practice
Judith Macpherson

Unconventional Wisdom
June Boyce-Tillman

Numen, Old Men: Contemporary Masculine Spiritualities and the Problem of Patriarchy
Joseph Gelfer

Forthcoming in the series:

For What Sin was She Slain? A Muslim Feminist Theology
Zayn R. Kassam

Our Cultic Foremothers: Sacred Sexuality and Sexual Hospitality in the Biblical and Related Exegetic Texts
Thalia Gur Klein

Through Eros to Agape: The Radical Embodiment of Faith
Timothy R. Koch

Baby, You are My Religion: Theory, Praxis and Possible Theology of Mid-20th Century Urban Butch Femme Community
Marie Cartier

Radical Otherness: A Socio/theological Investigation
Dave Harris and Lisa Isherwood

Catholics, Conflicts and Choices
Angela Coco

Telling the Stories of Han: A Korean, Feminist Theology of Subjectivity
Jeong-Sook Kim

Ritual Making Women
Shaping Rites for Changing Lives

Jan Berry

LONDON   OAKVILLE

Published by Equinox Publishing Ltd.
Unit 6, The Village, 101 Amies St., London SW11 2JW, UK
DBBC, 28 Main Street, Oakville, CT 06779, USA

www.equinoxpub.com

First published 2009

British Library Cataloguing-in-Publication Data
A catalogue record for this book is available from the British Library.

ISBN   978 1 84553 414 1 (hardback)
          978 1 84553 415 8 (paperback)

Library of Congress Cataloging-in-Publication Data

Berry, Jan.
Ritual making women : shaping rites for changing lives / Jan Berry.
    p. cm. — (Gender, theology, and spirituality)
Includes bibliographical references (p.   ) and index.
ISBN 978-1-84553-414-1 (hb) — ISBN 978-1-84553-415-8 (pb) 1.
Liturgics. 2. Feminist theology. 3. Christian women — Religious life.
4. Life change events — Religious aspects — Christianity. 5. Ritual. 6.
Women — Religious life. 7. Life change events — Religious aspects. I.
Title. BV178.B48 2009
264.0082 — dc22

                              2008055837

Typeset by S.J.I. Services, New Delhi
Printed and bound in Great Britain by Lightning Source, Milton Keynes, UK

CONTENTS

Chapter One

EXPLORING THE POWER OF RITUAL

Starting-points for the Journey

A group of friends gather in a home. Together they celebrate and give thanks for the fifteen years a woman has spent in ministry, and acknowledge her pain and anger at the oppression and injustice she has found within the church. They place stones in a bowl to mark the church's condemnation of gay sexuality and the concealment to which it leads, and then pour water over them as a sign of forgiveness and cleansing. The woman extinguishes a candle as she renounces the formal recognition of her ministry; then a new candle is lit as, with the support of her friends, she commits herself to 'an exploration into woman-centred faith and spirituality'. The group shares a wilderness meal of bread and honey, and the ritual ends with an affirmation of justice and healing.

The ritual described above is one that took place when I resigned from the Baptist ministry; a published form of it can be found in *Human Rites* (Ward and Wild 1995: 179–82). It marked a turning-point in a long period of struggle as I sought to hold together being lesbian, feminist and Christian. I still felt myself called to ministry, and to continuing in my chaplaincy appointment, but felt my denomination's guidelines on sexuality were such that I could no longer minister within it with integrity. I had written a letter of resignation, but felt that the struggle and turmoil I had been through, and the sense of loyalty and affection I still felt for many within the church, needed something more significant than a mere reply from a committee!

With the help and support of a close friend, I planned the ritual and gathered together a group of friends who knew something of my journey, and the agonising of the decision-making process. Together we shared in the ritual, and the meal that followed. At the time it was an attempt to mark an important transition in my life; to resist the sense of vulnerability and oppression, and to claim my own freedom and choice in leaving. As I look back I see how it has also shaped my subsequent path in spirituality and ministry; although I did not realize it at the time, the origins of this book were there on that evening.

Since then I have shared with friends (mostly women, but sometimes men as well) in a variety of rituals — to mark the ending of a job, blessing a relationship, house-blessings, and the closure of a difficult and painful working situation. I have read or heard about rituals for celebrating same-sex relationships and healing from abuse. I have shared with circle-dancing friends in rituals that mark the seasonal cycles, often focusing on themes of loss, remembrance, desire, and re-creation.

Throughout this period I have been part of small groups of women meeting, sometimes for sharing and discussion, but often including the celebration of liturgy and ritual. We have marked the Christian festivals or seasons of the year, we have explored themes through sharing in symbols and symbolic action, we have celebrated or grieved transitions in our lives. Often I have not only participated, but written or created the material for such groups to use. These groups have been set in a broadly Christian context, but in the circle-dancing network I have shared in rituals that draw on pagan and Goddess elements to mark the Celtic festivals and transitions in our lives.

In pastoral ministry and in counselling, I have become increasingly aware of the importance of imagery, symbol, and symbolic action as people work through the impact of significant, life-changing events in their own experience.

Through this varied experience I have realized the vital part which ritual plays in helping us to handle transitions in our lives. Ritual provides a framework in which powerful emotions can be confronted and expressed. It allows participants to enter a space beyond words, where symbols, bodily movement and symbolic action are the vehicles of meaning. It provides a physical and time-limited space, made safe by a structure which provides shape and boundaries to experiences and feelings which can otherwise feel dangerously chaotic and overwhelming. Although some rituals are solitary, most are performed communally, either relating to a shared experience, or allowing an individual to express and negotiate her own experience in the company of others who support and care.

Most rituals are in the framework of some kind of religious or spiritual belief, and so provide a wider context of meaning for the individual's journey or narrative.

My own theological background is in the non-conformist tradition, which has tended to be suspicious of ritual, seeing it as mechanistic and 'empty', the polar opposite of sincerely-held beliefs and convictions. In my first pastorate, I was rebuked for lighting a candle during a church service because this was 'papist'. Ideas have changed dramatically, and an increased appreciation of the importance of the visual and symbolic aspects of worship is now much more common in Free Church and many other traditions, whilst liturgies from the Taizé and Iona Communities have made the use of symbols such as candles and stones a regular part of many people's prayer.

Feminist theology has added to my appreciation of the importance of symbolism. The emphasis on the sacredness of the body, sexuality, and our senses found in feminist theology (and even more strongly articulated in Goddess thealogy) has led to a more holistic approach to liturgy and worship, replacing the Christian dualism which opposed flesh and spirit, body and mind, with a sense of the holiness of all life and the embodied presence of God/dess in the earth.

However, it remains true that some rituals have become so familiar that they have lost much of their power to move or to convey authentic belief and conviction. Some are out-of-touch with every day experience, some reiterate dogma to which the participants can no longer subscribe, and some elements of contemporary experience are not touched by ritual at all. There is therefore a need for what Driver (1998) calls 'liberating rites' in two senses of the word. Our familiar rites and liturgies need liberating from out-worn formulae or archaic symbols which no longer resonate with contemporary experience; and women and men in modern Western society need rites which are liberating and life-giving.

This book explores the ways in which women are using liturgy and ritual to mark and construct transitions in their lives. I have accompanied women in the process of planning and devising their rituals, I have kept journal entries of ritual occasions in which I shared as a participant, and I have listened as women have told me their stories of ritual and symbolic action. I have reflected with the women on their own understanding of their rituals and their significance and meaning, sometimes still unfolding for them months and years after the event. Using their stories and conversations, and my own practice in constructing ritual, I look at the ways in which ritual uses space and symbol, the role played by others in making ritual and symbolic action into a shared, communal process, and the ways in which participants use ritual to give meaning and shape to their experiences. Using feminist theology and social anthropology as interpretive frameworks, I show that ritual not only marks what has happened retrospectively, but plays a part in the construction of meaning and theology—not only expressing, but creating story and transformative action.

Mapping the Territory

My focus in this book is on rituals that women have created—written, put together and enacted—for themselves. This is not to deny that there is much creativity in ritual going on elsewhere—one of the most creative writers on ritual (Ronald Grimes) that I have discovered is male. But my own experience and practice is rooted in women's groups, and as a feminist I wish to take women's experience and stories seriously. Of course, it is impossible to talk in general terms of women's experience as if it were a homogeneous whole; rather, I pay attention to the diverse experiences of particular women as they engage in the process of creating ritual. Not all of the women I have worked with would describe themselves as feminist, although most have been influenced to some degree or another by feminist thinking. But the interpretive framework with which I work, and in which I inevitably set their stories, is provided in part by feminist theologians, researchers and scholars. Most of the participants are Christian, many of them theologically educated, and highly articulate about their faith; others have a strong spiritual awareness that they would describe in various ways. My own background is Christian theology, but strongly influenced by a feminist theology of liberation which is eclectic in drawing on pagan and Goddess traditions.

I have limited myself to rituals which have been created and enacted by women in relation to transitions in their own lives. This means that although men have sometimes been participants in the groups, I have not looked at rituals such as weddings, or naming of children, where men have shared in the planning. Because I have been quite opportunistic in my selection of rituals, there is a wide variety of life-events described here. What they have in common is that they are events not usually marked in the formal liturgy and rituals of the church. This is in keeping with the claim of feminist theology that women's experience is often invisible or marginalized — for many of the events of our lives there are no existing rituals. Where rituals do exist, they are often out of touch with women's lived experience — and so they have felt the need to create something for themselves, shaped and enacted in a way that gives meaning and a sense of structure to the transitions they are going through.

There are of course many possible definitions of ritual, and in chapter five I discuss these and some of the accompanying theory in more depth. The rituals discussed here, however, are not repeated, formulaic rituals, but one-off creative events, limited to a specific context and group. They are often playful and experimental, and the rituals themselves are part of a wider, more extensive process of reflection and creativity. Whilst they have common elements and themes, and sometimes draw on a similar pool of resources, each is unique; and often for the women themselves, the process of planning and creating is as significant as the ritual act itself:

> and it is noticeable that it is not only participating in liturgies and rituals that helps people to change in creative ways — the process of creating liturgy, and the theological effort involved, itself changes lives (Ward and Wild 1995: 2).

The Nature of the Journey

This book is based on the research which I undertook for my doctorate, looking at women's practice of ritual making through the lens of practical feminist theology. But the research itself was part of a larger journey, a personal and interactive process, in which my own understanding of ritual changed and developed as I moved towards a goal as yet not totally defined.

I used qualitative and ethnographic methods to engage with my research. I relied on interviews and participant observations, backed up by journal entries recording conversations, observations, notes from supervisions and research groups as well as my own insights and questions. Many of my interviews were with people already known to me — others formed the basis for new friendships, and the process was one of personal discovery. I was greatly encouraged in this approach by Amanda Coffey's book, *The Ethnographic Self* (1999), and have discovered within myself something of the passion for research of which she writes. Early in the process I entered the following note in my research journal:

> a conversation today with Rachel, in which she said, "You've got a passion for research". And with a kind of surprise, I think she might be right! ...She was also very touched when I said she had a lot to do with it, inspiring me! But I do feel excited about what I'm doing...(Journal entry, 29.2.04).

I carried out my research on a part-time basis, alongside a demanding teaching job, and so at the time it felt somewhat fragmented, snatching at opportunities for interviews and observations, often looking with slight envy at colleagues who were able to undertake full-time research or an extended period of field work. But there were advantages to this — it meant that study, conversation, relationships and my own practice were integrated into a holistic exploration that is consistent with both feminist and practical approaches to theology. There were of course times of frustration, when the space to read or write was squeezed out entirely by other pressures, and times of excitement as new ideas took shape and were formed into words and arguments. But women's lives and experiences do not fit neatly into discrete compartments!

It was not a lonely journey either. My reflections on ritual were shared with my supervisor, with research groups, in conference papers and sessions with students, and in conversations with friends. The image of the isolated researcher writing alone in her study (although I love the times when that is possible!) goes alongside a collegial and collaborative process of learning and reflecting with others which helped me to remain motivated and excited. I continue to work with others to create and shape rituals. Some of them are rituals that feature in this book; others are part of the pattern of a regular group meeting monthly. This process involves me in continuous reflection on the ritual process and my own practice, refining my skills and awareness of myself not only as a researcher but as a reflective practitioner as well.

In particular, this book owes its existence to those who shared their stories and their rituals with me. Some told me of rituals they had created in the past, others invited me to participate in rituals they were planning, some entrusted parts of the planning to me. Alison, Andrea, Clare, Cora, Nicola, Runa and Sue have chosen to be named; Carol, Jackie, Jane, Louise, and Rebecca are known by pseudonyms that they or I have chosen: but all have given generously of their time and creativity, and have been prepared to share their feelings with honesty and courage. I am grateful to all of them for the privilege of sharing in their journeys.

There are many others who are not named, and whose stories are not told; but whose support, encouragement, and sharing of rituals and liturgies have shaped my thinking far more than they, or I recognize: members of my feminist research group, of the women's spirituality groups which I have been part of over the years, those I have shared with in circle dancing rituals and events, have all been part of my journey.

My partner Alma, who came into my life when I was approaching the end of my research, has been a steady encouragement and support, always believing in this book and the thesis which preceded it.

A Plan of the Route

In the next chapter I look at the roots of women's ritual in what Teresa Berger (1999) has called 'the Women's Liturgical Movement', the creating of liturgy by women's groups, shaped by feminist theology. I survey the growing literature relating to feminist liturgy, and refer to theoretical insights from other disciplines which also inform my thinking. Chapter three looks at methodology, analysing some of the advantages and difficulties of ethnographic research, the questions of validity and objectivity raised by interpreting women's stories of ritual, and the importance of reflexivity. In the following five chapters I look in more detail at the rituals themselves, exploring them in the light of theoretical perspectives and data drawn from the other rituals I have studied. Interspersed between the chapters are stories of some of the rituals; they can stand alone as case studies in themselves, attempting to capture something of each woman's voice and story; but each one also serves to introduce the themes in the chapter which follows. In chapter four I examine the nature and process of the transitions which the women are experiencing, set in the context of rites of passage theory as it has been developed by Arnold van Gennep and Victor Turner. Chapter five looks at the practice and theology found in the women's rituals, and sets this alongside ritual theory, drawing out both the parallels and the distinctiveness of women's ritual making process. Chapter six argues that ritual is a process of story-making, and draws on narrative theory to show how ritual plays a part in constructing identity and agency. In chapter seven, I explore the communal dimension of women's ritual, and reflect on the tension between private and public. Chapter eight looks at feminist theologies of embodiment and sacramental theology, and how this links with ritual theory on performativity. In the final chapter I draw out the implications and issues for Christian pastoral liturgy, feminist theology, and my own practice and reflect on the possible future directions which may be taken by women's practice of making ritual. The journey takes me from my own experience, through the stories of other women and critical engagement with theory, to the recognition of the power of ritual making as a liberating and transformative process.

Chapter Two

'SISTERS ARE DOING IT FOR THEMSELVES'[1]

Women's Experiences of Exclusion and Marginalization

My interest in women's rituals stems from my broader involvement in feminist liturgy. Over a period of about eighteen years I have been discovering the power of liturgy written and created by and for women. As a white Western woman ordained in the Protestant non-conformist tradition I have found some freedom of expression and equality in worship; but in Christian feminism I have found a theology which speaks more directly to my own experience and identity. I have been involved in writing feminist prayers, shared in the development of liturgy in on-going groups, and introduced and used feminist images of God in my own leading of worship.

Women's ritual making does not arise in a vacuum, and in this chapter I look at some of the writing about the creation and analysis of 'women's liturgy'. This is the rich soil in which the diverse rituals, liturgies and ceremonies which women are developing to mark transitions in their lives are rooted.

For many white western women, the experience of the church's liturgy has been one of exclusion, marginalization or invisibility.

In many Christian traditions, there is a long history of women being denied the authority to preach or preside at the Eucharist. In the Roman Catholic church women may still not be ordained to the priesthood, and in the Church of England the ordination of women has been a recent and strongly-resisted development. In the non-conformist traditions, there have been more possibilities for women. Gertrude von Petzholt was ordained as a Unitarian minister in 1916, and Constance Coltman as a Congregationalist in 1917 (Wootton 2000: 52). Nevertheless, there has continued to be opposition to women's leadership and preaching, particularly in those churches

1. The title of a song recorded by Annie Lennox and Aretha Franklin on Atlantic, 1984.

which hold to a more fundamentalist view of scripture and so object to women taking up positions of authority. Within the United Reformed Church, which has an official policy of affirming the ministry of women, there are still anecdotes of women finding it hard to find pastorates, or encountering sexist or patronizing comments from male colleagues.

For much of Christian history women's voices have been silenced, as Janet Wootton (2000) shows in her account of women's involvement in both preaching and church music. Whilst women have often been involved in private and domestic rituals surrounding birth and death, as formal and institutionalized religion has taken over, their agency has decreased; and Susan White (2003) argues that we hear little of women's stories as participants because most liturgical history is text-based, and so portrays women as the passive recipients of worship led by men. Her retelling of the social history of worship seeks to recover the story of women's active participation of women as agents in worship.

Furthermore, women are often not visible in the words and images of the liturgy. Christian liturgy is primarily androcentric, with a male Father/Creator, a male Son/Saviour, and a Holy Spirit who is occasionally described as female, but is more often referred to in masculine or non-gendered terms. This male God 'lords' it over 'mankind' with hierarchical power, or stoops to rescue victims with benevolent, paternalistic care—although some liturgical material is now beginning to replace such terms as 'mankind' and 'brotherhood' with more inclusive language. Generally, the language of liturgy reflects a patriarchal theology which emphasizes maleness, hierarchy, and self-abnegation. Whilst many worshippers (male and female) accept this as the norm, there are increasing numbers of women who feel alienated and marginalized by it.

Women's voices are not included in official liturgical texts: for example, Susan Roll claims that up until the time of Vatican II there were no words of women in the official liturgical texts of the Roman Catholic church (Roll 1994: 387–88). Frequently women feel that they are not active subjects of liturgy. Male experience is taken as the norm; or where women's experience is central, it is portrayed in negative or stereotypical ways (e.g. the associations of women's bodies with 'uncleanness' in childbirth and churching rituals; or the idealization of women's role in home and family on Mothering Sunday). Although there are pitfalls in generalizing about women's experience, the realities of gender inequality and injustice, violence against women, and the limitations placed on women's roles in leadership in church and secular spheres have not traditionally been subjects of liturgy. Women's bodies have been feared and negated rather than honoured; and the language and imagery of liturgy has perpetuated women's submission, rather than encouraging them to seek liberation. There has been little opportunity for women to see themselves as made in the image of God, or to hear stories, sing hymns or offer prayers in which their own experience and spirituality is the subject.

In *Defecting in Place* the authors describe the results of a survey of over 3,000 women (Winter, Lummis and Stokes 1994: 30). Since they deliberately sought respondents from feminist sources this is not a random or representative sample, but it indicates profound dissatisfaction amongst many women with traditional worship and liturgy. For some women this leads to leaving and withdrawing from institutional forms of religion:

> The lack of ritual/symbol that can speak to me as a woman accounts for my withdrawal from religion and my increased attention to spiritual maturity (Winter, Lummis and Stokes 1994: 27).

Mary Daly used the image of exodus in calling for a walk-out in a sermon in Harvard Memorial Church in 1971 (Daly 1986: 144), and since then women have used this image for the leaving-behind of patriarchal forms of church. The title *Defecting in Place*, which the authors have chosen, suggests an alternative model for those who remain to some degree or another involved with institutional religion, whilst at the same time creating their own forms of worship and liturgy:

> I believe women can find creative alternatives for ritual and prayer without giving up totally the connection with tradition. I think women creating their own forms/rituals will make a powerful contribution to the future understanding of church (Winter, Lummis and Stokes 1994: 101).

Feminist Liturgical Responses

The responses to these experiences of marginalization and exclusion are varied, and it is hard to make generalizations. Nevertheless, there has been what Nicola Slee refers to as a 'great outpouring of feminist liturgies in recent decades' (Slee 2004a: 178). Much of the liturgical development has taken place in small, grass-roots groups, usually with shared leadership. Most liturgies are created as one-off events, and until relatively recently there have been few published sources. Early resources included *Sistercelebrations* (Swidler 1974), *Images: Women in Transition* (Grania 1976), *No Longer Strangers* (Gjerding and Kinnamom 1983) and *Women-church* (Ruether 1985). Other resources were published in leaflet or booklet form on a small scale by groups such as The Movement for the Ordination of Women and Women in Theology. Janet Morley's *All Desires Known* (1988, 1992) and the *Celebrating Women* collection (Ward, Wild and Morley (eds), 1995 [1986], which both began in this way have since been published by mainstream religious publishers. In 2004, SPCK published *Praying Like a Woman* (Slee 2004b) followed by Susan Durber's *Preaching Like a Woman* (2007).

In addition to the response from Christian feminist theology, other books were published (mostly in the United States) which sought to rediscover and reclaim ancient matriarchal or Goddess rites, such as Z. Budapest's *The Holy Book of Women's Mysteries Parts I and II* (1979, 1980), Starhawk's *The Spiral Dance* (1979), and Merlin Stone's *The Paradise Papers* (1979).

Janet Wootton (2000) and Jenny Daggers (2002) are both useful sources for historical accounts of developments within Christian feminist liturgy in the United Kingdom. The Christian Women's Information and Resources Project (CWIRES) began in 1979, following the vote against the ordination of women at the Synod of the Church of England in 1978. At about the same time the Movement for the Ordination of Women was formed in the place of two existing groups—the Anglican Group for the Ordination of Women and the Christian Parity Group (Daggers 2002: 28–29). Catholic Women's Network (CWN) and Women in Theology (WIT) began in 1984 (Daggers 2002: 41). WIT began as an Anglican, London-based movement, working in parallel with the Movement for the Ordination of Women, with the aim of encouraging the theological education of women in preparation for the time when the Anglican Church would ordain them as priests. WIT quickly broadened out into a network of individuals across the country, with some groups incorporating liturgy as part of their programme (for example in London, Manchester, Birmingham and Sheffield).[2]

2. I was involved with 'Women in Theology' from about 1988–97, and for part of that time served as the Chair of the Core Executive.

The Britain and Ireland School of Feminist Theology began by planning a summer school in 1989. The first school was held at Lampeter in 1992, and schools have been organized every two years since. The *Journal of Feminist Theology* was launched with Sheffield Academic Press in 1992, and was followed by a series of publications introducing various aspects of feminist theology. Although these organizations had an interest in feminist theology generally, worship usually formed part of the programme of conferences, summer schools, and local groups; and gave members the opportunity to explore different liturgical forms and patterns.

Other groups had a stronger liturgical focus. The story of the St Hilda congregation in London is told in *Women Included* (St. Hilda Community 1991). This group formed in 1986 around the issue of women's ordination in the Anglican Church and the celebration of Eucharist. It was not restricted to Anglicans, and unlike most groups described here, also included men, although leadership and liturgy were women-centred. In Sheffield the Womanspirit group, of which I was a part, grew out of a WIT group as four of us felt the need for a stronger ritual and liturgical focus. We met fortnightly over a period of about three years, sometimes with one member planning a liturgy; at other times with all members bringing contributions on a previously-agreed theme. I am currently part of a group in Manchester which meets monthly for a ritual or liturgy and a shared meal.

There have been similar developments in the United States. The term 'women-church' was coined by Elisabeth Schüssler Fiorenza as 'ekklesia gynaikon' in 1981 (Procter-Smith 2003), and later translated as women-church by Diann Neu (Schüssler Fiorenza 1992). It became more widely-known with the publication of Ruether's book *Women-church* (1985), a collection of feminist liturgies. It is used as a self-description by a number of groups, although Schüssler Fiorenza argues that the translation loses some of the radical meaning of 'ekklesia' as the free democratic assembly as well as church, and therefore has a less political resonance than first intended (Schüssler Fiorenza 1992). 'Sisters Against Sexism' began in the Washington DC area over twenty years ago as a group of women religious gathered in protest at the treatment of women in the Catholic Church on the occasion of a papal visit. The group, originally composed of Roman Catholic sisters, has now expanded to include women from a variety of traditions. Members meet monthly for a ritual prepared by one or two members in turn, and a shared meal; and the group is now part of a wider women-church movement.³ Diann Neu and Mary Hunt are also founders of WATER (Women's Alliance for Theology, Ethics and Ritual) which has a resource centre and programme in Silver Spring, Maryland.⁴ The story of the Women's Liturgy Group in New York City is told by Cindy Derway (2001). This group has also been in existence since February 1981, and again all the founder members were Catholic nuns or ex-nuns. The group follows a similar pattern, meeting in members' homes, preparing liturgy together, or sharing the task amongst different women in turns. Both groups include Eucharistic and Seder celebrations amongst their programmes, although for some women the Eucharist is too strongly associated with patriarchal church to be reclaimable. Whilst many women are involved in these groups and others like them, for others the main experience of women's liturgy will be at conferences or workshops, such as the Re-Imaging Conferences in the United States, the End of Decade conference in Durham in 1998 or the conferences of the European Society for Women in Theological Research described by Susan Roll (1993).

These are just some of the stories of groups emerging in what is broadly a Christian or post-Christian framework. They show common elements of dissatisfaction with traditional liturgy, informal structures, and shared leadership. However, they are only part of the diffuse picture of what Northup (1997) describes as 'ritualizing women'. She argues that groups celebrating women's liturgy can be described as Christian feminist, women-church, Goddess spirituality, or as consciousness-raising groups incorporating spirituality. Eller (1993) also points to links with paganism, New Age and Therapy movements, although the latter are not usually feminist, or exclusive to women.

In practice, however, these groups are not mutually exclusive, and there are many overlaps. Jenny Daggers argues that Christian feminism in the United Kingdom was dominated by its agenda of

3. Based on personal conversations with Diann Neu and members of Sisters Against Sexism.

4. In 2001, I spent part of a sabbatical as Visiting Scholar at WATER, and much of this information was gathered during this period. I am grateful to Mary Hunt and Diann Neu, and members of SAS for their hospitality and sharing of resources.

transforming the institutional church (specifically the Church of England) and so did not develop into a separate women-church movement as in the United States. Groups such as Women In Theology, and Catholic Women's Network, she argues, saw themselves as models of a transformed church encouraging the full participation of women:

> When CWN and WIT built up their group life, inclusive of liturgical experiment, they created a model of reformed church, not an alternative to the institutional churches (Daggers 2002: 84).

While there may be some truth in this in relation to the founding and early days of CWIRES and Women in Theology, I believe she overstates the case, and as Christian feminist liturgy grew it broadened out both denominationally and in attracting women who found no home within traditional denominations. For some, even the terms women-church and worship had too many associations with patriarchal institutions, and they preferred to talk of feminist or women's spirituality. For others, although remaining within the denominations, Christian feminist groups became the safe spaces which nurtured their personal spirituality and creativity in a way which the institutional church was unable to do.

For some women Christian theology and spirituality is irredeemably patriarchal. They turn to rediscovered or reconstructed images and practices of the Goddess, finding their spirituality nourished by a female sense of the divine which is immanent in nature and embodied in human existence (Starhawk 1979; Roberts 1993). Although there are groups which are specifically devoted to Goddess spirituality and practice, there are some Christian feminist and women-church groups which draw on Goddess imagery and language, and celebrate the seasons and cycles of the year in addition to Christian festivals.[5] For Nicola Slee, the challenge which the Goddess Movement brings to orthodox Christianity is an important one which needs to be heard:

> Whilst at first sight a long way from orthodox Christian belief and practice, the Goddess movement represents an important challenge to and critique of the church, for it affirms the "underside" of Christian orthodoxy: those aspects of human experience (such as the body, the senses, sexuality, femaleness per se) and cosmic reality (the earth, the

5. For an example, see my 'Prayer for Midsummer' in Ruth Burgess (ed.), *Bare Feet and Buttercups*, 2008: 142.

seasons and cycles of growth and decay) which have been neglected and even demonised by an overly cerebral, word-based and male-based religion (Slee 2003: 32).

Other women come to feminist liturgy, ritual or spirituality by a totally different route, finding that their self-esteem and awareness of their agency as women grows through consciousness-raising, experiences of therapy, or new age beliefs. For some, this leads to a search for an adequate spirituality in which to express their sense of self, and they participate in women's groups or liturgies as part of this personal and spiritual exploration, while not claiming any particular religious allegiance.

The variety and the developing nature of this movement make it difficult to categorize and even to name! Northup (1997) points out the difficulties facing researchers: the difficulties of definition, the lack of paper evidence due to the emphasis on flexibility and adaptability, and the lack of clear line of a development, with no central organization. Nevertheless there have been some attempts to analyse and reflect on developments in women's/feminist liturgy; and I want to review the major contributions to this debate before going on to articulate my own understanding of what is meant by feminist liturgy.

Naming Feminist Liturgy

Teresa Berger (1999) probably uses the most general and inclusive terminology. She prefers the term 'Women's Liturgical Movement' to describe a process emerging in the twentieth century, following the Liturgical Movement, which although it sought to renew the liturgy of the church, failed to address its gendered and male-dominated nature. She encompasses within this women's groups devising liturgies as and for women, whether or not they define themselves as feminist; women rediscovering and claiming their participation in traditional liturgy; and those working for gender justice within liturgy.

Other writers, however, are more specific in talking about feminist liturgy. Marjorie Procter-Smith (1990) talks of the feminist liturgical movement, and again compares it with the liturgical movement, drawing out both the similarities and differences. Both movements, she argues, have a concern to transform liturgy; both stress participation and the importance of speaking to particular pastoral need; both explore the need for greater expressiveness in ritual and symbol. The feminist liturgical movement, however, differs in its attitude to the authority of tradition; liturgical tradition is constructed, and the gendered nature of that construction must be recognized and challenged. There is therefore a need for feminist reconstruction, and the hermeneutical principles of suspicion, proclamation, remembrance and creative actualization that Schüssler Fiorenza (1985) uses must also be applied to the analysis and revisioning of liturgy.

Some writers are unhappy with the use of the term liturgy at all, seeing it as too tied to institutional religion. Cynthia Eller (1993) writing specifically about Goddess spirituality, rather than Christian theology, prefers to talk about spiritual feminism. Diann Neu (1993a) uses the term liturgy but also talks of ceremonies, particularly with reference to liturgies and rituals relating to specific times or events in individual lives. Mary Collins (1993) argues that liturgy suggests something that is too ordered, and too narrow, with primarily Jewish/Christian associations.

Most writers cited here use a feminist analysis, and writers such as Janet Walton (2000) and Diann Neu (1993a, 1993b) talk of feminist rather than women's liturgy, specifically analysing liturgies and rituals according to feminist principles, asking the question 'is this liturgy feminist?' Apart from the title of Teresa Berger's book (1999), the word 'worship' is rarely used; for many, it has too many connotations of subservience to a transcendent, hierarchical, powerful being. Northup (1997) talks of women's religious communities trying to establish their own patterns of worship, but prefers to use the term 'ritualizing women', so stressing the activity of women and the process of creating ritual rather than a finished product or norm.

Characteristics of Feminist/Women's Liturgy

In spite of the diversity and difficulty of categorizing feminist or women's liturgy, certain characteristics appear frequently in the liturgies and rituals that are created as part of this movement. A number of writers produce their own lists (Northup 1997, Neu 1993, Procter-Smith 1990, Berger 1999), generally based on observation and experience of actual liturgical events or (more rarely) texts. Although their lists vary slightly, certain common ground emerges.

Women's Experiences and Stories

Not surprisingly, at the centre of women's liturgies is a sharing of women's experiences and stories. These may relate to women's embodied experience, celebrating, marking or grieving experiences in relation to birth, sexuality, menstruation or menopause, and ageing that are often ignored or stigmatized in the dualism of patriarchal liturgy. Often there is a sharing of events in a woman's life, or recalling experiences of women's suffering. Much of the sharing of stories is autobiographical, as women tell their own stories, in a way that has echoes of consciousness-raising groups in the secular women's movement. In fact, for some, the sharing of stories is a ritual in itself:

> We knew it was a very special time but we had not thought of sacred ritual as being as mundane and ordinary as our own talking and listening about our lives (Goldman 1988: 21).

More often, however, the telling of stories will be an element within the liturgy, as women share experiences, feelings or insights in relation to a particular theme. The telling of stories may also include the remembering of other women — reclaiming biblical stories, or recalling women from history. Marjorie Procter-Smith (1990) talks about the process of liturgical anamnesis, which critiques the patriarchal tradition through reclaiming and reconstructing the traditional texts and stories, comparing this use of 'liturgical imagination' to Schüssler Fiorenza's 'historical imagination' (1985). Many women's liturgies also make use of poetry and fiction, and writers such as Adrienne Rich and Alice Walker acquire almost canonical status, as their words take the place once filled by scriptural texts.

The Use of Space and Time

Very few women's liturgies seem to take place in churches, although occasionally a conference liturgy may make use of a chapel. This is no doubt partly because women do not always have access to or permission to use religious buildings; but also because many groups prefer the informality of a home, the flexibility of a room without fixed seating or, when weather and climate permit, the outdoors. Nevertheless, in women's liturgy there is an attention paid to space, colour and arrangement that forms an integral part of the liturgy. There is a strong sense of sacred space — made sacred not by the associations of a holy building, but by the embodied nature of the liturgy and its symbols and activities:

> The ritual space was also made sacred by the women themselves. We gathered to worship in a way authentic and liberating to us, not as in a church but in a semicircle around a large common earthen bowl (McDade and Longview 1988: 125).

Marjorie Procter-Smith (1995) argues that the knowledge and awareness of women's suffering leads to the importance of creating a safe space; and for many women there is also the present fear of opposition and ridicule from male colleagues. This does, however, raise questions of accessibility; many women's liturgies are not open to outsiders, or are publicized only by word of mouth; and Roberts points out that some Goddess celebrations which take place in the open are only accessible to those who have transport and/or are physically fit (1993). What is inclusive for some becomes in other senses excluding of others—but this is justified by the need for some kind of boundary which gives a sense of safe and sacred space to the participants.

Whatever the location, the arrangement within the space almost invariably takes the form of a circle or semi-circle. In goddess rituals, the power of the circle is made explicit as they begin and end with casting and opening the circle, putting a space-and-time boundary around all that happens within the ritual:

> When we enter the circle, it is said that we enter a "world between the worlds", a sacred liminal space where it is possible to enter into communion with the divine, step into the mythic, and actually alter the fabric of reality, if we enter it with perfect love and perfect trust (Roberts 1993: 140).

For Susan Roll (1994), the circle marks the non-hierarchical nature of women's liturgy, and stresses the participation of all. Lesley Northup (1993) develops this theme, arguing that women's liturgy rejects the 'dominance of verticality' found in traditional liturgy, in favour of a horizontal orientation. Through this horizontal orientation the liturgy stresses community and shared participation, nature and the earth, and helps the process of integrating liturgy with the domestic and mundane, and with the world of politics and culture.

The understanding of time is another significant feature of women's liturgy. Lesley Northup (1997) argues that modern consciousness is dominated by a linear view of time, whilst in women's liturgy the dominant image is that of a circle or spiral. This is particularly true in pagan/Goddess ritual, where the cycles of the seasons and the pagan festivals associated with equinox and solstice are celebrated, and the wheel of the year is a determinative symbol for both space and time (Roberts 1993). Susan Roll (1994) points out that women's liturgy uses both the seasons of the church year and the seasons of the calendar year; and in the northern hemisphere these can often resonate, so that Easter celebrations draw on themes of spring and rebirth, and All Saints is linked with the dying of the year. She argues that, although solar time is often seen as male, and the lunar cycle as female, women's liturgy more often follows the solar cycle. I, however, would see this as more applicable to Christian feminist liturgy than to Goddess ritual which tends to be lunar in its orientation. The other main way in which women's liturgy makes use of time is in reclaiming seasons and cycles of women's lives which are often neglected in traditional liturgy and rites of passage—so Diann Neu (1993a) talks of rituals to celebrate first menstruation, and croning rituals.

Symbol and Symbolic Action

A common feature of women's liturgies is their use of symbols or symbolic action. Feminist theology is holistic and embodied in its approach, and this is reflected in liturgy in the use of symbols that make use of all the senses, and in embodied action, gesture and movement. Susan Roll (1991) describes how traditional symbols of fire, water, food and oil have been used and reclaimed in women's liturgy. Lesley Northup lists a whole variety of sources for symbols and images:

> Cooking, cleaning, parenting, bathing, dressing, managing, sewing, networking, creating, teaching—the endless host of women's unglorified daily activities are being mined by women seeking a distinctive spiritual expression (1997: 33).

Many of these symbols are drawn from everyday activities or crafts commonly seen as women's work or women's crafts, although Marjorie Procter-Smith (1995) points out the dangers in this. First, there is the risk of reinforcing patriarchal stereotypes—there is a thin line between valuing the activities and roles normally assigned to women, and stereotyping women as the sole performers of these roles. A similar argument can be made in relation to imagery and symbolism drawn from birth and child-bearing; for some women it is a powerful affirmation of their experience; for others, it reinforces stereotypes of women's role and excludes those who are not mothers. Second, she cautions against using objects without regard to the exploitation either of nature or of women's labour; the source and history of objects used as symbols must be considered carefully. Others have expanded this into a critique of the co-optation of symbols and symbolic practices of other cultures — rather than an affirming or empowering acknowledgement, this runs the risk of becoming an exploitative colonization of others' spiritual resources. In a scathing critique of what she describes as the 'postmodern neo-colonialism' of New Age Native Americanism, Laura Donaldson challenges the 'close association between some constructions of women's empowerment and such emerging forms of consumption as the rummaging through of imagined histories and the social practice of imagined nostalgia' (Donaldson 2001: 250).

Many symbolic actions such as anointing, movement and touch involve the use of the body, and so play an important part in reclaiming the sense of women's bodies as sacred. In spite of the emphasis on mothering, few writers make mention of the inclusion of children in liturgy. Diann Neu is the only writer I have come across who states this as a specific principle of feminist liturgy, and most of the liturgies I have come across have not sought to include children (in fact, for some, the women's group is their one space away from family responsibilities).

Much liturgy uses everyday objects as the focus of symbolism and metaphor (bread, stones, water). This strengthens the sense of integration of ritual with everyday domestic life, and is part of the horizontal expansion referred to by Northup (1997).

Female Images of the Divine

For many feminist writers, seeing women's experiences and bodies as sacred and in the image of God requires language and imagery which speaks of God in female terms. The dominance of the imagery of God as father in Christian tradition, along with the hierarchical notions of lordship and submission which accompany it, has led to many women feeling excluded, and seeking different ways to talk about God. There are a number of different strategies for doing this. Sometimes a simple use of the female pronoun for God can be a consciousness-altering experience, initially producing resistance, but then often a sense of inclusion and empowerment.[6] The predominance of the imagery of God as Father has led many to think of God as mother, or to use imagery associated with giving birth. Inspired by the parable of the woman searching for a lost coin, women search the scriptures for the places which speak of God in female terms. The work of feminist biblical scholars such as Schüssler Fiorenza has drawn attention to the imagery of Wisdom as a female figure in Proverbs 8, and Wisdom, or Holy Wisdom, has become a popular designation of God in feminist liturgies. Equally, the Spirit of God (a female noun in Hebrew, neuter in Greek) has been embraced as a female personification of divinity, and is often linked with that of Wisdom. Other strategies speak of God in terms of activities or crafts traditionally associated with women—so God may be pictured as Weaver, or Breadmaker, or as making or mending patchwork, or wielding a broom to sweep the house clean.

For Christian feminists the male figure of Jesus presents a particular challenge. There are a number of attempts to deal with feminist Christology, but in liturgy often there is an emphasis on retelling the stories of women associated with Jesus, stressing their active agency and discipleship, rather than their victimhood, or their sinfulness. The use of female imagery in Christian feminist liturgy is founded in the assertion that all (male and female) are created in the image of God, and to live out the reality of this in worship we must be able to image God in female terms as well as male.

Feminist theology and spirituality has a strong emphasis on creation or connectedness with nature, and so there is a strong sense of God's presence as found immanent there. This may be expressed by using gender-neutral imagery, for example of light and darkness, stones, water, to convey something of God. In Goddess spirituality this is more explicit, and so the Goddess may well be identified with the moon, or mother earth.

Diann Neu (1993a, 1993b) argues that seeing women as imaging the divine is a key feature of feminist liturgies. Teresa Berger (1999) also recognizes the importance of female images and forms of address for God, arguing that although initially imagery of God as

6. See, for example, the poem *A Revelation* by June Pettitt in *Celebrating Women* (Ward, Wild and Morley 1995: 122).

mother and nurturer predominated, there is a critique of such language as reinforcing stereotypes and an ideology of motherhood which is not necessarily liberating for women. Marjorie Procter-Smith (1990) also discusses the use of language, identifying three approaches to androcentric language. The first is the use of non-sexist language, which is non-gendered or gender-blind. This she argues is useful but may still be heard as male; terms such as friend, creator, and healer, whilst not necessarily masculine are likely to be understood as such by women who have grown up with images of a male God and male pronouns. The second is inclusive language which balances male and female, and opens up a range of images and metaphors; but she argues that this assumes an equality and symmetry which does not actually exist in society. She argues for a third category, emancipatory language, which specifically and proactively sees God identifying with women in their struggle for liberation. In practice, women's liturgies draw on all three approaches, but Procter-Smith argues that only the third is truly feminist, rather than simply inclusive.

Pain and Anger

Over the years exclusion and marginalization by the church has led many women to experience a deep sense of hurt and anger. For some this is compounded by experience of suffering or abuse, whether in childhood, or in violent relationships as adults. For those who have experienced violence or abuse at the hands of men (including clergy) and fathers, worship addressed to a male Lord and God, or the glorification of suffering and submission, can add to the layers of oppression. Alongside those who have personal experiences of abuse, there is a growing awareness of injustice and oppression against women, against children, against vulnerable people or minority groups, and against the natural world. Feminist liturgy needs not only to change the ways of addressing God, but to find a way of acknowledging the pain and anger. Although many of the Psalms and some of the prophetic writings of the Old Testament cry out to, or even against, God, there has been little room for acknowledgement or expression of anger in traditional Christian liturgy. Feminist liturgy seeks to articulate the anger felt by many women in the context and framework of worship and prayer.

For Marjorie Procter-Smith, women's liturgy is carried out in the context of the suffering and abuse of women, and women urgently need to reclaim and use the form of the lament to express this anger and rage at a patriarchal God:

> The feminist reconstruction of prayer builds on the necessary conditions for women and other oppressed people to say no and therefore to say yes. It recognizes the anger and grief of women and the necessity of ritualizing that anger and grief (1995: 54).

Diann Neu commonly uses the form of the litany as a kind of exorcism of the evils of patriarchy. Frequently it is from this anger and rage at the injustices suffered by women that a broader awareness of social justice and a sense of solidarity with other women arises.

A Communal Dimension

Another feature of women's liturgy is a rediscovery of the community of women. Whilst there are prayers, poems and blessings which are highly personal, and most likely to be used by individuals, liturgy by its very nature is the public worship of the church. Feminist liturgy, however, is more often celebrated in small groups of women, or at conferences or special services, rather than forming part of the regular worship life of a congregation. There is a strong sense of connection with other women, and although this may sometimes be romanticized in a way that does not pay sufficient attention to diversity and power politics, there is a genuine attempt to stress equality and solidarity amongst women. There is often a rejection of hierarchical positions and leadership, and frequently the process of planning is a communal and collaborative one, with a pooling of ideas and resources, and the leadership of the event shared. Within the liturgy itself, there is often opportunity for spontaneous contributions or for everyone present to participate in a symbolic action.

Procter-Smith (1990) refers to the absence of hierarchy and shared leadership. Diann Neu (1993) sees the sharing of power and involvement expressed in a number of ways—in a collaborative process of planning, through leadership styles and a rotating leadership, through spontaneous responses within the liturgy itself, and in the creation of a space which encourages participation.

What Makes a Liturgy Feminist?

While there are many common features to women's liturgy, such shared characteristics do not really address the question of 'what makes a liturgy feminist?' As Berger (1999) and Procter-Smith (1990) point out, many of the concerns of feminist liturgy are shared by the earlier liturgical movement—which also encouraged greater participation and more flexible use of space. The use of symbols and symbolic acts has been developed within a number of Christian groups, such as the Iona Community, and is now more common in mainstream liturgy. Groups and networks such as 'emerging church' and 'fresh expressions of church' are experimenting with alternative forms of worship and liturgy, including more flexible use of space, a holistic approach, and use of symbols—many of them adding to this a greater use of technology to produce multi-media imagery and sound. Inclusive language for human beings—what Procter-Smith (1990) calls 'horizontal inclusive language'—is now much more common in published liturgies, even if it meets with some resistance from those who see it as a sop to political correctness; although female language and what Procter-Smith would call emancipatory language is probably still restricted to feminist groups and conferences. Therefore, although it is possible to list the common features and characteristics of feminist liturgy, they cannot be claimed as unique or totally distinctive.

More digging beneath the surface is required to define feminist liturgy, and some writers have attempted this. Diann Neu (1993b) analyses her own liturgies, and lists many of the elements that occur in other writers' descriptions. Again, however, many of these characteristics are not unique to feminist liturgy, but can be found in other expressions of worship arising from liberation theologies or a concern to relate liturgy to the contemporary context. Janet Walton (2000) gathers her thoughts on 'feminist liturgical tasks and principles' into three categories: 'Honoring one Another and God', 'Correcting the limits of patriarchy' and 'Doing Liturgy Differently'. Mary Collins (1993) sets out five principles of intentionally feminist liturgy: it should be emancipatory and empowering of women; it must be the product of community; it should critique patriarchal liturgies; it should use distinctive symbols and strategies; and it should take the form of liturgical events rather than texts.

In a more recent article Procter-Smith addresses this question specifically. She summarizes the various lists of characteristics and goes on to argue that these are not necessarily restricted to feminist or 'woman-identified' liturgies. While feminist liturgies may be seen as those which resist patriarchal forms, she argues that defining them in this way can also perpetuate the stereotypes and dichotomies which originate in patriarchy in the first place:

> the patterns chosen for feminist ritualizing often replicate patriarchal gendered dichotomies. Patriarchal dichotomies associate women with nature, relationships, and mutual sharing (Procter-Smith 2003: 502).

She argues that feminist liturgy needs to be seen within the context of women-church—the 'ekklesia gynaikon' of Schüssler Fiorenza. She argues that just as Schüssler Fiorenza uses 'ekklesia' to mean not only church, but also a free rational assembly, so 'leitourgia' (liturgy) needs to be understood with a political connotation as representing the political and social work of women-church; it needs to take account of the multiple and complex layers of oppression denoted by the word kyriarchy rather than patriarchy, and carry with it the potential for social change and transformation.

This is an understanding that is shared by other writers too. Northup sees feminist ritualizing as a form of discourse, and therefore about power—while ritual is often conservative, it may also construct an alternative reality and help to bring about social change:

> What does seem clear, however, is that women's ritualizing comprises, in its very nature, a political activity that seeks variously to redress grievances, alleviate suffering, overturn inequity, and elevate the position of women (Northup 1997: 103).

Teresa Berger, in an article addressing the issue of liturgy as a source for theological reflection, argues that whilst much liturgical study has been gender-blind, feminist theologians need to recognize the power of liturgy in shaping and constructing theology. As such, it is a site of struggle and a means of negotiating power:

> The importance of liturgy as a site of struggle over what shapes Christian women's lives cannot be over-emphasized. For the Christian tradition in which liturgical authority seemed to be the prerogative of a male priesthood, or more recently, a caste of (mostly male) liturgical experts, the fact that women themselves now actively construct and

interpret their liturgical world is a primary mode of claiming power (Berger 2001: 73).

Each of these writers, although they express it somewhat differently, moves beyond listing the characteristics of feminist liturgy to explore and analyse its underlying principles and way of operating. Drawing on their work, I propose the following principles of feminist liturgy.

First, in order to be described as feminist, such liturgy must be affirming and empowering of women. This is the first criterion, and is essential to distinguish women's/feminist liturgy from other alternative and inclusive approaches. It specifically excludes those forms of liturgy by women which still use patriarchal concepts. It carries with it an implicit criticism of and challenge to patriarchy, and so I would not define this as a separate category, which makes women's liturgy sound predominately reactive, but see it as one aspect of liturgy which is empowering and liberating for women. This empowering will be reflected in the characteristics of the liturgy which we have examined earlier, but it is the empowering and liberating nature of the liturgy itself rather than these characteristics which make it feminist. It includes the recognition that women's lives, bodies, experiences and relationships are to be valued and can be images of the divine and divine activity, whatever name is used. It is not entirely unproblematic, as it still raises the question of who defines what is empowering and liberating, and what empowers one group may ignore or contribute to the oppression of another; nevertheless the intention of liturgy to be empowering for at least a particular group or community of women is a useful starting-point.

It is this particularity which leads on to my second criterion, in that feminist liturgy is explicitly contextual. This applies both to the process and the content of liturgy, written or enacted. Most feminist liturgies are created for specific situations; if they are transferred to other occasions, it is usually with adaptation; liturgies which use written or published material tend to select from a variety of sources to construct something to fit their own needs; and in some instances it is hard to find anything written down. There is nothing in feminist liturgy corresponding to fixed liturgies of the church, or official service books. It may be argued that this is because women do not have the power or authority to impose universal norms; but it is at present in the nature of women's liturgy-making to be highly resistant to any process of generalization or imposition. It arises both from the broad context of women's oppression and exclusion, and the particular context of the group or community. It could be argued that all liturgy is contextual, even when it claims universal validity or application; but in feminist liturgy (as in other expressions of feminist and liberation theologies) the context is named and made explicit; it is the particularity of the liturgy which gives it its empowering and liberating dimension.

Third, women's liturgy has its origin and expression in the community of women. Frequently the process of producing the liturgy is a shared one—by a group, by two or three individuals, or by one person drawing together the contributions of the group. Even when one person is actually assigned responsibility for the task, it is usually with a particular group in mind, and with some opportunity for others to contribute ideas, insights, or prayers, either beforehand or spontaneously during the ritual itself. Most liturgies are celebrated in groups; although the Wicca tradition includes blessings and spells which may be used in private. In the liturgies themselves, there is usually an awareness both of global and historical community of women; frequently we find acknowledgement of women in the past who have been oppressed, or who have been inspirational in their leadership and power; and there is an attempt at solidarity with other women across barriers of race, class and colour. There are dangers in this of a false romanticizing of sisterhood, or a co-opting of the traditions of others—but there is a growing awareness of the community of women, with all the ambivalence and contradiction that phrase implies.

Finally, there is in feminist liturgy a strong focus on social justice. Unsurprisingly, this usually stems from a concern for gender justice, and protest and anger at the oppression and exclusion of women. Roberts (1993) notes that this is sometimes less apparent in Goddess liturgy, which because of its emphasis on participation, can lack a critical prophetic voice; however, other Goddess writers, such as Starhawk (1982) would argue strongly that ritual and magic can be political actions. In the past feminist liturgy has been accused of being too white and middle-class in its concerns; but an examination of current liturgy suggests that if this ever were the case, there is a process of expansion of consciousness taking place. Women's liturgy frequently shows an awareness of other oppressed or excluded groups — women of colour, those with disabilities, the inclusion of children, a recognition of violence against women, of poverty, and of discrimination due to sexual orientation. Sometimes liturgies will be explicitly linked with protest or social action for justice; even where this is not the case, there is frequently an indication, in litanies, stories, symbols or prayers of intercession, of a wider world-view.

Taking these as the criteria for feminist liturgy, I would argue that there are some forms of liturgy which are explicitly and intentionally feminist, in that they set out to affirm and empower women, they arise from and address a particular context and situation, they show an awareness of the diversity and complexity of the communities of women, and they are a site for political and social change. In addition, there are other liturgies which share many of the features of feminist liturgy, and show the influence and impact of the feminist liturgical movement in their use of space, language or symbolism, but are not intentionally feminist or woman-identified, although they may aim to be inclusive in a more general, broader sense.

Many of the liturgies and rituals I describe here are intentionally feminist; others may best be described as 'women's liturgy/rituals'. In some ways this term is imprecise, and therefore includes rather than excludes (for example, some groups and individuals who would not define themselves as feminist, even if they use some feminist insights and values); but it puts the focus on women and on their active agency and participation. Although I work from a feminist perspective and use feminist tools of analysis, I recognize that not all of the participants in my research would define themselves or their rituals using that term. Similarly, although I tend to use the term 'liturgy' for my own work, with the understanding of its derivation as 'the work of the people', this is a term that is less familiar to those outside a Catholic or Anglican tradition of worship, and has little meaning for those not from a Christian background; some women would prefer to use the term ritual, or ceremony. But what emerges is a movement in which women, often but not always acting out of a feminist theological framework, are demanding the right to shape liturgy and worship, placing their own experiences at the centre, and imaging God and divine activity in female, or at least non-gendered, ways.

Women in Transition

Feminist liturgy is a broad category, and may include eucharistic worship, celebration of Christian festivals, liturgy relating to specific themes or based on reclaiming biblical stories, characters or texts. Within this, there are some rituals which relate specifically to change and transition. Many of the experiences and passages of women's lives are not marked in the rituals of the church. Elizabeth Gray asks:

> How are women to name as sacred the actual physical birth, which comes with no sacred ritual, while lurking around the corner of time are the long-established rituals of circumcision or baptism? (Gray 1988).

While women are participants in much of the ritual life of the church, established liturgy does not put their experience at the centre or allow them to define the terms in which their lives are described. Traditional marriage ceremonies originate in and continue to reflect patriarchal notions of ownership; initiation and funeral rites are usually gender-blind or neutral, not taking note of the particular experiences of women. Areas of pain, abuse and trauma are not recognized – until relatively recently there has been little recognition of the pain of miscarriage in liturgy – although the work of SANDS (Still-birth and Neo-natal Death Society) and hospital chaplains (Smith 1998–1999) have begun to rectify this. There is still little ritual that relates to abortion or the pain of abuse, rape or violence against women; and little attention paid to women's experiences of paid work, child-rearing, or home-making.

There is therefore within feminist liturgy a growing concern to recognize such events and critical passages in women's lives through appropriate liturgy or ritual. The collection *Human Rites* (Ward and Wild 1995), although not restricted to feminist liturgy, was compiled by two members of Women In Theology, and includes a high proportion of liturgies created by women, including rituals relating to menarche, miscarriage and abortion, divorce, and healing from abuse. Winter *et al* (1994: 187) recognize the place of rites of passage amongst the women participating in their survey. Diann Neu, who is a therapist as well as a liturgist, writes of the therapeutic power of women's ritual and aims to 'examine the function of ritual in feminist spiritual support groups and describe its therapeutic potential to empower women to make and face transitions' (1995: 186). She has published a collection of women's rites relating to times of transition (Neu 2003). Nicola Slee lists some of the occasions which women include within their rites and liturgies:

> new rites of passage—for menarche, menopause, setting up home, entering into partnerships, same-sex as well as heterosexual—and rites of healing—for abortion, miscarriage, the end of a relationship, rape or domestic violence—are created, and no aspect of life is considered beyond the scope of prayer and worship (2003: 90).

The importance of transition and of marking it liturgically has always been recognized by the sacramental life of the church, particularly within the Catholic tradition. Feminist theologians, however, argue that women's embodied experience has been excluded from the traditional sacraments and that in many cases women are not permitted to administer or preside at them. Susan Ross argues for the development of a feminist sacramental theology, in which our sacramental understanding is expanded to include the embodied existence and realities of women's lives:

> Rituals for a girl's menarche, for the loss of a child due to miscarriage, abortion, or neonatal death, for recovery from rape, or familial sexual abuse, for menopause, for childbirth, are all ways of deliberately inserting the embodied presence of women into the liturgical life of the church (Ross 2001: 167).

Dialogue with Other Fields

Whilst my main focus is on feminist theology and liturgy, there is considerable work on transition in other disciplines such as psychology and social anthropology. Christian pastoral care has long recognized the relationship between life events and liturgy. Willimon (1979) argues for the importance of forging a stronger connection between worship and pastoral care, but whilst recognizing the importance of pastoral sensitivity to the needs of individuals, places emphasis on the objective liturgy of the church as the symbolic vehicle for meaning, and has no critique relating to gender. Ramshaw (1987) on the other hand, writing about the way in which ritual and liturgy function in relation to pastoral care, stresses the importance of 'ritual honesty' and recognizes the particular nature and context of women's experiences. Roger Grainger sees the need for creating new rites of passage, but does not include a gender critique, instead arguing for a universalizing approach to religious ritual:

> Religious ritual is the timeless location for the identification of the human with the divine, just as human life is experienced historically as narrative, in the ritual format divinity is itself given a story, so that our human stories may be touched and changed by contrast with the focussed imagery of the divine (Grainger 1994: 6).

Anderson and Foley (2001) also talk of ritual as interweaving the divine and human story. They talk of the importance of integrating worship and pastoral care, and recognize the many contemporary situations which need new, alternative rituals.

In the secular world, there is growing recognition of the therapeutic power of symbolic action and ritual. There is not scope here to look in detail at all the therapeutic literature, but writers such as Imber-Black (1988) and Janine Roberts (1988) recount the importance of ritual in family therapy, and Joan Laird recognizes the specific need for women's ritual:

> Since rites of passage are important facilitators in the definition of self in relation to society, there is clearly a need for women to reclaim, redesign, or create anew rituals that will facilitate life transitions and allow more meaningful and clear incorporation of both familial and public roles (Laird 1988: 338).

From a religious perspective, writers such as Griffith and Griffith (2002) argue for the need for psychotherapists to recognize the importance of ritual, ceremony and spiritual practices; and Valerie DeMarinis (1993) includes ritual as a stage within her model of feminist pastoral psychology. Most women's rituals are not carried out within a therapeutic framework or as part of the pastoral ministry of the church; but they do fulfil something of the same function in helping women negotiate the transitions in their lives in a supportive context.

Ritual and rites of passage clearly form a major element in social anthropology. Durkheim's (1976) understanding of ritual as an expression of religious belief which promotes social cohesion is foundational; and writers such as Rappaport (1979) and Tambiah (1985) also stress the social functions of ritual. Catherine Bell (1992) gives a thorough survey of ritual theory, arguing that much of it is founded on a dualism of thought and action. She argues instead for an approach to ritual which analyses it as a social practice in itself, rather than an expression of belief or thought, and her perspective is helpful in looking at women's rituals. Unlike ritual in the thought of Durkheim (1976 [1915]) and many of the scholars who have followed him, these rituals are not well-established, repetitive and formalized actions, but one-off occasions, created and enacted for a particular context. As such, they do not fit some of the classic definitions of ritual, but need to be analysed as particular examples of a contemporary social and religious practice. They are instances of what Mitchell (1995) calls 'emerging ritual', and Ronald Grimes and Lesley Northup describe as 'ritualizing'.

Much thinking about rites of passage derives from van Gennep's scheme of classification, which uses the metaphor of the threshold (limen) to talk of rites as pre-liminal, liminal and post-liminal. His thinking is developed further by Victor Turner, who focuses on the concept of liminality and the state of 'communitas' which accompanies it. Whilst his thinking gives a helpful framework for looking at these rituals, the feminist critique of Caroline Walker Bynum suggests ways in which women's rituals do not always fit the pattern so neatly.

The growing emergence of newly-created or emerging ritual has led to the recently-developing field of ritual studies. Ronald Grimes (2000), like many feminist writers, draws attention to the lack of ritual for many of life's passages, and speaks of the importance of creating and enacting new rites. He draws on social anthropology, theology, sociology and psychology to examine existing practice and develop new rituals in relation to the traditional passages of birth, coming-of-age, marriage and dying. He argues for the need for ritual criticism (1996), and writers such as Driver, and Anderson and Foley draw on his work, particularly in relation to Christian liturgy and ritual. Within this writing there is a recognition, similar to that within feminism, of the inadequacy of many existing rituals in Western society, and the creative activity of women and other marginalized groups in addressing this. Lesley Northup (1997) also draws on Grimes' work, and has written a thorough account of women's ritualizing, looking at many of the issues (such as the use of space and symbol, and the political and social dimensions of ritual) that are raised here.

Reclaiming Ritual

The liturgies and rituals which women are creating for themselves have not originated in a vacuum, but are part of a wider context of a growing awareness of the need for new, reclaimed, and creative ritual. The emphases on the experiences of women's lives, the need for liberation from oppressive stereotypes and the potential for female imaging of the divine in feminist liturgy provide the context and environment in which women are creating rituals to mark life-events, whilst the growing attention to ritual in the process of transition in other fields provides additional tools for analysis. Women who are creating and enacting their own liturgies are insisting on the importance of their life-events and significant transitions being the subject of liturgy and ritual; not in androcentric terms which reflect the idealization or stigmatization of dualism, but in women-defined ways which are holistic and embodied in the language and symbolism they use. In their making of ritual, sisters are claiming the power to 'do it for themselves'.

Chapter Three

WHOSE STORY IS IT ANYWAY? AN EXPLORATION OF METHODOLOGY

When I began my research into women's ritual I had a (deceptively) straightforward aim — I wished to hear and tell the stories of rituals, liturgies and ceremonies which women had enacted in relation to transitions in their lives, in order to explore the meaning these rituals held for them and the part played by ritual in negotiating change. Although I recognized that the early feminist emphasis on the primacy of women's experience was an over-simplification, hiding many diverse and complex layers, I still believed that the particularity of some women's experiences was worth uncovering and recounting. Moreover, I believed that telling one's story could be empowering and liberating — finding words to narrate significant life passages in the presence of attentive listeners who could analyse and reflect on the material would make visible dimensions of women's experience and theology that too often remained hidden or marginalized. Nelle Morton's phrase 'hearing into speech' (1985) rang true for me in my own feminist theological journey, and I knew it resonated with many of my friends and colleagues too. But as my research progressed my understanding of the process developed; my reading interacted with my experiences of participant-observation and interviewing in an action-reflection cycle, raising methodological questions that invited me to explore issues of interpretation, validity, reflexivity and theological reflection.

Hearing the Stories

My approach to hearing the stories drew on the techniques of ethnographic fieldwork combined with what practical theologians have begun to call 'reflective practice' (Lyall 2001). I gathered data on twelve case studies of women's ritual, through a combination of interviews and participant observation. Some of the women told me their stories of rituals they had enacted in the past, describing the circumstances surrounding them, and sharing their subsequent reflections on the meaning and significance. Sometimes I was invited to be a participant in the ritual group; on these occasions I drew on journal entries made immediately afterwards, and a subsequent interview with the woman who had created and enacted the ritual. On other occasions I was invited to help plan the ritual, and then I was able to accompany the woman concerned through the whole process, sharing in the planning, participating in the ritual itself, and reflecting on it in interview afterwards. In addition, I have interviewed women who work with others in creating ritual through spirituality, art or drama; I have recorded observations and snatches of conversation in my research journal; I have participated in and written 'thick descriptions' (Geertz 1973) of rituals in conventional church settings, conferences, workshops, and circle-dancing networks; and I have regularly participated in, planned and led rituals on a variety of themes for a group of women meeting monthly. The overall effect has been that I have immersed myself in the theme of women's ritual, and the different observations, interviews and conversations form a patchwork of women's experiences, pieced together in a pattern shaped by my interpretation and understanding.

I found interviewing easy and relaxed. In line with Ann Oakley's early article (1990; [1981]) on feminist research, which challenged the objective, positivist approach in which the interviewer remains strictly neutral, I aimed to establish an equal, mutual relationship. The research interview is a co-construction of knowledge, in which researcher and participant collaborate in seeking to produce understanding. Hospitality played a great part in the process; most of my interviews took place in a home setting (mine or the participant's) and were usually accompanied by at least a cup of coffee, and I found that in most cases our prior knowledge of one another and shared theological background created trust and eased communication. I found also that most participants enjoyed talking about their rituals and the events that surrounded them, and that the process of conversation helped to shape their own understanding:

> I think it has been really good actually that you've come to do this
> [interview]...And it has been quite a good experience to sort of

remember and think about why, and what my hopes were, and again
I think that's part of that awareness I carry forward (Interview, Andrea).

Feminist writers such as Ann Oakley (1990), Janet Finch (1993)
and Maxine Birch (1998) all argue for the importance of genuine
empathy and the establishment of trust. The creation of rapport is
not about an effective interview technique, but a genuine interest
in and engagement with, and attempt to understand the life
experiences of an other. Kathleen Gerson and Ruth Horowitz argue
that successful in-depth interviewing requires the ability to create
trust and mutual commitment within a relatively brief time-span,
and draw parallels with therapeutic conversation:

> Indeed, the intensive, in-depth interview more closely resembles the
> therapeutic interview of clinical practice than the highly controlled,
> closed-ended questionnaire used in social surveys...The best interviews
> become a conversation between two engaged people, both of whom
> are searching to unravel the mysteries and meanings of a life (Gerson
> and Horowitz 2002: 210).

I find the parallels with therapeutic interviews helpful to a point—
as a counsellor trained in the person-centred tradition my listening
skills were an asset, but at times I felt afterwards that more pro-
active questioning might have been helpful; and I had to remind
myself of appropriate boundaries if I were not to follow paths that
would take me too far into personal exploration of the events that
led to the ritual rather than focusing on the ritual process itself.

In telling their stories, women are constructing their experience
and meaning; their stories are socially-located, and what can be
said depends upon the concrete and material realities of their lives,
as well as the dominant social or cultural discourses. Stevi Jackson
makes the point that no story-telling recounts 'raw experience' (1998:
48). Stories have political implications, and can confirm or challenge
the status quo:

> Some narratives can be seen as supportive of the existing *status quo*;
> others have subversive potential. Hence narratives can be an arena of
> political struggle (1998: 60).

Telling the stories of women's experiences is not necessarily
liberating in and of itself; they may be told in such a way that they
reinforce gender stereotypes. Women may tell stories of passion
and romance which conform to heterosexual ideals of love and
marriage; or stories of abuse and violence which reinforce notions

of patience and submission. It is the way in which women's stories are told and interpreted to challenge or subvert conventional norms — what Riet Bons-Storm (1996) calls the dominant psychological or socio-cultural narratives — that makes them politically empowering.

Most of the women who participated in my research are educated at least to graduate level, many with an academic background in theology. As women who are consciously and intentionally creating their own rituals, they tend to be articulate and imaginative, and with a strongly-developed sense of self-awareness and expression. Many, though not all, are practising Christians, and most have some awareness of feminist perspectives, whether or not they would define themselves as feminist. Their stories, as told to me in interview, are therefore constructed within that framework; and their interpretation of their own experience often carries, quite consciously, that bias. Clare, for example, expresses her own sense of ambivalence and marginality in relation to her academic work, her ministry, and her work within a local community:

> And again the feeling in the thesis was very much being on the edge of the academic community and needing to conform to a certain amount but still be different. And I think I'm still very much in that place of being a minister and being on the edge of what those churches would recognize as ministry or as Christianity, and actually feeling that's the place I think I'm meant to occupy. But also being on the edge of community in terms of bridging the gaps between the powers in the community and the local people (Interview, Clare).

Moreover, the experience which women are recounting to me is not only of the life-events they have experienced, but of the rituals which they have created. As I shall argue later, the ritual itself is a story, a construction and interpretation of experience, so what I am hearing in an interview is often not only a story, but a story of a story, a reflection on and interpretation of a construction of experience that has already been shaped in a conscious and intentional way.

Just as Oakley and other feminist writers have challenged the traditional notion of objective, neutral interviewing, so they have called into question the notion that the researcher must remain distant and detached. The naturalistic paradigm of research (Lincoln and Guba 1985) recognizes the importance of the person of the researcher as an 'instrument', but feminist writers take the argument much further in developing the idea of the importance of the relationship between researcher and researched.

Traditional views on research stressed that the researcher must remain detached and distant in order to retain critical distance. Even in ethnography, where it is necessary for the anthropologist to immerse her/himself in the field, and to form relationships of trust and empathy with key informants, there are concerns about establishing too close a relationship. Hammersley and Atkinson whilst arguing for a naturalistic paradigm, reflexivity and an acknowledgement of the role of the researcher as research instrument, nonetheless argue:

> Ethnographers, then, must strenuously avoid feeling "at home". If and when all sense of being a stranger is lost, one may have allowed the escape of one's critical, analytic perspective (1995: 239).

Whilst coming as a 'stranger' into a situation may have the advantage of critical distance, for me this was outweighed by the benefits of mutual collaboration which grew out of relationships of trust and personal involvement. Amanda Coffey (1999) argues that the portrayal of the task of ethnography as that of a stranger gaining entry into the field, gradually gaining enough familiarity and immersion to facilitate accurate understanding and representation, whilst maintaining an appropriate professional and critical distance is a 'pedagogical simplification' (1999: 20) that does not do justice to the complexities of negotiating relationships and one's own identity in a demanding, embodied, emotional process:

> Our own sense of personhood—which will include age, race, gender, class, history, sexuality—engages with the personalities, histories and subjectivities of others present in the field. Our own subjective personality is part of the research and is negotiated within the field (Coffey 1999: 57).

In practice, feminist researchers take up a variety of positions along a continuum between observation and full participation (Reinharz 1992). On the whole, the trend is for feminist ethnographers to value genuine relationality which builds friendships and has the potential to change their own understandings and consciousness:

> In general, feminist participant observation values openness to intimacy and striving for empathy, which should not be confused with superficial friendliness. Rather it means openness to complete

transformation. This transformation—or consciousness-raising—lays
the groundwork for friendship, shared struggle, and identity change
(Reinharz 1992: 68).

For some, particularly those seeking to understand a religious
belief or value system, it is only complete immersion, or initiation
into the tradition, which can give genuine understanding. In the
Journal of Feminist Studies in Religion Karen McCarthy Brown
describes how she moved from her training in the 'importance of
objectivity and value-free interpretation' (1985: 77) to a more active
engagement with, and eventual initiation into, Haitian Voudou. She
developed a feminist methodology incorporating empathy and a
willingness to trust her own intuition. She challenges the
conventional assumptions of her training, that a religious system
can only be studied with objective neutrality and implicitly raises
the question as to whether, in fact, participation is a prerequisite
for authentic understanding and interpretation.

In choosing the topic for my research, I consciously wanted to
explore something that was relevant to my own context as a feminist
liturgist and contextual theologian, rather than exploring a 'foreign'
(in a literal or metaphorical sense) field. My writing therefore has
many parallels to educational, social, or health research, located in
the researcher's own professional or occupational setting. I began
my search for participants amongst my own friends, colleagues and
networks; and although this widened out a little, the constraints of
part-time research and the limited opportunities for travel, plus
the nature of the field itself (feminist theology in Britain is a small
world!) meant that very few of my participants were strangers to
me; and those who were relatively unknown at the beginning for
the most part became friends as we shared the stories of their rituals.
This has given me a foundation of shared knowledge which would
not have been accessible to me so easily if, for example, I had
attempted to examine Jewish or Hindu ritual. It has allowed trust
to be established quickly, providing a foundation for deeper
sharing of personal information, beliefs and convictions. The basis
of this research, then, has not been the distance of the stranger,
but the 'at home-ness' of interviews based on close personal
relationships characterized as far as possible by mutuality and
equality, and observation in which I am fully a participant and
sometimes practitioner.

In all of this the aim of hearing others' stories has remained, although with a far greater awareness of the complexities of that process. Practically, though, I had to place limits on my research and there are some stories that have not been heard. I chose to focus on rituals created and enacted by women—so there are no stories here of men's rituals, or those of heterosexual couples (although there are many creative and exciting ones I have heard of). Most of my participants are from the Christian tradition, or if not professing Christians, have some cultural awareness of Christianity. Whilst there are some who would not claim any religious label, there are no participants from major world religions such as Judaism, Islam or Hinduism. All of my participants are white—and while I could claim that this 'just happened', that would be naïve—it is much more likely that it reflects the white middle-class dominance within church, academy and Western feminist theology. Thus, whilst the 'at-home-ness' of this research has many strengths, I have to recognize also that it lacks something of the tension and ambivalence of engagement with the strangeness of 'the other' which characterizes some ethnographic writing. This book emerges out of a process of research carried out in my own setting and context, lived out alongside a full-time teaching post and attempts to maintain friendship networks and relationships; often it felt fragmented, seizing opportunities, squeezed into odd snatches of time; at the same time it was never wholly absent from my day-to-day life, but grounded in my daily activities and integrated with my relationships and feminist theological/spiritual practice.

Interpreting the Stories

As I have listened to women's stories, I have become aware of my own perspective not only in hearing, but in representing them. It is impossible to tell or retell a story, or describe a culture, or give an account of religious beliefs or value systems, without some interpretation—there is no such thing as simply telling the story.

The term 'thick description' was used by Clifford Geertz (1973) to convey his understanding that any anthropological description included interpretation. Geertz, however, is still working with what is basically a modernist assumption that it is possible to give a realistic and accurate account, albeit an interpreted one, of what has taken place. In postmodern writing on ethnography there is a considerable shift, which places much more emphasis on the production of the written account than on accurate and realistic observation. The publication of the anthology *Writing Culture* (Clifford and Marcus [ed.], 1986) shifted the focus within the discipline from the concern with accurate representation of another culture to the nature of ethnographic texts themselves and the process of producing them. *Writing Culture* placed much more emphasis on the way in which knowledge was gained, and the role of the ethnographer in writing and producing a representation of the culture s/he had studied. Ethnographic texts were seen not as realist representations of other cultures but as 'inherently partial—committed and incomplete' (1986: 7).

Ethnography is not so much a naturalistic account of an alien culture, but a story of the ethnographer's journey into new territory. How that journey is begun, the feelings that it evokes, the tools and techniques that are used to convey it to the reader, become the focus of the ethnographic writing. Ethnography is telling a story, and the way in which that story is constructed and told becomes the object of scrutiny. The two dimensions of fieldwork, the scientific observation of another culture as if in a laboratory, and the personal impact on the ethnographer undergoing a personal rite of passage, exist together in an uneasy tension of objective and subjective; postmodern ethnography is beginning to pay more attention to the latter:

> The new tendency to name and quote informants more fully and to introduce personal elements into the text is altering ethnography's discursive strategy and mode of authority. Much of our knowledge about other cultures must now be seen as contingent, the problematic outcome of intersubjective dialogue, translation, and projection (Clifford 1986: 109).

This inevitably raises questions of authority. In another article (Clifford 2003) Clifford examines issues of authority in the postmodern approach to ethnography. Authority no longer resides in the public and professional validation of the fieldworker, whose scientific observation and analysis have enabled him or her to get to the 'facts' of the culture. Authority is now seen in multi-layered ways, as a negotiation between experience and interpretation, involving both researcher and researched, their locations, experiences, relationships, and politics. It is the production of that written text which creates or constructs the culture, and the process of that production needs to be the subject of analysis and critique:

> It [textualization] is the process through which unwritten behavior, speech, beliefs, and traditions or ritual, come to be marked as a corpus, a potentially meaningful ensemble separated out from an immediate discursive or performative situation (Clifford 2003: 132)

Writing Culture was seen as marking a ground-breaking turn in ethnography, but was also criticized at the time of its publication for its exclusion of feminist perspectives. James Clifford's justification of this shows all the elitism of a male-dominated academy: the book grew out of an advanced seminar with limited participation, and there were no women writing in sufficiently innovative and experimental ways. The hidden agenda of 'old boys' networks' which work to exclude women is acknowledged, but with no attempt to discuss the underlying political implications:

> The seminar was small and its formation ad hoc, reflecting our specific personal and intellectual networks, our limited knowledge of appropriate work in progress. (I shall not go into individual personalities, friendships, and so forth, though they are clearly relevant.) (Cliffford 1986: 20).

According to Clifford's own argument, if ethnographic text is an allegory, referring to other stories, a construct influenced by political, cultural, and socio-economic factors, then it seems his analysis of the production of text needs to go much further in examining gender issues, alongside other forms of exclusion and marginalization. What is not said, and the process by which it is omitted, is as significant as the finished text.

A feminist critique of the experimental ethnography of Clifford and others is offered by Kamala Visweswaran (1994). First, whilst she welcomes their emphasis on the personal and subjective writing of ethnographic writing, she argues that they ignore earlier work of women writing 'confessional field literature'; these first-person narratives questioned positivist assumptions, and exposed the disjunctions and misunderstandings of fieldwork in a way that pre-dates experimental ethnography — they were radical before their time, but marginalized because they did not fit the accepted genre of fieldwork studies. Second, whilst Clifford claims ethnography as a co-production or construction of culture, he pays little attention to the voice of 'the other', whether 'woman' or 'native', and does not analyse or critique patriarchal authority. It is in the storied form of novels by writers such as Hurston and Deloria that we find an analysis of power between cultures that is absent from much ethnographic writing:

> These 'anthropological novels' address relationships of power not only within culture, but also between cultures, something the bulk of ethnography, experimental or otherwise, has been slow to undertake (1994: 38-39).

Since the publication of *Writing Culture* others have argued that since ethnography is recounting and constructing lived embodied experience, the representation of that needs to be embodied too, and so speak of the performative nature of ethnography. Dwight Conquergood argues against the dualistic separation of theoretical and bodily knowledge, and for an understanding of ethnography as embodied performance rather than the simple collection of data:

> The performance paradigm privileges particular, participatory, dynamic, intimate, precarious, embodied experience grounded in historical process, contingency, and ideology (2003: 363).

The performance of ethnography moves further from being a straightforward reporting of observations into an intersubjective dialogue with the subjects of ethnography. As such, it can never be neutral, but is a political and potentially transformative activity:

> Because subjectivity is formed through a range of discursive practices — economic, social, aesthetic, and political — and meanings are sites of creation and struggle, subjectivity linked to performance becomes a poetic and polemic admixture of personal experience, cultural politics, social power, and resistance (Madison 2005: 174).

The process of writing or performance, then, does not simply express what the observer has witnessed and understood, but helps to construct or shape reality; it is a performance that is co-created between researcher and participants.

> Cultural performances range from plays and operas to circus acts, carnivals, parades, religious services, poetry readings, weddings, funerals, graduations, concerts, toasts, jokes, and story telling. In all these examples, self-conscious and symbolic acts are presented and communicated within a circumscribed space. Meaning and affect are generated by embodied action that produces a heightened moment of communication (Madison 2005: 154).

There is a performative dimension to ritual, not necessarily in the sense that it is staged for an audience (although this may apply to some rituals) but in the performing of embodied actions which focus and carry much of the meaning. This performative dimension is particularly difficult to convey in written text; verbal descriptions of action, movement and symbol can easily seem flat and lifeless. My retelling of the story of the performance of a ritual is like taking the script and attempting to recreate the subjective meanings, significances and nuances that give colour, shape and vitality to the performance. At the same time I interweave my own interpretation of and response to the rituals described, with the awareness that I am telling and performing my own story as well as those of the research participants; and that my own understanding and practice shapes not only 'what happened', but how that is recorded, retold, and embodied in the act of writing.

Re-presenting the Women's Stories

Retelling the stories of women's rituals is not a straightforward matter. In my journal I attempted to write 'thick descriptions' of rituals I attended, being as accurate and realistic as memory allows. At the same time I know that, even at that stage, I was interpreting; what I remembered was selective, depending on what struck me as significant, or moved me emotionally, at the time. As a participant observer, I know that my presence and agency consciously and unconsciously shaped some of the rituals themselves. In some instances I was invited to help construct the rituals by the women themselves. Sometimes this was a conscious element in the initial negotiation; my skills and creativity were made available, and I would gain material for my research—one woman felt less guilty about taking up my time because she knew my research would benefit from the process:

> I mean, I'm just so grateful to you for—I know you're going to use it for your research—but for the time that went into it, the creativity that's here, I think it's just brilliant (Interview, Jackie).

So the rituals in which I shared in the planning were very much a joint performance, and that process of interpretation is carried through into my retelling of the story.

Where I did not participate in the rituals, but simply heard the story in interview, my own interpretation and agency was less immediate; nevertheless, in the process of recording, transcribing, selecting material for inclusion in the research, I was already interpreting—even before I began any conscious analysis of the data. In transcribing material from tapes, the way I punctuated a participant's speech, the number of 'ums', 'you knows', and pauses I included in my written transcript, the material I selected to quote, and any 'tidying-up' of speech in quoting material reflected my own interpretative choices.

There is therefore a process of interpretation at work in the production of data; the observing and recording, the transcribing and editing, the selecting and quoting, all reflect my bias, and my way of hearing and telling others' stories. In telling the women's stories I am telling my own; the challenge is to be aware of that process of interpretation, and to own it; to recognize the fictional and constructed nature of my accounts, and to explore and make transparent the process of co-construction that leads to a written text.

The stories of women's rituals which I heard form a kind of undercurrent throughout the book. Some of them are told in detail, others provide the data for analysis. But I want to introduce the stories here, giving a brief description of the circumstances and context, and the symbolic actions used in each case.[1]

A number of the rituals relate to various kinds of endings; three of them specifically to redundancy. Alison was a friend of mine who had been made redundant, after a difficult and stressful time at work. She wanted to mark the ending of her work, and invited me to help plan a ritual. She discussed some ideas with me, and then invited some of her close friends to a ritual in her home which she had constructed. She asked us to remove thirty silver coins, as symbols of the betrayal and disappointment she felt in the job, and in their place to light thirty candles as symbols of hope and justice. Rebecca was also made redundant, although her redundancy coincided with the beginning of a period of study. She felt the need for ritual to help her let go of a job she had loved, and which she had hoped to continue on a part-time basis whilst studying. She

1. A summary of this material, with the women's names listed alphabetically, can be found in table form in Appendix One.

held four rituals through the autumn, using leaves to symbolize letting-go in a variety of ways — burning them, burying them, dropping them in water, and finally releasing them on the wind. When Jane was made redundant, she felt angry and let down. She decided to lead a ritual in a group that met regularly to help her come to terms with her feelings. She discussed ideas with me beforehand, and focused on the symbol of the shell to represent the sense of identity she felt she had lost along with her job. Glass beads and fishes represented the positive aspects of work; all were placed in water and transformed by lighting a floating candle above them.

Another two rituals marked endings, but with a clear element of celebration and moving on. Clare was a doctoral student, who wanted a ritual to mark the completion of her thesis, feeling that traditional graduation would not meet her needs. She asked me to work with her in planning it, and we decided to tie knots in ribbons to symbolize feelings of struggle and ambivalence, then weaving them into a dreamcatcher. She invited the people who had supported her during the writing of the thesis to a ritual and a party in her home. Carol wanted to mark ten years in ministry, but the anniversary coincided with her departure from her pastorate without another post to go to. Although she discussed her feelings and ideas with me and chose the people she wanted to invite, she wanted me to plan the ritual and conduct it in my home. I felt it needed to include thanksgiving and celebration, which we symbolized with a mosaic made of coloured tiles to affirm her gifts, but also to acknowledge her pain in leaving and the uncertainty of her future.

Two of the rituals were house-blessings. Louise had built a new extension to her house; it had been a costly and disruptive process, and she felt the need of a blessing to 'redeem' it. We progressed through the house, with appropriate words for each room, and sprinkling water as a sign of blessing. She and I were both part of the group that shared in the ritual; later, Louise offered to be interviewed and sent me the notes she had made at the time. Andrea, too, wanted a house-blessing; she asked her local minister to lead it, and I was invited to be part of the group. We moved round the house, with words of blessing and small gifts in each room, finishing with Andrea's own commitment using words from the Methodist covenant service.

Another two rituals involved renaming. Jackie was a friend who asked me to help her plan a ritual marking her change of surname, after the ending of her marriage. We met together on three occasions to plan it, and the ritual itself included elements of letting go of the past, the making of her new name, and a symbolic movement into another room for the declaration of her name. I met Runa through circle dancing networks, and when she heard about my research, she offered to be interviewed about a ritual she had conducted earlier, taking a new name as she worked through and moved on from her experience of childhood abuse. She had gathered friends around her, and enacted a symbolic exchange of gifts representing different aspects of her identity.

The remaining three rituals related more closely to bodily passages and changes. Nicola, whom I have known for some time, responded to my request for research participants at a conference, and offered to be interviewed about a Eucharist she had celebrated just before her hysterectomy. I met Cora through one of my other research participants. She had experience of ritual work on sites sacred to the Goddess in Crete, and as a teacher of the five rhythm dance movement of Gabrielle Roth.[2] I met her and interviewed her about a ritual she was planning for her birthday the following day; but she also told me about a menopausal ritual she had shared in a year earlier. Circumstances meant that I was unable to return to interview her afterwards, but nevertheless the interview gave me much interesting material on ritual, from a somewhat different perspective from most of my participants. I had known Sue through women's networks for some years, and she agreed to be interviewed about a ritual she had arranged to mark her sixtieth birthday, and also sent me some of the written materials from it.

There is, of course, much overlapping of themes and material. In analysing the rituals I have tried to draw out common themes, and reflect on them in relation to theoretical work drawn from social anthropology and ritual studies. To a certain extent, however, this fragments the data and loses the integrity of each woman's voice. I would have liked to keep the data whole and present a coherent story in the form of a case study interwoven with interpretation for each woman—but this would have been too lengthy and

2. More details of Cora's work can be found on her website http://www.thirteenthmoon.f2s./com

repetitious. What I have done, therefore, is to introduce each of the next five chapters with a more detailed case study of one of the rituals, allowing the other stories to emerge as part of the overall reflection. The rituals I have chosen to describe in more detail are mainly those in which I have participated most fully, sharing in the planning, and attending (sometimes constructing) the ritual itself.

Telling Better Gendered Stories

As I have retold the women's stories, I have become increasingly conscious of the process of interpretation. However, the possibility of differing interpretations means that there needs to be some ground for choosing particular interpretations and an awareness of the process involved in doing so. Relativism and postmodern rejections of the idea of a meta-narrative raise questions for feminist methodology; and in the light of feminist ethics and politics, it is important that we have grounds for committing ourselves to one story over another:

> In general, however, feminists have wanted to distinguish between better and worse accounts of gendered lives, and so have needed to justify some form of systematic investigation, reasoned argument, and rules of method (Ramazanoğlu and Holland 2002: 37).

If stories are interpreted, then some interpretations have more positive implications for women than others. Feminists have sought to establish, if it is no longer appropriate to talk in terms of neutral objectivity, how we justify what is valid knowledge and choose between competing claims.

Donna Haraway recognizes the partiality of our vision, but does not accept that we should abandon all claims to objectivity and validity. She sees feminists as trying to climb a greasy pole, with objectivity at one end and relativism at the other. She critiques the tendency of feminists to privilege subjugated positions, claiming that no positions are 'innocent'. What is important is to recognize the particularity and situatedness of knowledge, for that is actually the best route to objectivity. The claim to universal knowledge and vision is, in fact, unsustainable — an illusion, the 'god-trick'. It is situatedness and particularity which form the foundation for objective claims to knowledge:

> I am arguing for politics and epistemologies of location, positioning
> and situating, where partiality and not universality is the condition of
> being heard to make rational knowledge claims. There are claims on
> people's lives; the view from a body, always a complex, contradictory,
> structuring and structured body versus the view from above, from
> nowhere, from simplicity (Haraway 1991: 195).

However, to assert the value of partial and subjugated knowledge
does not mean that we should abandon claims to objectivity and
validity, and feminist thinkers struggle to hold the two in tension.
Caroline Ramazanoğlu and Janet Holland suggest that rather than
the 'greasy pole' analogy, we should see feminist methodology as
a continuum, on which different writers position themselves in terms
of objectivity and relativism. Feminist researchers are dealing with
the political and social lived activities of women's experiences, and
it is important that we should be able to 'tell better stories of
gendered lives' (Ramazanoğlu and Holland, 2002: 106).

Feminist research may be seen as research about women's lives,
research conducted by women, or research which benefits women
in some way. For Liz Stanley and Sue Wise (1993), all three are
important. Research *on* women's lives has an important descriptive
function in filling in some of the gaps in existing knowledge of
women's lives; but it runs the risk of establishing a women's ghetto,
and is not necessarily, in and of itself, feminist. Feminist research
must be done *by* women, they argue; an essential element in feminist
research is feminist consciousness, rooted in the experience of being
female in a patriarchal society, and therefore not available to men.
Feminist research is not tied to any particular method, but lies in
the way of seeing and interpreting reality, and the relationship
between the researcher and researched:

> And while we see "feminism" as a particular way of seeing reality, we
> also feel that "feminist research" can be identified as something more
> than this. This "something more" is to be found in the nature of the
> relationship between the research and the researched, as well as in the
> researcher's own "feminist consciousness" and her experience of being
> a woman (1993: 44).

Finally, feminist research must be *for* women — it must be research
that in some way has positive and useful implications for women;
and whilst I agree that this is an important aim, I also consider it
the most problematic of the three.

Feminists engaged in action research argue for conscious partiality and a view 'from below', rather than the hierarchical perspective of a researcher who has power over the researched. For example, Maria Mies (1993) sets out positive methodological guidelines for feminist research, and describes her attempt to apply these in a project undertaken by an action group setting up a house for women who had experienced domestic violence. She argues that feminist research must be rooted in a desire for change and be an active part of a political movement or struggle; the research process must be a process of conscientization for both researcher and researched (1993: 68-73). Mies' principles clearly fit her action research project and arise from her political agenda. However, feminist research will not always be a conscious-raising process, nor can it always be clear that research is directly related to a particular movement for change. To argue that the search for knowledge must always begin with a desire for change in the status quo seems to imply a predetermined outcome of research which detracts from its exploratory open-ended character. Therefore, although many feminists would want to go along with some of Mies' criteria, they cannot all be applied to all feminist research.

There is clearly a political agenda to feminist research, in that it arises from a particular value system, and as such it is liable to be criticized for its lack of objectivity by those who fail to acknowledge that all research and knowledge has a bias (Helen Roberts 1990). Whilst I would agree that bias on the part of the researcher is inevitable, and that it is important to be clear about one's own agenda, the principle that feminist research should be of benefit and value to women raises difficulties in practice. Firstly, if research is an open-ended and interactive process, it is impossible to predict its results; and to attempt to do so seems to be to prejudge the outcome of the research in a way which compromises a genuine spirit of inquiry. Secondly, the complexities of women's lives and social realities mean that it is impossible to talk in general terms of empowering women; the empowering of some may mean the continued oppression of others.

Another value or principle that is held by many feminists is that as far as possible there should be a sense of equality and mutuality between the feminist researcher and the research participants. The idea of the researcher as the expert in a hierarchical relationship, possessing knowledge and information which she withholds from her participants is one which many feminists resist (e.g. Oakley 1990, Helen Roberts 1990). Roberts, for example argues that feminist research should be readily presented in ways that can be understood by those who do not have a formal academic background, and in particular by less powerful groups who are the participants in research projects. However, while this is important, feminists also need to be able to negotiate and claim status within the academic community; and so are caught within the tension and ambivalence of establishing credibility in academic terms on the one hand, while remaining accessible to those who have less educational background.

I am in sympathy with the position of DeVault (1999) who argues that while earlier feminist writers stressed the importance of collaboration and equal partnership with participants, this is not always possible and realistic, and that there is a danger of feminist researchers setting themselves impossibly high standards in a kind of quest for moral purity. Therefore she has a possibly lower, but more attainable goal of ensuring that participants are not harmed by the research, and have as much control as is possible and feasible given the circumstances. She envisages the voice of the author as:

> a voice that is thoughtful and self-reflective. I imagine a voice that is not imposingly authoritative, but clear and personal—the voice of an author who invites others to listen and respond, aiming more toward dialogue than debate. My aim is to write about others carefully, in both senses of the word—with rigor and with empathic concern (DeVault 1999: 190).

In my own research, I attempted to apply some of these principles. I focused specifically on a particular area of women's lives (in this case their theology and practice of ritual) and sought to make visible areas of life often excluded or marginalized. I listened and interpreted from a feminist theological perspective, believing that the situated knowledge and partial perspective of feminist methodology is consistent with the principles of contextual or liberation theology.

One issue that confronts many feminist researchers is that they are often working with material that is personal and private. If this is to be used in research, then there are issues involved in making public knowledge, emotions and perspectives that are often hidden. This can confront the researcher with a dilemma; on the one hand, there is the objective of making visible what has often been hidden and marginalized; on the other, the dominance of public and/or academic knowledge is extended further into personal and social life:

> The central dilemma for us as researchers is that we are seeking to explore such privately based knowledges and personal understandings, but to then reconstitute them within publicly based disciplinary knowledge. In doing so, are we extending the dominance of publicly based knowledges and expertise, and colluding into its intrusion into every nook and cranny of social life? (Edwards and Ribbens 1998: 13).

However, the feminist dictum that the 'personal is political' means that there can be no rigid distinction between personal and public; feminist researchers have to be prepared to work with blurred boundaries of what is private and public, and to tolerate some ambiguity and tension into bringing hidden aspects of women's lives into more public arenas.

The tension of making public what is private is present in my research. The rituals which the women describe often carry this tension within themselves. They are semi-private, often with a few specifically-chosen guests; and yet they are bringing personal events and emotions into a more public arena. In talking and writing about those occasions, not only the rituals, but the events that lie behind them, become more public and visible. I offered my participants the chance to use pseudonyms to protect their identities — some accepted this, others chose to keep their own names as part of the process of telling their stories. But even where pseudonyms are used, I am aware that feminist theological circles are relatively small, and some participants may be identified by others — although probably only by those who know them well, and have already heard something of the story.

Another major area of concern to feminist researchers is that of reflexivity, or the use of the self in research. Stanley and Wise (1993) argue strongly that, as feminist research is based on feminist consciousness and a relationship between researcher and the research participants, the person of the researcher is crucial to the process. This awareness needs to be made evident in the research, and the feelings, reactions, and processes of the researcher made an explicit subject of the research.

The research process is not simply the gathering of data to construct and retell the experience of others, but a process which involves the researcher's own identity at every level, and acts as a process of construction of the self:

> What is central ... is the recognition that fieldwork is personal, emotional and identity *work*. The production of self and identity occurs both during and after fieldwork. In writing, remembering and representing our fieldwork experiences we are involved in processes of self presentation and identity construction (Coffey 1999: 1).

This is demanding work, and requires an awareness of our own histories to enable us to listen sensitively and effectively to the stories of others. While I would not go as far as Walkerdine *et al.* (2002) in arguing that the researcher needs an awareness of psycho-analytic concepts of transference and counter-transference in order to understand her own reactions and emotions adequately, I do believe that reflexivity, far from being a self-indulgent personal outpouring, demands a high degree of self-awareness and emotional discipline:

> We suggest that far from opening up the simple confessional, an engagement with emotions and unconscious processes is absolutely crucial for understanding not only how multiple subjectivities are held together, but also the tricky place of emotions, ours and the participants, within the research process (Walkerdine *et al.* 2002: 193-94).

Although reflexivity has become a major emphasis in feminist (and other forms of qualitative) research, often little attention is paid to the process of self-analysis, including an analysis of the researcher's own social location and politics, and that of the participants in the research. Beverley Skeggs argues that the ability to reflect on self is a cultural resource that is taken for granted in academic circles, but is not available to everyone, and therefore there is the potential for a considerable power differential between researcher and participants:

> The skills which are accessed through research, produced through reflexivity and authorized through writing are the means by which the research self comes to be formed and known...The ability to be reflexive via the experience of others is a privilege, a position of mobility and power, a mobilization of cultural resources (2002: 361).

Reflexivity should be seen not as a self-indulgent reflection, but a critical analysis of the process and an acceptance of responsibility and accountability to others.

Several researchers stress the potential power differential between researcher and participants. This is particularly the case when there are differences in social location, education, or economic resources. Because many of the participants were friends, colleagues, or members of a peer group, I did not feel conscious of a strong power differential in the research. Ann Gray, however, points out that some researchers can feel anything but powerful:

> The raft of belief and self-worth, therefore, must be constructed and reconstructed daily in order that the research can continue and develop, that the next interview be set up or that the word processor can be faced. It is often extremely difficult, in these circumstances, to identify with or see ourselves as the "all powerful researcher" figure posited by critiques of research politics (Ann Gray 1995: 155).

In the early stages of my research, I was very conscious of the educational and academic achievements of some of my participants, and could identify with the sense of vulnerability expressed by Gray! Part of the reflexivity of the research process was my awareness of my own identity as a researcher, and my own growth in confidence both in the coherence of my research project and my own ability and motivation to carry it out. But however vulnerable I may have felt at times, I am aware that there is still a power of interpretation invested in the researcher — however much I seek to represent my participants accurately, seek feedback from them, co-operate with them in the research, the final process of interpretation rests with me. I hope and believe that this is a collaborative process, but am also aware that that collaboration can only go so far; in the end what I make of their material is my responsibility, and writing is powerful.

Throughout my working with this material the idea of reflexivity is one that has excited and moved me. Research, for me, is about personal involvement, and my awareness of my own position, reactions and development, is crucial. I became personally involved with the women whose rituals I shared, and entered into the stories of others. I found my own ideas developing as I listened to others' stories, and even more so as I retold and rewrote them, finding the writing process itself to be an important tool in reflexivity. In my journal, and in work-in-progress papers that I wrote, it was as I found words that my analysis and ideas took shape — writing is a constructive process. In preparing to talk about the research process in a seminar at Glasgow I wrote:

> Writing—helps me focus—don't know what I think until I write it—
> writing for me formative process rather than summative (Journal entry
> 14.12.04).

Trying to tell better gendered stories became an exploration of
my understanding of feminist theory, a reflection on my own context
and location, a developing awareness of my own identity within
the research process, and an integration of research experience,
theory and theology.

A God's-Eye View

Donna Haraway uses the phrase 'the god-trick' for the illusion that
it is possible to have an objective, overall view of truth. In the closing
section of this chapter I want to explore the connections between
method and theology, arguing that the feminist methodology
described above is consistent with a feminist liberation theology.

The discipline of practical theology is increasingly drawing on
social science for its tools and methods but the connections between
methodology and theology are rarely made, although the publication
of *Practical Theology and Qualitiative Research* (Swinton and Mowat
2006) begins to address some of the issues. Similarly, while gender
issues often have a high profile in secular disciplines, Ursula King
and Tina Beattie (2005) argue that they are often ignored in
theological studies:

> There exists what I call a *double blindness*: on one hand most
> contemporary gender studies, whether in the humanities, social
> sciences or natural sciences, remain extraordinarily "religion-blind";
> on the other hand many studies in religion continue to be profoundly
> *"gender-blind"* (King and Beattie (ed.), 2005: 1-2).

Nevertheless, particularly in the disciplines of practical theology
and feminist theology, there are connections to be made. Themes
of interpretive story-telling and the disclosive nature of experience
and practice are developed in practical theology and congregational
studies.

In his work on congregational studies James Hopewell (1987),
argues that an effective way of describing and interpreting the life
of a congregation is to find and tell the story that 'fits' their self-
understanding. As he makes his argument, he interweaves his study
of congregations with his own story of serious illness. The categories

of stories which he chooses to use (comic, tragic, ironic and romantic) are taken from literary criticism, and his stories are drawn mainly from Greek and Roman mythology. A postmodern approach would probably be much more eclectic in its use of stories, and less inclined to look for over-arching themes; nevertheless in Hopewell's work we see a use of interpretation through retelling of stories, and something of the reflexivity of the writer found in feminist methodologies.

A similar approach is taken by Leonora Tisdale (1997) in her work on 'exegeting the congregation'. She describes how in her own congregational ministry she moves from traditional biblical exegesis to a determination to preach in a way that takes seriously the experiences and stories of her congregation. She uses a much wider range of story and popular culture than Hopewell, arguing that for many congregations their stories may be drawn from films, novels or even songs. But again, it is often in story that a congregation's experience, conviction and theology can best be expressed, interpreted or constructed.

The notion of 'thick description' originating with Geertz is taken up by Don Browning in his account of practical theology. He argues for a process of critical correlation—of movement from practice to theory and back to practice again. Theology has four dimensions; the descriptive, the historical, the systematic, and the strategic or fully practical. Descriptive theology consists of thick description of practice which gives rise to theological questions in a way analogous to social science research:

> Cultural anthropology and ethnography are extremely useful for uncovering the interplay of the narratives, signs and symbols that make up the visional and cultural dimensions of practical theology and action (Browning 1991: 122).

In Browning's method, the questions raised in this way are placed in juxtaposition with the historical Christian tradition and systematic themes to arrive at a theology which is fully 'strategic' or practical. In its attempt to create systematic categories, Browning's scheme imposes a framework on the material that loses something of its immediacy; but his recognition of the importance of interpretive description and his insight that practice is a way into understanding ideas and theology is a key concept in the development of congregational studies. Practice is 'theory-laden' — by describing and interpreting practice we uncover underlying ideas and concepts that may not be fully articulated in words and dogma by the practitioners. Moreover, he has an understanding of reflexivity — the 'social location of the researcher is...an extremely important component of descriptive analysis in the larger practical theological task' (1991: 22). He rejects the positivist, detached view of research and sees it as a process which is dynamic and potentially transformative:

> Those proposing the hermeneutic view of descriptive research believe such detachment is impossible; both researcher and subjects are influenced and changed by the research itself (Browning 1991: 48).

Practice however, not only reveals and expresses theory, but may be seen as disclosing and shaping new insights and understandings. Elaine Graham looks at the three areas of feminist preaching, spirituality, and liturgy (using written texts rather than ethnographic observation) to examine claims that through privileging women's experience, feminist praxis provides a challenge to patriarchal values and assumptions (Graham 2002).

Such practices are not only disclosive in revealing practitioner's values and beliefs, but in their posing of an alternative and challenging the homogeneity of patriarchy, potentially transformative of the Christian tradition. Here again we see a rejection of neutrality in favour of a consciously chosen feminist perspective or standpoint.

The partial and committed nature of feminist methodology reflected in feminist standpoint theories and the situated knowledge of Donna Haraway has its parallels in liberation theology's 'bias to the poor' and its emphasis on the contextual nature of theology. Linell Cady (1997) draws attention to the construction of identity in a specific historic and social context, and argues that a contextual theology needs to take account of the multiple and shifting forces that shape people's lives. Mary Fulkerson makes explicit the parallels between feminist theory and liberation theologies:

> The argument of historical-material feminism that *standpoint,* or position in the social formation, is epistemologically significant is consonant with what liberation feminists mean by the positive work. Women's situation as the oppressed gives us a vantage on the failures of the system and is developed constructively in the fact that a positive bias *for* women helps to recuperate women's agency from accounts that render them invisible (Fulkerson 1994: 38).

There is little direct use of feminist theological method in liberation theology, but an interesting article by Mary Savage (2003) draws on her experience of liberation theology and the work of Paulo Freire in Nicaragua to argue that ethnography has a potentially transformative and liberating role to play:

> Neighborliness, then, is a child of praxis, a practical activity having a complex intellectual dimension, exercised for the sake of assisting the marginalized on a journey toward greater freedom and participation in common life (2003: 342).

Mary Fulkerson (1994) argues for a feminist liberation epistemology that takes seriously postmodern understandings of the construction of identity. She argues that feminist theology needs to move beyond liberal theories of the autonomous self, and recognize the construction of the subject. The diversity of women's experience must be recognized, and we need to move beyond inclusion to the transformation of structures. She proposes five characteristics of a liberationist epistemology. First, there is need for a hermeneutic of suspicion in any use of the theological tradition, recognizing that it can be either oppressive or liberating. Second, theology is never politically neutral, and the connections between theology and economic, cultural and social interests must be noted. Knowledge must not be reified as an ultimate vision, but seen as a production within the concrete and material realities of life. There is a need to recognize multiple layers of oppression and the possibilities for change; and finally the constructed nature of the self in its social location must be taken seriously. Such an epistemology, she argues, is rooted in an understanding of the limitations of theology and a dependence on God's grace for our salvation; not in any triumphalist way, but in a way that acknowledges and works with the brokenness of human relating:

> What is clear about feminist theological practice is that it takes up a calling or vocation to support the vision of God's realm as a realm of justice in light of which social arrangements of hierarchy and domination, whether of gender relations, race or other forms of human togetherness, must be resisted and transformed (1994: 25).

Nicola Slee, (2004a), whose research on women and faith development is theological and educational, draws on similar principles in expounding the principles underlying her methodology. Slee argues that research should be grounded in women's experience, but recognizing the impact of diverse forms of feminism and of deconstructionism, she also stresses the importance of listening for difference. She carries out her research within a commitment to liberating and empowering women, and along with many other feminist researchers stresses the importance of reflexivity.

Elaine Graham, Heather Walton and Frances Ward (2005) set out methods in theological reflection, arguing that while the term 'theological reflection' is much used, the process often suffers from insufficient engagement with biblical and historical tradition. Of the seven methods which they suggest, there are two that are closest to the methodologies I use here. Constructive narrative theology, with its emphasis on human experience and story has resonances with my desire to 'tell women's stories'; and theology in action, or praxis with its stress on the roots of theology in performed action, takes up the commitment to justice and bias towards the marginalized of liberation and feminist theologies.

There is therefore some overlap between feminist methodologies in the social sciences and approaches which have been developed in practical, feminist and liberation theologies. I have drawn on these sources to develop my own principles of a feminist theological methodology.

A Feminist Theological Methodology

As I progressed through my research, my own understanding of a methodology that is consistent with a feminist theology of liberation grew and developed. First, I am aware of the partiality and bias of my own interpretation. I have developed a feminist standpoint through working as an ordained woman in a patriarchal church and society, and I bring that perspective to my writing. Although I have a relatively privileged position, as a white woman with a university education and a full-time post in theological education, I also know the marginalization of being female in a male-dominated society, and lesbian in a heterosexist society and church. In Haraway's terms, then, my knowledge is 'situated' in my own social and theological location, and is both partial and committed. As a feminist I make no claims to objectivity and detachment; as a theologian I bring a confessional stance which is based on my conviction of a God/Goddess immanent in the world and human activity, and of Gospel values of liberation and justice.

I began with a desire to 'tell women's stories'. While I still believe that I should tell those stories as faithfully as I am able, as part of my accountability to the women who have shared in my research, I am now much more aware of the complexities of such retelling. There can be no story without interpretation, both the interpretations of the narrators themselves, and my own interpretation as I listen, record, and retell. I am conscious that, in Ramazanoğlu and Holland's phrase, one of my objectives is to 'tell better stories of gendered lives'. In an aim that is consistent with liberation theology's bias to the poor, I want to tell stories that make a difference to women, that if possible are empowering and liberating, and at the very least do not cause harm, shame or even embarrassment to the women who have participated in my research or to other potential readers. While I would like to claim that my research will be of value to women, research, like all human social practice, is an intersubjective process with no predictable or guaranteed outcome. I write in the belief—or hope—that anything which makes visible the realities of women's lives in a patriarchal church and society, and which strengthens the awareness of women's creativity, must contribute to empowering and liberating them.

Third, I maintain a conscious awareness of my own experience and process in the research. I am aware of my involvement in empathy, often in friendship, with the women whose stories I tell. I trace my own role and development, aware that this is a journey and a process in which I learn and change as I engage with others, through interview, observation, and written texts. I am aware that while I cannot predict, much less guarantee the outcomes of my research, I want it to be of liberating value to women. I am aware of what Beverley Skeggs (1995) has called the messiness of ethnography, with its mixture of realism, interpretation, and intersubjectivity; and the messiness of my own research, with its loose ends, its fragmentation and opportunism. For me this echoes with incarnational theology, in which God/dess is embodied in the material and concrete realities of women's lives, experiences, and struggles for justice.

I have discovered that many of the themes of my methodology are mirrored in the research itself, and recur later in my analysis of and reflection on the material I have gathered. Just as I have wrestled with my role in telling and interpreting women's stories, so their rituals form an enacted narrative that tells and interprets their stories, constructing their identity in relation to their context and relationships. As feminist methodology becomes aware of making private knowledge public and visible, so the rituals in this study negotiate the tension between private and public. As I seek to find a methodology that is embodied both in women's lives and in my own interpretation, so these rituals embody and perform a theology of a God rooted in women's bodily actions and transitions. There is a coherence between methodology and the feminist theology and spirituality emerging from women's practice of making ritual. It is a methodology and theology that is fully in keeping with the story of a God committed to the poor and marginalized, risking all the messiness of incarnation.

Case Study One

LETTING GO AND MOVING ON — CAROL'S STORY

Carol is a friend whom I first met some years ago through networks of women ministers. She has a creative approach to ministry and worship, loving to use colour, poetry and music. Like many creative women, she has sometimes struggled with the institutional church that can threaten to stifle creativity with bureaucracy and meetings, and be resistant to change and innovation. Nevertheless, her leadership of worship and her pastoral sensitivity are appreciated by many in her congregations and beyond.

Carol first talked about wanting to do something to mark ten years in the ministry, although she was uncertain what form this would take:

> I know I'd had it in mind for a long time that when — if — I reached ten years in ministry I wanted to mark it in some way...Whether it was with a few people, or a short service at church, that would actually just be mindful of that — that ministry and me had been living together for ten years (Interview, Carol).

As events unfolded, however, the ten year anniversary coincided with Carol coming to the end of her appointment, without a clear direction for her future ministry. The significant date went by unmarked except by a few friends and family, and the focus instead was on the process of leaving and saying goodbye:

> The getting to 10 years faded into a degree of insignificance — I was a bit shy of — in fact I never mentioned it to the churches...I didn't feel it was the right thing to be focusing on and we were actually focusing on leaving so it wasn't — it wouldn't really have been a celebration any more (Interview, Carol).

It became clear, however, that for Carol there was a sadness and sense of loss about this lack of marking, which was undermining her already-fragile sense of confidence in herself and her ministry:

> Bit sad. Yes, as if it was sliding away — I did have to keep trying to remind myself it's ten years, it's actually ten years of life, isn't it, and

everything, and what had happened in those ten years was significant, it was OK, and it wasn't all a failure...because I didn't feel it was something to celebrate anymore. I did feel I'd failed—that I'd only just made the ten year point which may or may not have had some significance (Interview, Carol).

After a conversation in which I suggested that the uncertainty of the future might be a reason for doing a ritual rather than not, Carol decided she would like to go ahead with what might be a smaller, more informal occasion, and asked me to plan it for her. This was a rather different process for me—I was used to working with others on creating their ritual, but Carol simply wanted to leave it to me, and I was very conscious of the responsibility entrusted to me:

And I trusted you. I knew it would be—um—things would happen from it really. I didn't anticipate at all what it would be like—but that you'd make it happen...I knew it was going to happen, I was really looking forward to it, and I hadn't got anything to do (Interview, Carol).

After talking with Carol about her feelings, gaining some ideas of readings or poems that she would like, the shape of the ritual began to emerge for me:

So I can feel a shape of a ritual forming; some celebrating for past, grieving for loss, letting go, moving into unknown future—call of ministry still strong—but shape of it unclear (Journal entry, Carol's ritual).

The challenge in creating Carol's ritual was to recognize the complexity of her feelings; to acknowledge the sense of failure without reinforcing it, to celebrate her gifts and the contributions she had made in ministry, to affirm her sense of calling even though she had no clearly-defined ministry to move into, and to build her confidence as she faced an uncertain future.

The ritual was held in my home, at Carol's request, and I had arranged the room with purple cloths and candles in the centre. We began with a song and some opening responses, then moved into a time of celebrating ten years of Carol's ministry.

I produce cards and glue and newspaper from under the table, and invite people to stick coloured tiles on for the aspects of Carol's ministry that we want to celebrate (Journal entry, Carol's ritual).

This became a sharing of people's own stories and memories, as they talked of Carol's friendship, her generosity of spirit, her ability to enable others to make music, her support in times of difficulty. It resulted in a colourful and random mosaic of tiles, and at the end Carol too joined in, thanking her friends for their support of her. We joined in a litany of thanksgiving, and then the Iona song 'Take this moment, sign and space' acted as a bridge into the next part of the ritual, 'Letting Go and Moving on'.

We began this with lines from a poem by R.S. Thomas, using the image of gravel thrown at a window for prayer to express something of Carol's feelings of stuckness and frustration, followed by a prayer and the hymn 'I dream of a church' using the imagery of God as a weaver, and written by Kate Compston (Duncan 1995). A passage from Deuteronomy which had been used at Carol's ordination was followed by another hymn, written by one of the participants, using the image of Exodus and being ready for a journey. The final section I called 'New beginnings', linked with the season of Advent by a reading of the Magnificat. We used a prayer I had written for another occasion and adapted, using the imagery of being on the threshold, each section ending with the response:

In the patience of waiting
and the courage of moving
God of Wisdom, be with us.

One of the other participants contributed a blessing she had brought, and then we lit candles in the centre of the room for new beginnings. We closed with a final song, which I had written for Carol's farewell service, and a prayer.

Carol brought an almost overwhelming mixture of feelings to her ritual. When we met beforehand she talked of her sense of lack of energy, of weariness, her difficulty in sleeping. She wanted to recognize the many good things about her time in ministry up to that point, and the friends she had made, and was thankful for them, but was also conscious that she had struggled with strong personalities. She still felt conscious of her calling but very uncertain of the direction it should take, and although she had chosen to leave her present appointment and move to another city, she was scared of feeling isolated and of not finding opportunities for future ministry. She hoped that the ritual would 'put to rest some things and open up others' (Interview, Carol).

As she looked back on it just over a month later, she had very little memory of the content of the ritual, but a strong impression of its atmosphere and the feelings surrounding it:

> in all honesty I can't remember any of the written liturgy...I just
> remember where I was sitting, where other people were sitting, the
> candles, the feeling...almost a—not near death experience, but this
> sort of out of body experience where you sort of, you're part of
> something but you can't quite take on board that the people round
> there are directing what they're saying at you or reflecting about their
> relationship with you sometimes (Interview, Carol).

What the ritual has done for her is give her a very strong sense
of the affirmation of others:

> But it has given me—I'm still totally overcome by the affirmation that
> people gave me. I mean, That's the thing. If ever anyone needed to be
> reminded that she had God-given gifts, that in some way at some
> point, in some people's lives were important and that they should be
> used, not hidden away—then it's me. That's what I'm saying, It's
> affirmation that—affirmation that I wasn't misguided in believing
> that God was and is calling me along in ministry (Interview, Carol).

At the time of the interview Carol was still living with uncertainty,
unsure of her future direction, but wanting to reaffirm her call to
ministry in some form:

> And did I have to be in the church, or out of the church?...So I still think
> because of the frustration, because of the pain, because of the disbelief
> that some people who call themselves Christian can behave in the
> way that they do, that my ministry may still be in the church. Because
> I still want...I still want some of this stuff...that we share, the colour,
> the texture, the encouragement, the belief in each other, the use of
> each others' gifts, in a way that gives, affirms people in the church,
> that then means they're able to go out, they're able to share all that
> with the people outside the walls (Interview, Carol).

For Carol, the fact that this took place within the framework of
her Christian belief and in the form of worship adds a different
dimension, in which God is seen as immanent, very much present
and amongst the relationships and the process of the ritual:

> But the fact that that was said in a setting which was actually recognised
> and someone was like—as given by God and that we did it in the way
> we did, in actually quite at root a traditional way...that these things
> wouldn't have happened if it wasn't—or that these things wouldn't
> have been drawn out of me if it wasn't for all the people there. And the
> fact that God in all of us was doing that...it still had a beyondness
> about it (Interview, Carol).

Chapter Four

THRESHOLDS AND PASSAGES: NEGOTIATING CHANGE IN
WOMEN'S RITUAL MAKING

Like Carol, all of the women whose stories I share here were
undergoing transitions which brought up powerful feelings; and
the rituals they constructed and created played a powerful part in
their process of working through those feelings and experiences.
People have always developed rituals to help in the process of
negotiating change and transition, and the classic ritual theory
developed by Arnold van Gennep and Victor Turner in relation to
rites of passage has given a theoretical framework for explaining
the role of ritual. But for women, the nature of transition and the
ways in which it has been marked are different; a feminist critique
of the nature of change and the ways in which women experience
and negotiate it, gives a gendered perspective on the process.

Making Women's Experience Visible

The life passages described in this book, and the rituals which
accompany them, are not those we commonly think of as 'rites of
passage'. They are not related to birth, to marriage or death; these
passages are commonly ritualized within church and society, and
so perhaps there is less need for women to create their own. That is
not to say that existing rituals and liturgies are always relevant and
appropriate to women's experiences—many still draw on patriarchal
ways of relating and view women's experiences in stereotypical
ways. There are however, many attempts to provide new resources
for such occasions. I have known couples devise their own naming
ceremonies in place of baptism, write their own promises or
marriage vows, and have participated in poignant and moving
funerals. These rituals fall outside my particular focus on women's
liturgy, but am aware that there is much creative work outside the

women's liturgical movement and the various expressions of feminist spirituality.

There are also those within the church who are willing to offer or devise liturgy for transitions which have not traditionally been recognized. Many ministers in pastoral charge are willing to work with individuals to create appropriate liturgies in a church setting. But for the women here, although they may have drawn on existing resources, there has been a need to create something for themselves; the rituals and liturgies to fit their experience either do not exist or are not widely available:

> Women's small-group liturgies express realities and passages for which no formal Christian ritual exists in the sacramentary — menarche and menopause, the sealing of commitments, a young person leaving home and parents, or an older person entering a nursing home, to name just a few. Such liturgies serve to acknowledge, express and heal pain left unrecognized and untouched in official rites (Roll 1994: 393).

Many writers within feminism have argued for the need for a spirituality that makes visible women's experience. Joann Wolski Conn (1986), in one of the earliest works on feminist spirituality, argues that any reconstruction of feminist spirituality must take account of women's experiences. Lizette Larson-Miller argues that this inclusion of experience within spirituality must extend to ritual:

> women will continue to ritualise their deepest memories and hopes, circling in an energising and inclusive dance which continues to have the ability to create communion where there has been discord and to embody corporately the image of God (Larson-Miller 1998: 77).

Whilst women's experience is diverse and multi-layered, these rituals grow out of particular experiences of marginalization, exclusion or conflict.

Women's experience of paid employment is one of the areas in which few rituals exist. Whilst women's participation in the workplace is increasingly recognized, and there is attention in the secular world to such issues as women and the glass ceiling, or bullying and harassment, the stereotyping which sees the public sphere as predominantly male and the domestic as female contributes to the fact that there is little liturgical material relating to women's experience of work. For several of my participants, issues surrounding work are important, and feature directly or indirectly in their rituals. Alison's ritual at redundancy is based on an unhappy working experience, which leaves her feeling compromised and guilty:

> In that job there were periods when I was extremely unhappy by what I witnessed in the job and more importantly what I felt the job was doing to me as a person. And when the job came to an end — not of my choosing — I was actually made redundant... there was a sense of...guilt of being part of that setting, and as I felt colluding with it to a certain degree (Interview, Alison).

For Rebecca, her work gave her not only identity, but a status she has now lost:

> I actually felt considerable concern at the end of my role. You know, status issues, I no longer had a badge, I no longer had a simple way to describe who I was, and I never really realised 'till I lost it just how much I gained from the kind of image of the job I had (Planning session with Rebecca).

Alison, Jane and Rebecca planned their rituals specifically in relation to work and redundancy, but Sue, who celebrated her 60th birthday, also felt the loss of work at retirement, a loss which she continued to feel for some time afterwards:

> I'm not used to being retired — I'm still in — feel in that ending phase now really, trying to fathom out what it's all about. So I didn't realise it would take that long really, you know, to settle — perhaps one never settles — the shock never wears off. But, you know, it's very different (Interview, Sue).

An issue which is at the centre of Clare's ritual is her relationship with the academic world. Although the tensions and problems for women in education are not new, I have come across only one other published example of a woman using ritual in relation to an academic environment. In an article in the *Journal of Ritual Studies*, Jane Simpson tells of her sense of a need for a rite of passage in taking up her first teaching position in the University of Canterbury, New Zealand. She felt the need to draw on her Pakeha (non-Maori) roots as well as affirming Maori culture and recognizing injustice; and the need to affirm her own educational values in the face of economic and social assumptions about the running of a modern secular university. She had to face the tension of enacting a confessional ritual in a secular department and university, but her ritual of room blessing signalled an important transition:

The passage from the known to the unknown required its own rite which expressed in symbolic form and action the way in which the academic community would give me life, and how I would in turn give life back in a spiral dance of life. Any such ritual needed to be public, unselfconscious, and prophetic, calling forth to new partnership, new ways of being, new visions and dreams (Simpson 1999: 55).

The tensions she felt were different from those experienced by Clare, but both rituals show the need to mark rites of passage which usually remain invisible in academy and church.

Joan Laird (1988) writing in relation to rituals in family therapy, argues that whilst most women's rituals have been familial and domestic in nature, there is a need for rituals that mark important transitions for women in public roles. Diane Bell (1996) argues that in traditional Aboriginal society, women's ritual activity tends to express, but also to shape, the gender and social relationships they live out. In the rituals that I have described above the experience that has been excluded is that relating to the public world of work or academy.

For some women in this research, part of the context for their rituals is the recognition that as single and childless women, they do not conform to patriarchal stereotypes. They comment on their awareness that many existing rituals are built around family patterns and systems. Alison, for example, is aware that many of the rituals she has participated in for other members of her family or her friends are not available for her:

and the sense as a single person I think a lot of liturgies are bound up with personal events — events in personal life...you know the birth of a child, end of a relationship, beginning of a relationship, houses, nesting — all of which for various reasons haven't been that relevant to me (Interview, Alison).

Sue, too, feels that her life has been different from accepted patterns, and in sending me the 'script' for her ritual writes:

I felt this was needed because as a single woman, who latterly has mostly worked at home, no one was going to provide any ceremony for me. I have none of the usual wedding anniversaries, or ceremonies for my children which I could preside over as a mother or grandmother (Letter, Sue).

For both Alison and Sue, their rituals are not specifically related to their singleness or lack of children; Alison is marking her redundancy, and Sue a 60th birthday and retirement. But both see their rituals as significant and necessary partly because other, more familial rituals are not available to them.

The blessing of a new home is not a liturgy or ritual that is restricted to women, or is specifically feminist. For women, as Young (1997) points out, the relationship with domestic, home space is a complex and ambivalent one. Traditionally women have been associated with the home and the domestic sphere, while the world of work and public life has been reserved for men. As women are beginning to reclaim the public sphere, so they are rethinking their relationship to home and domestic life. In some instances this leads to what some feminists have called a 'valorisation' of the domestic, romanticizing and idealizing it as women's space. It can be seen also as a place of privilege, reserved for those of a certain status, wealth or class. But Young argues that there are certain 'critical values' of home which should be available to all—safety, individuation, autonomy, and preservation; and the home can become a place for the construction of identity:

> Home is the site of the construction and reconstruction of one's self. Crucial to that process is the activity of safeguarding the meaningful things in which one sees the stories of one's self embodied, and rituals of remembrance that reiterate those stories (1997: 163–64).

For Andrea, the blessing of her home represents a new beginning after a period of loss:

> It was a kind of being together with my family so furniture and stuff that I'd had at my dad's house for all those years. It was the first time— I think I remember saying to you it was the first time I'd had everything in one place really since that time when I was 18 (Interview, Andrea).

She also has very clear ideas about how she wants her home to be used, in a way that arises out of her Christian commitment:

> It was a recognition of God's part in it I suppose. And God's part in my life I suppose in bringing me through various things to this place and in seeking God's blessing for the house and seeking God's part in whatever follows in the house (Interview, Andrea)

For Louise, the blessing is not so much of her home, but of an extension she has recently had built. The building work was costly and disruptive, and the experience had been one of loss which she feels needs 'redeeming':

I needed to find a way of it feeling like something that was positive in
the end, as opposed to a just very expensive waste of money...So it was
about—maybe as much reclaiming what was good about it and trying
to put aside the less good (Interview, Louise).

For both Andrea and Louise, the blessing of home and domestic
space is closely linked with their journeys of loss and new beginning.
The home space is not something that restricts their role and activity;
rather, it is about their sense of identity, independence and
autonomy.

In other rituals, however, it is private, intimate experience that
is made more visible. The acceptance of women's bodily experience
is a major theme in feminist theology and spirituality. For Nicola,
facing a hysterectomy, although she can find a considerable amount
of secular literature, there is little to help her in theology or liturgy,
and she creates her own eucharistic liturgy as she prepares to face
her operation.

Cora speaks of her need to mark the menopause, again a bodily
passage in a woman's life that is usually ignored in Christian liturgy;
although in the shamanic tradition of which Cora is a part, it is
more commonly recognized and honoured:

I'm beginning to realise menopause has felt like a sort of like a descent
myth...Even though you always know you're going to get old and die
you don't actually imagine what it's going to be like—all right—and
so I want to really have a sense of both facing that and honouring the
process I've been in...(Interview, Cora).

Feminist liturgy makes the bodily experience of women, which
has often been invisible or marginalized, central:

In liturgical experiences, bodies are present in their material, actual
dimension. Liturgy recovers the importance of the body as a place of
salvation, and in liturgy we celebrate the awareness and joy of being
body, body that is good from its origin in creation (Silva 2000: 124).

For Nicola and Cora, although the body is a site of pain and
loss, ritual is also a way of honouring the bodily processes they
are undergoing, and affirming that the female body is a place of
envisioning the divine.

The two rituals of renaming reflect not so much a familiar
experience that has been invisible in ritual, but a new experience
itself. Women have been given names by their parents in infancy,
taken their husbands' names in marriage, and may occasionally have

chosen to use nicknames or different versions of their given names. But for women to choose their own names (at least in modern Western society) is still relatively uncommon. For Runa, the choosing of three new names represented a complete break from the family who had abused her, and the possibility of writing openly about that abuse:

> it meant I could publish what I liked and I could claim that freedom for myself to write within a sort of...it was sort of within the cover of a name my family wouldn't recognise...(Interview, Runa).

For Jackie, her surname signified a link and a connection with her ex-husband which she no longer wished to retain. While keeping her two first names, she chose a last name from within the history of her family that would enable her to create a new sense of autonomy and identity.

While these two rituals have their origins in past experiences of abuse and pain, this is not the focus of the ritual—for both women it is the choosing and constructing of a new identity that is the point of transition: 'claiming the name and claiming an identity of my own' (Interview, Jackie).

In making ritual these women are taking personal experiences of change and transition which often remain invisible and unrecognized, and finding strength in sharing their stories with others:

> But whether a woman relates her most painful experiences to a silent group or leaps over a steaming cauldron and makes a wish to cries of 'Blessed Be'! the basic impact is the same: ritual is personalized. Every participant is given the opportunity to inject something of herself and her concerns into the ritual, and to see these met with the support and encouragement of her group (Eller 1993: 101).

Naming the Feelings

Frequently as women planned or remembered their rituals alongside me, they talked as much of feelings and emotions as of the content of the ritual, and saw one of the functions of the ritual as helping them to express or acknowledge those feelings. For all of them, their rituals arise out of strong feelings and the need to express, work through, or negotiate them. They reflect complex and multi-layered emotions, and an ability to articulate them in both words and symbolic actions.

Some of the rituals begin, as did Clare's, in a sense of celebration and thankfulness. Jackie, in her renaming, wants to give thanks for the friends who have supported her, and to celebrate the singleness and potential creativity of her new identity:

> Celebration—singleness, friendship. Creativity, spirituality, connectedness with environment—things that had been denied, stifled in marriage (Journal entry, planning session with Jackie).

Carol feels it is important to celebrate significant milestones on her journey, and amongst all the pain she has known in ministry is still thankful for what she has received:

> Thankfulness—realisation I do have so much to be thankful for—ministry's been rich (Planning session with Carol).

However, by far the predominant feeling named by the women is that of loss. For Rebecca, and Jane, there is a clear loss of identity which goes along with redundancy:

> And then as I explored more deeply I realised that I was also experiencing a kind of sudden loss of my identity and it was that had led us to think, Mmm, maybe creating a ritual around this change in my life might actually help to ease things. (Planning session with Rebecca).

For Rebecca, that loss also includes a loss of status; for Jane, of the creativity she had found in her work. For her, the loss is parallel to that of bereavement:

> Because redundancy is a bereavement. And that's why I've done a lot of work therapeutically on linking redundancy to my experience of bereavement so that I have some idea of what's going on (Interview, Jane).

For Carol and for Nicola, the loss is a bodily one, of weariness and lack of energy and choice:

> So it was all tied up really with a lot of loss and I think for me the loss of my womb and the ceasing to bleed were both actually very significant things and I think at one level, you know, at one level I had known it was highly likely I wouldn't have children and it's not that I ever really thought that I would—well, in any specific way I hadn't wanted children. But there was something about knowing the finality of that—that I could not have and that choice was taken away (Interview, Nicola).

She describes her experience of multiple losses — of job, income, flat, as well as illness — as 'a time of immense kind of tearing down and stripping' (Interview, Nicola).

There is a considerable amount of literature on loss and grieving, and this is clearly not unique to women's experience. The church has traditionally been associated with loss through death, and is still probably the major provider of funeral liturgies, although that is changing in an increasingly secular society. It is also not new to associate other forms of loss — such as redundancy or the breakdown of relationships, with bereavement, and to find parallels with the grieving process. It is more unusual however, to find liturgical expression of the feelings of loss associated with illness, loss of work, or relationship; and the recognition and expression of such feelings in these liturgies is significant.

The two rituals around blessing a home, which in many ways were rituals of celebration, also had elements of loss associated with them. For Louise, it was the cost of a building process which had been much more expensive, lengthy and disruptive than she had anticipated and the loss of a potential relationship; for Andrea, it was the recent loss of her parents and her family home.

This highlights another feature of these rituals — frequently women's feelings are mixed and ambivalent, with thanksgiving and loss, anger and celebration, inextricably interwoven.

Carol's ritual is the one that most clearly combines ambivalent feelings — of thankfulness and celebration, but also of loss and grief; conviction of her calling, but uncertainty about the future. She felt a sadness and sense of loss, which was undermining her already-fragile sense of confidence in herself and her ministry:

> I did have to keep trying to remind myself it's ten years, it's actually ten years of life, isn't it, and everything, and what had happened in those ten years was significant, it was OK, and it wasn't all a failure...because I didn't feel it was something to celebrate any more (Interview, Carol).

Cora, too, expresses ambivalent feelings about her experience of menopause:

> It's a sort of fullness and an emptiness at the same time — the emptiness of letting go and — but also an honouring of — sort of — yeah, sort of everything that has brought me to the place I'm at — my sort of gifts and achievements and what I've received and what I came into this world with (Interview, Cora).

One of the functions of ritual is to enable us to deal with ambivalent feelings (Ramshaw 1987). Women in these rituals are insistent that the negative or painful feelings are acknowledged:

> The next—the ambivalences—there needs to be something done at that point. There's a sense in which although I don't want to burn the thesis, there's a sense of wanting to destroy some of those other feelings of anger (Planning session with Clare).

In Christian feminist liturgy there is a deliberate attempt to overcome the dualism or splitting of negative from positive which allows for the expression of difficult and painful feelings. This is probably even more pronounced in Goddess spirituality which seeks to honour and celebrate the whole cycle of natural and human experience:

> It is fundamental to feminist thealogy and liturgy that we honour darkness and death, alongside light and birth, as intrinsic to the regenerative process (Roberts 1993: 149).

One of the emotions that the church has found most difficult to acknowledge is anger, and this has often been particularly true for Christian women, socialized into being 'nice girls' who do not protest loudly, but conform to stereotypes of the tender, nurturing woman. Therefore for the women whose rituals are described here, the ability to name and express their anger is a crucial element in working through transition. Rebecca is angry at being made redundant, and Jane is angry not only at her redundancy, but at the events and experiences in her working life which preceded it:

> But yes, I am still angry—I'm angry at the waste. I'm angry at what I see to be a lack of appreciation of the work I was doing but I think that anger was always there even when I was working (Interview, Jane).

Clare, although she is celebrating the completion of her thesis, is angry at what it has cost her in terms of compromise and relationships, and what she sees as the game-playing of academia. Louise was angry at the cost (personal and financial) of building her extension, and saw her ritual as an important element in coming to terms with that.

In therapeutic settings the importance of giving expression to anger and finding creative ways to channel it has been commonly recognized, but this has been less apparent in Christian theology. One of the main emphases in feminist liturgy is the insistence that there must be a place for anger, and that this is not only pastorally and therapeutically important, but theologically and biblically grounded. Marjorie Procter-Smith (1995) argues that women can only pray at all if anger is externalized and expressed; far from being excluded from prayer, anger must claim its rightful place. Susan Roll claims that feminist liturgy has the potential to do this:

> Part of the potential of women's liturgies is the possibility finally to be honest about the anger and pain, to name it openly and to connect it with one's personal life-experience in a structured ritual setting. Ritual can offer a vehicle to express righteous anger before God, in the recognition that the Hebrew prophets and Jesus himself felt rage in the face of injustice and abuse (Roll 1994: 395–96).

In contrast to those definitions of ritual which see it as fixed and unvarying, taking a set form regardless of the feelings of the actors, the understanding of ritual here is one in which feelings are expressed, acknowledged, and consciously worked with. There is therefore an understanding of ritual which links it closely with pastoral care and with therapy, and several writers in the field of pastoral care recognize the value of ritual. Elaine Ramshaw lists a number of functions for ritual in the realm of pastoral care, and examines each of them in the context of Christian pastoral care, both for the individual and the church community:

> I will consider ritual as a way to establish order, to reaffirm meaning, to bond community, to handle ambivalence, and to encounter mystery (1987: 22).

Worship and pastoral care need to be integrated within the Christian community (Anderson and Foley 2001). Each is impoverished without the other; pastoral care without worship becomes flat and one-dimensional, losing any sense of the transcendent, whilst worship needs the pastoral dimension to ground it in lived human experience. Periods of transition particularly need ritual to help interpret and make sense of the conflicting and ambivalent feelings which accompany times of crisis:

> What happens, however, when there is no established ritual or acknowledged liturgical response to a powerful story of crisis, transition or loss? Most situations in need of ritualization, however, are a muddle between beginning and ending, between living and dying, between continuity and discontinuity (Anderson and Foley 2001: 128).

The power of ritual is recognized also in the therapeutic setting. Imber-Black (1988) working in family systems therapy, claims that ritual is important in dealing with themes of membership, healing, identity, belief, and celebration. James and Melissa Griffith (2002) see part of their work in psychotherapy as helping and enabling their clients to structure rituals and ceremonies:

> We help people to notice, honor, and make space for important rituals and ceremonies in their lives, staying curious about what the person's experience is and how that may be relevant to the work of the therapy. Our role is to support the person in "holding the mystery" as he or she participates in, learns from, and draws strength from a ritual or ceremony (Griffith and Griffith 2002: 177).

Anne Bewley (1995) draws on her knowledge of both feminist theology and psychology to argue for the importance of 'sacred ritual' in therapeutic work, in providing a framework in which symbolic objects or actions can work at an unconscious level. Such work needs to operate within the client's belief system, and to be a co-operation between therapist and client; but, used appropriately, can enable clients to negotiate changes in their lives:

> Sacred ritual can serve to heal, to empower, and to change consciousness and behavior. In my experience, a ritual that is carefully constructed between client and therapist will further the work of 'ordinary' therapy. The role of the therapist is to help the client reconnect with an understanding and experience of the sacred that works for her and to implement that experience into the therapeutic setting (Bewley 1995: 213).

There is therefore a general recognition of the value of ritual in pastoral care and in therapy. But just as women have often been invisible in liturgy, so they have often not been taken seriously in pastoral care. Although women are often seen as the recipients of pastoral care, Riet Bons-Storm (1996) argues that their stories have often been heard in stereotyped ways, as victims in need of rescue, and that their authentic experience of suffering, or of strength, has not been heard or believed. Kathleen Greider (1999) and others review the growing feminist contribution to the field of pastoral theology, care and counselling, and draw attention to a number of themes which are emerging, including a number of themes which also appear in these rituals, such as women's relationship to the church and ministry, the highlighting of female experience, women in theological education, and the place of theology alongside psychology and anthropology. Zoe Bennett Moore (2002) surveys recent work on feminist pastoral theology, and highlights not only the increasing attention paid to themes of violence and abuse, and embodiment, but also the agency of women in giving and receiving pastoral care, and the contextual, relational element of women's lives.

The rituals here are not only making women's experience visible, but in naming and acknowledging feelings of loss, ambivalence and anger they are claiming an agency and autonomy that resists patriarchal stereotypes of women as passive victims or submissive carers. I have already argued that some therapists, such as Anne Bewley (1995) use ritual as part of their therapeutic work; and Valerie DeMarinis (1993) includes the creating of ritual as one of the stages in her model of the pastoral psychotherapeutic process. Diann Neu, who works as both a liturgist and a therapist, makes a strong claim for the therapeutic power of ritual:

> Feminist rituals have therapeutic potential for women who seek empowerment and healing. They have the capacity to ease difficult life transitions, to provide a lens for looking at relationships, to tap wellsprings of individual and joint creativity, to heal personal pain, to celebrate life, and to transform the political (Neu 1995: 199).

The women whose stories are told here are not using ritual in formal or structured therapeutic settings, and I would not want to argue that the rituals are therapy. Nevertheless there are interesting comparisons to be made between their rituals, and the therapeutic process. Both have some sense of setting up boundaries, and both see the holding of a safe, clearly-defined space as an important element in personal change. In therapy, however, the boundaries are held by a professional seen as having expert power and knowledge; whereas in ritual the boundaries are defined and held by the women acting collectively as a group. More importantly, therapy has an expressed intention of working for personal change or healing; in ritual the intention is less explicit, and much broader. There is nonetheless a therapeutic aspect of ritual, manifested in the way in which the women taking part see some connections between the power of ritual to change and transform their lives and the healing potential of the therapeutic process.

The Process of Making Ritual

Traditionally, many rituals have been defined by religious authorities, and transmitted in families, tribes or cultures across generations. But in these women's making of ritual, there is a constructive and intentional process emerging, in which women use their agency to create a ritual relevant to their personal experience of transition.

The women had varying experiences of ritual before devising their own. Many of them (Alison, Louise, Nicola, Jackie for example) came with quite a wide experience of liturgy and ritual both in church and in more informal settings:

> I suppose a lot of that is upbringing and the sense that significant events in people's lives are marked in some way and the most basic being part of the church where you witness weddings and baptism and dedications and inductions and all those points of transition...also through attending much more informal liturgies (Interview, Alison).

Runa felt she had little experience of ritual before her name-changing ritual, but was able to draw on some experience of church liturgy and also her background and experience in therapy:

> I'd never done ritual before then. I'd witnessed sort of rituals in the Christian church, in my childhood...And maybe the other major thing is that the sort of therapy I was doing — the therapy that I later went on to train in myself — Gestalt — which has got this tradition of what was called experiment (Interview, Runa).

Others also draw parallels with the therapeutic setting. Alison draws on her training in Neuro-Linguistic Programming (NLP), and Sue compares the boundaries of a ritual to the setting of boundaries in her practice as a psychotherapist:

> The boundaries around therapy as I'm used to it anyway are very firm, and it's a very firm holding, and I think that's what ritual does in some ways, it's a holding, and puts boundaries around something. And once you've got a boundary, inside that boundary something can happen (Interview, Sue).

Some of the participants in the research were members of ongoing groups using ritual, similar to those described in chapter two. Although they did not all carry out their rituals with that particular group, they were part of a setting where ritual was a regular part of their spiritual practice:

I suppose I'm part of a—I consider myself to be part of a spiritual group and by that I don't mean my church, although I am a member of a church but it's a broader concept for me (Planning session with Rebecca).

Cora's involvement with ritual was strongly influenced by Gabrielle Roth's 5 Rhythm dance movement, and her creation of ritual began as part of a group of women:

when everything was changing in my life, when I went to Crete and first discovered the 5 rhythms and one of the first things that happened...was, I think we called ourselves, a matriarchal study group...We studied Wicca and the Goddess and we started making rituals and I think that was probably the beginning of conscious making of rituals for me (Interview, Cora).

Nicola at the time of her hysterectomy was living with a religious community with its own rhythm of liturgy, and so for her ritual was a natural presence within daily life:

cos in a way you know ritual was part of our daily life. And I was under no compulsion whatsoever to share their life of prayer but I did generally speaking...very informal, doing their own thing. So it felt the kind of place where creating ritual was part of women's community really (Interview, Nicola).

Although their backgrounds are varied, for all the women there seems to be some previous knowledge or experience of liturgy or ritual, whether in a church, spiritual, or therapeutic setting. Even Runa, who felt she had little previous experience at the time, had some prior knowledge to draw on. This is not surprising—while individual ritual or symbolic actions may seem to come naturally or intuitively to many people, constructing a ritual involving a group of people is a sophisticated process that requires some awareness of group process, of structure and boundaries, and the nature of symbol and symbolic action. It seems unlikely (although not impossible) that an individual would choose that particular format or process out of a vacuum.

An important part of the ritual is the planning, and most of the participants were actively involved in that process. Carol and Andrea gave much of the planning over to others, but even so their initial ideas and thoughts were key:

In a phone conversation with [her minister, who led the ritual] this morning, she said Andrea had written "loads" about what she wanted;

but some things (e.g. whether or not to have communion) she'd been
uncertain about right up to the last minute (Journal entry, Andrea's
ritual).

For others, the planning was part of a long period of gestation,
thinking and mulling over ideas:

> I can't remember when it began but I do remember...talking about it,
> and you encouraging me to think about what it was I wanted the
> liturgy to say and from that deciding there were really three stages...So
> once I got that structure I was actually less worried about what I put
> together (Interview, Alison).

Louise saw her ritual as the outcome of a much longer process of
thinking things over:

> although as I say I probably actually wrote what I was going to do that
> afternoon the words would have been quite carefully crafted and they
> would have come out of a process, albeit not conscious, of thinking
> quite carefully, I think, about what I wanted to say and how I wanted
> to say it (Interview, Louise).

For some, the physical preparation was an important part of the
ritual. Almost all the rituals involved sharing food afterwards, and
some of the women mentioned the preparation specifically in the
interview:

> I wanted to feed people, and part of the preparation was in the morning,
> shopping and cooking — I made a huge soup and an apple crumble and
> bits of cheese — that took most of the morning but that was an important
> part of it (Interview, Alison).

In line with much of the literature which sees feminist liturgy as
a collaborative process, many of the participants talked about the
value of planning with another person—in some instances myself
(although I have to recognize they may be saying what they think I
want to hear!), in other cases with a group or another individual:

> And it helped to sit down and have somebody else to say, actually,
> what are you doing here, what do you want to do, what's the purpose
> of this, because often when you're very involved in something it's
> hard to take a step back and actually ask those questions—so for me
> it's helpful having somebody else that can actually reflect so it's not
> just put together but it's actually thought through (Interview, Clare).

Ward and Wild (1995) make the point that planning is an integral
part of the ritual process at the beginning of *Human Rites*, and Janine

Roberts defines ritual as including both the planning and the collaborative elements as part of the process:

> Rituals are coevolved symbolic acts that include not only the ceremonial aspects of the actual presentation of the ritual, but the process of preparing for it as well (Janine Roberts 1988: 8).

Ronald Grimes (2000) uses two models for the work of creating ritual. One is the diviner, who uncovers people's meanings, intentions, and feelings, to create or almost discover the ritual. The other is that of the plumber, who is aware of the technology of symbol, structure and process. He argues that both are necessary for the creation of effective rituals, and both are evident in the planning processes described here. For example, Jackie talks of how I was able to help her find a shape for some of her half-expressed ideas and feelings (the diviner model):

> I think the planning was incredibly important because it helped me to shape and name what it was I was actually doing. As you know, when I first asked you, I'd got this idea but I hadn't a clue what I wanted to do. I just knew it was an important marker. But to have those two sessions where you were asking me about, it was about those things, you know, what are you, what I was wanting to do, what I was wanting it to do for me, which enabled me to think more deeply about what I was hoping, what this kind of transition was that I was attempting to engage in (Interview, Jackie).

But at the same time much of the planning included discussions of what was practical and feasible in the time and space available (the plumber model):

> I think that apart from you and me there would be enough people to take one letter each...and give people free rein—a letter, a piece of card—a free rein to do what they want with it—to make the letter in any kind, any creative form at all...so what I thought is if they did that on small pieces of card then we could actually put them together to create the surname and I could write my first name (Planning session with Jackie).

For these women, then, the ritual is not only the 'ritual moment', but a long process of gestation, planning, preparation, enacting and subsequent reflection, which is itself a part of the much broader process of transition in which they are caught up. It is one aspect of their process of negotiating change in such a way that they can let go and move on.

Letting Go and Moving On

The ritual enactment itself is often described by the women in terms of letting go and moving on; an acknowledgement of the past, and looking to a new future. For Jane, this took the form of letting go of some of her despair at redundancy:

> Cos I'd felt quite hopeless and that nothing would change no matter how hard I tried. I think those were the main things — the despair and the hopelessness — that I let go (Interview, Jane).

Sometimes the letting-go was explicitly symbolized. Rebecca developed four separate rituals over a period of time as she worked through her feelings about redundancy, and used the symbol of a stone washed in a stream for letting go of her negative feelings whilst not wiping out the past:

> So we talked and thought and we walked, and in the end we decided to choose a stone each to represent elements of the past that we wanted to see washed clean, but with acknowledgement that they were still going to be with us. And for me particularly that was an incredible response to my negative thinking about my job cos I didn't want my job to end and I had really nasty niggly feelings about it (Interview, Rebecca).

For Alison, the acknowledgement of the past is an important step before she can move on:

> I just remember that it was something to do with recognising the significance of it — wanting to draw a line under it in my own way — in a way that's much more fundamental than a leaving do and I think it was also something to do with moving on. I think there was a connection there (Interview, Alison).

For Clare her ritual marked the end of a process which had been ongoing, although there is also a moving-on to the next stage:

> I think it's [the ritual] much more end process, but recognising that the end is open-ended. So it was the end of something, but leaving it open. And it was very important in the ritual, and in putting it together to talk about sort of moving on and looking on to what happens next and the sort of community idea (Interview, Clare).

For Cora, rituals are part of a much wider cyclical process:

> They mark a stage in the process, either a beginning of something you want to start, you know, or the end of something you want to finish, or something that strengthens you along the way. They're part of a

journey, they're not the whole thing. Though they can help to complete a cycle (Interview, Cora).

Others expressed a sense of completion, or closure, through the ritual. For Rebecca, the four definite moments in her ritual, over a period of months corresponded to stages in her own process, so that by the end of the autumn she had a sense of completion:

> Although I left at the end of September there were things I was still doing for the organisation and I think the ritual's helped me think, OK, I did some of this, I've done these events, but I won't do it again, you know, that's it, I am definitely stopping. But it's like allowing me to kind of re-enter into this kind of place (Interview, Rebecca).

For some, the moving on was expressed in concrete terms. Both Jane and Alison were appointed to new jobs shortly after their ritual, and although neither would argue for a direct cause and effect, both saw the ritual as playing a part in that process through helping to bring about a change or a shift in their attitude:

> I'm very careful about who I say this to and how I say it but I'm convinced there was a connection between what happened in the liturgy and getting the job—I don't know what that is but the way I would like to see it is about—that it did close something off and release me to do something else...But I do feel on a more serious level, there is some kind of connection between the liturgy and moving on (Interview, Alison).

For some, the meaning and effect of the ritual continued as they reflected back on it:

> But it is very pleasurable to be taking the time to go back over it with an interested person—because it makes it significant again and that was the point of it, wasn't it really? And it's a reminder I suppose of actually why we were there, what it was we were supposed to be doing (Interview, Carol).

Reflexivity is seen as one of the characteristics of women's ritual, often found within the ritual enactment itself (Northup 1993). Here the reflection was subsequent to the ritual, and was prompted by my interviews; it is impossible to say whether the women would have engaged with it otherwise. Nevertheless, those, such as Cora, who use ritual regularly, see the ritual process as a continuing uncovering of meaning:

> I remember reading somewhere that the full meaning of a ritual is often not known 'till years afterwards and I think that's right as well.

You know, the bigger, the more significant the ritual is, the more mystery there is in it as well (Interview, Cora).

Rites of Passage

Some of the earliest work on rites of passage is that of Arnold van Gennep (1960 [1908]), with whom the term (*rites de passage* in French) originated. Although the term rites of passage is widely used nowadays in relation to birth, marriage and death as individual, universal human passages, van Gennep's work originally related to the negotiation of changes of status through ritual within tribal societies. He argued that, whereas in contemporary Western society we tend to hold to a distinction between sacred and profane, in tribal societies all is holy, and therefore transitions from one state to another are marked by rites or ceremonies (1960: 1-2). Often transitions have a territorial dimension—a move from one place to the other, and so the doorway, or threshold, is seen as a marginal, holy, place between two states:

> Precisely: the door is the boundary between the foreign and domestic worlds in the case of an ordinary dwelling, between the profane and sacred worlds in the case of a temple. Therefore to cross the threshold is to unite oneself with a new world. It is thus an important act in marriage, adoption, ordination, and funeral ceremonies (1960: 20).

Each transition involves three phases. First, there is a separation from the old, a relinquishing of the existing status or family ties. Second, there is the transition phrase itself. In this the person (or group, say, of initiates) is between two states; they belong nowhere, and are therefore marginal, but also in a sacred space. Third, there is the incorporation into the new status, as adult, or husband or wife, recognized not only as a personal transformation of identity but a public assuming and acknowledgement of a social role and status. Each of these stages is marked by its own rite or set of rites, although they vary in length and complexity. Van Gennep uses the Latin word for threshold (limen) to describe these stages:

> Consequently, I propose to call the rites of separation from a previous world, *preliminal rites,* those executed during the transitional stage *liminal (or threshold)* rites, and the ceremonies of incorporation into the new world *post-liminal* rites (1960: 21 Author's italics).

Although van Gennep's work is developed in relation to human passages, and this is how it is now most widely used, he saw his understanding of the nature of transition in relation to seasonal passages too—it was a scheme, or an image, that could be used of the whole of life:

> For groups, as well as for individuals, life itself means to separate and be reunited, to change form and condition, to die and to be reborn. It is to act and to cease, to wait and rest, and then to begin acting again, but in a different way. And there are always new thresholds to cross; the thresholds of summer and winter, of a season or a year, of a month or a night; the thresholds of birth, adolescence, maturity, and old age; the threshold of death and that of the afterlife—for those who believe in it (1960: 189–90).

Van Gennep's work has been widely influential, and has had considerable influence on contemporary understandings of Christian liturgy and rites of passage. Although van Gennep saw the stages usually worked out in three different sets of rites, his scheme is more often used now to represent stages within one ritual or liturgy. So, for example, in Christian baptism there is a renouncing of evil, or the old life, a threshold moment marked by the sprinkling of or immersion in water, and an incorporation into the faith community; a wedding is the threshold between the single and the married state. However, whilst in van Gennep's work the different stages are used to refer to social status or role, in contemporary thinking they have often become individualized, and are used to refer to personal or psychological changes in a sense of identity.

In the rituals here there is some evidence of van Gennep's framework. In their use of ritual to help them let go of the past, the women make a separation from their previous status or emotion. Sometimes this includes a change of status, as in redundancy for example, but more often the emphasis is on letting go of negative or angry feelings. The reincorporation into a new status is less clear; but what does emerge is the sense of moving into a new psychological or spiritual space, certainly with a sense that this has wider social and communal expectations, but with no clarity about what form that might take. However, because van Gennep's thinking on rites of passage is so widely used (even if people do not always know its origin) it is impossible to say whether these rituals confirm his thinking, or whether his theories have (consciously or unconsciously) shaped their construction. Ideas of letting go and moving on in relation to rites of passage have become so inscribed in our thinking that it is difficult to conceive of rituals of transition which do not show something of this process.

The liminal, or threshold, moment in these rituals, however, while it is evident in some, is less clearly-defined; and so I want to turn now to some of the theory on liminality, in particular as developed by Victor Turner.

Liminality and Communitas[1]

Victor Turner's work on ritual has developed van Gennep's scheme further, particularly in relation to the liminal phase. Because being on the threshold is to be between two worlds, belonging in neither, it is a space separated out from normal everyday life, characterized by ambiguity and a collapse of the normal categories of identity and status. It is a space, or state, usually depicted or described in terms of metaphor, image or symbol:

> Liminal entities are neither here nor there; they are betwixt and between the positions assigned and arrayed by law, custom, convention, and ceremonial. As such, their ambiguous and indeterminate attributes are expressed by a rich variety of symbols in the many societies that ritualize social and cultural transitions. Thus, liminality is frequently likened to death, to being in the womb, to invisibility, to darkness, to bisexuality, to the wilderness, and to an eclipse of the sun or moon (1969: 95).

Because there is a loss of the normal, or previous identity or role, and the new one has not yet been assumed, it is an opportunity for those entering the liminal space to lay aside pressures, responsibilities and the weight of office or social expectation:

> In this interim of "liminality", the possibility exists of standing aside not only from one's own social position but from all social positions and of formulating a potentially unlimited series of alternative social arrangements (1974: 13-14).

The liminal phase is characterized by what Turner calls 'communitas'. Turner argues that there are two possible models of human inter-relatedness, one in which society is highly structured and differentiated, another in which there is individual equality

1. This argument was first developed in my article 'Whose Threshold? Women's Strategies of Ritualization' in *Feminist Theology* 14.3 (May 2006: 273–88).

and a lack of structure. It is this latter model which emerges in communitas, hence the term 'anti-structure', which Turner also uses. Here there is a lack of status and differentiation; it is a state of equality and mutuality, in which normal hierarchies and distinctions are dissolved.

It is characterized often (amongst a comprehensive list of other qualities) by anonymity, nakedness or uniformity of clothing, an absence of status or rank, an absence of property and distinctions between rich and poor, and an all-pervasive sense of the sacred and of mystical or divine powers (1969: 106).

Although Turner talks about a lack of status in communitas, he also talks in terms of status-reversal and elevation within the liminal state:

> The strong are made weaker; the weak act as though they were strong. The liminality of the strong is socially unstructured or simply structured; that of the weak represents a fantasy of structural superiority (1969: 168).

Most rituals relating to life-crises or to the taking on of a new office or identity share a pattern of the reversal of status. Before assuming authority a king or a chief first undergoes ritual humiliation — taking on in ritual form poverty, nakedness, or a female role; or submitting to those of lower status. This ritual humiliation does not undermine his authority; rather, by providing a contrast, a gap, a brief experience of anti-structure, it acts to reinforce the status quo. Society moves in a dialectic process, what Turner calls a 'social drama' between stability and structure, and the freedom and mutuality of 'communitas':

> From all this, I would infer that, for individuals and groups, social life is a type of dialectical process that involves successive experience of high and low, communitas and structure, homogeneity and differentiation, equality and inequality (1969: 97).

Whilst Turner acknowledges that communitas can allow new ways of thinking to emerge, for the most part these are contained within the core world view of society. There is a movement or tension between the two which allows the social structure to survive periods of change and transition which could otherwise threaten its stability:

> Communitas cannot stand alone if the material and organisational needs of human beings are to be adequately met. Maximization of

> communitas provokes maximization of structure, which in its turn produces revolutionary strivings for renewed communitas (1969: 129).

Turner's description of communitas is often seen as an idealized form of community, which has many attractions for feminists. It challenges status and hierarchy, argues for role reversal, and seems to suggest a utopian realm where distinctions of race, age and gender no longer apply.

His understanding of liminality also has resonances with contemporary queer theory, which in its insistence that gender and sexuality are culturally constructed, challenges and subverts conventional notions of role and gender, in a way that destablilizes cultural expectations:

> This is then the 'essence' of queer theory, that there is no essential sexuality or gender. 'Queer' then is not actually another identity alongside lesbian and gay...but a radical destabilising of identities and resistance to the naturalising of any identity (Stuart 2003: 10).

However, in Turner's scheme liminal space and communitas are inherently conservative, in that they act as a kind of safe, ritualized outlet that subsequently enables the re-establishment and maintenance of social hierarchy. Both feminist and queer theories, however, want to see the destabilizing of traditional roles and hierarchies as a challenge to, rather than a way of reinforcing, the status quo. Therefore, attractive and useful though Turner's work is in many ways, it has a functionalist aspect.

A Feminist Critique

Caroline Walker Bynum (1992) uses her research on medieval female mystics to develop a feminist critique of Turner's model. She argues that his scheme is based on men's experiences and looks from a male perspective. Where he attempts to describe or visualize women's rites and experiences, he inevitably looks 'at' women rather than 'with' them:

> Turner's ideas describe the stories and symbols of men better than those of women. Women's stories insofar as they can be discerned behind the tales told by male biographers are in fact less processual than men's; they don't have turning points. And when women recount their own lives, the themes are less climax, conversion, reintegration and triumph, the liminality of reversal or elevation, than continuity (1992: 32).

Women's experience of social change is often less sudden and dramatic than men's, and the social realities of women's lives do not always permit a sudden reversal or change:

> Women could not take off all their clothes and walk away from their fathers and husbands, as did Francis. Simple social facts meant that most women's dramas were incomplete (1992: 43).

Turner's scheme is developed in relation to a male elite, and it is high-status men (and the exclusive language is apposite here!) who on the whole gain from the reversal of liminality:

> Now men who are heavily involved in jural-political, overt, and conscious structure are not free to meditate and speculate on the combination and oppositions of thought; they are themselves too crucially involved in the combinations and oppositions of social and political structure and stratification...But in ritual liminality they are placed, so to speak, outside the total systems and its conflicts; transiently, they become men apart (Turner 1974: 241).

Turner, when he does attempt to look from a woman's perspective, assumes a symmetrical correspondence; that for those of low status the experience of communitas will be one of reversal and elevation. In fact, Bynum argues, this is not generally the pattern we see with oppressed groups — they do not envisage or ritualize a reversal of power and exploitation, but a different ordering of society, in which hierarchies are not reversed but abolished; and the imagery is not that of humiliation and triumph, but struggle. Status reversal is of particular relevance to those of high status who have something to lose:

> Thus liminality itself — as fully elaborated by Turner — may be less a universal moment of meaning needed by human beings as they move through social dramas than an escape for those who bear the burdens and reap the benefits of a high place in the social structure...As recent liberation theologians have pointed out, it is the powerful who express imitation of Christ as (voluntary) poverty, (voluntary) nudity and (voluntary) weakness. But the involuntary poor usually express their *imitatio Christi* not as wealth and exploitation but as struggle (1992: 34).

Bynum is writing primarily about the experiences of women medieval saints and mystics, but her argument is relevant to contemporary women. Anderson and Hopkins (1992), who interviewed a number of women about their spirituality, argue that the recurring imagery of 'leaving home' in male accounts of the spiritual quest is replaced in women's stories by a more interior shift in consciousness, integrated with their daily relationships and work of home-making. Similarly *Defecting in Place* (Winter, Lummis and Stokes 1994) describes how many women have chosen to remain within the church or Christian tradition, whilst questioning patriarchal dogma and shaping their own symbols, imagery and spirituality. While this is clearly not true of all women, there is some indication of a pattern which bears out Bynum's claim that women's stories show more continuity than the 'processual social drama' of Turner's theories.

In the rituals of the women whose stories are told here, there is often no dramatic turning-point, but rather a process, in which the ritual itself is a part—often a significant one, and sometimes a decisive moment. The threshold is a powerful image and it is used specifically in two of these rituals. Carol's experience, of having left her pastorate, but uncertain of the future, suggested some of the loss of status in Turner's view of liminality, and I consciously used the image of being on the threshold in one of the prayers in her ritual.[2] But unlike Turner's liminality, this was not a temporary and symbolic loss of status, assumed during a ritual enactment. Rather, for Carol, the sense of liminality and uncertainty continued; and when I interviewed her a couple of months after the ritual she was still uncertain as to her future:

> And did I have to be in the church, or out of the church?...some do make the decision ...that it's going to be out. So I still think because of the frustration, because of the pain, because of the disbelief that some people who call themselves Christian can behave in the way that they do, that my ministry may still be in the church (Interview, Carol).

In Jackie's re-naming ritual, the movement from one room to the other suggested the symbolism of the threshold, which became very powerful. But for Jackie, there is also a continuity—she keeps her first two names, she remains rooted in her home, her friendships, and her work. The ritual is a decisive moment in taking on her new identity, but set within a process which has also involved telling others and signing legal documents:

> I've realised that in doing the legal stuff and thinking about "This will be my name for next year" I've realised the enormity of it and what

2. I am grateful to Elizabeth Baxter for the inspiration provided by the 'threshold theology' she is developing based on her work at Holy Rood House in Thirsk, Yorkshire.

I'm doing—all the more reason to have that ritual...It's a certain fear about, it's not fear, it's irrevocable. OK, it's not irrevocable, but actually it is. I've made the decision, I've signed all the documents (Planning session with Jackie).

In some ways, these rituals mark decisive turning-points in a process of separation and letting-go, of negotiating change and transition, and discovering new beginnings. However, the process of change is ongoing, and the ritual so inextricably interwoven with it, that for some it is hard to separate the two:

Well, it's hard to say what was the ritual and what was the act of changing my name. You know, I mean, to change your name it's like every day, so many times a day I'm reminded that I changed my name. So that reinforces who I am. So in one sense it's hard to say I had a new sense of self dating from the ritual but I'm convinced that it did really help (Interview, Runa).

This fits with Bynum's description of change and transition in women's lives—there is often not one dramatic moment, but a process of transition, worked out in women's daily lives and relationships, in which the ritual forms one stage. There may be a liminal or threshold period, but the imagery is primarily of ongoing struggle and journeying rather than decisive change.

Neither do these rituals enact a reversal or elevation of status. A ritual may mark or arise out of a change of status or role (as in redundancy), but rather than re-enacting that, tells the story and enacts a claiming of agency or empowerment. In Turner's thinking the experience of liminality ultimately works to reinforce the status quo and promote social cohesion, by allowing a period of communitas in which normal hierarchy and status are overturned. The period of liminality, or communitas, seems subversive, with its role reversal, and abandonment of norms and conventions. However, it is the intervals of liminality that allow the normal structure of society to persist and to survive the forces of change which threaten. The liminal phase, in Turner's theory, contains change, rather than promotes it:

Both these types of ritual [i.e. status elevation and reversal] reinforce structure...The gaps between the positions, the interstices, are necessary to the structure. If there were no intervals, there would be no structure, and it is precisely the gaps that are reaffirmed in this kind of liminality. The structure of the whole equation depends on its negative as well as its positive signs (1969: 201).

It would be possible to see the women's rituals here in this light, as specific times or 'intervals' which safely contain women's desire for change in a way which allows patriarchal norms to continue unchallenged. There is certainly an awareness of the possibility of this within feminist theology. For example, Pam Lunn reviews literature on Goddess spirituality and argues that some forms of ritual can 'undoubtedly change the participants' emotional states, internal imagery and subjective perceptions of their own capacities'. But, she claims, unless this leads to concrete action and change in the external world then 'this whole movement may be nothing but an emotional opiate, a consolation prize for women who are powerless in the rest of their lives' (Lunn 1993: 30).

For the women here, their rituals are not simply a safe outlet, but an attempt to envisage and enact the changes in their lives within a symbolic framework which enables them to interpret change and transition on their own terms. Their rituals make a difference — they do not simply mark change, or contain it; they also help to effect changes in their lives that continue after the ritual has ended. There is not a period of liminality followed by a return to the status quo, but a definite and significant step in a process of ongoing resistance to patriachal norms. Alison articulates it very hesitantly, in terms of a theology she is half-reluctant to own:

> So I think I would say it is one of the most life-changing experiences I've ever had in liturgy...even though some of the conclusions I draw from it are not entirely comfortable with my theology, but it did work — and that's what fascinates me — it did work and I've never had that before or since. I think maybe one of the reasons was I was so determined to do it, and it was so important to do it (Interview, Alison).

For the women, their rituals are not a reinforcing of social structure, but a conscious negotiation of change, in a way which challenges patriarchal norms and values:

> Whilst the symbolic actions of ritual alone are unlikely to be sufficient to overthrow patriarchy, rituals allow transformed perspectives on reality and potential. They expose the ill-formed ideologies of patriarchy and also envision concrete changes that would embody values and principles consistent with feminist visions of justice and well-being (Caron 1993: 103).

Case Study Two

KNOTS AND DREAMS—CLARE'S STORY

At the time of her ritual Clare was a student training for the ministry and working on her doctorate. As she drew nearer to completing her thesis, she began to talk about needing a ritual which would mark that ending for her. We agreed that I would help her to plan the ritual, and we met for the first planning session at her home.

The major element which Clare named was celebration and thanksgiving: thanksgiving to God, and to those who had supported her through her work on the thesis—family and friends, the first nation people amongst whom she'd done her research, tutors at college and the research group.

Significantly, she also named two women whose contribution and role would often remain unrecognized and invisible. The first was:

> a single mum with three children...she wouldn't know it but she's been a real support—showing me how much you can manage to do as a woman juggling things (Planning session with Clare).

Second she named her childminder:

> because she's actually been one of the key people in the thesis though you wouldn't know it...without even realising it she's played a huge part in giving me the time to do the work (Planning session with Clare).

The theme of community and the involvement of other people was key to Clare throughout the planning of the ritual; not only in giving thanks to people, but in their participation in the ritual itself. There was also a strong sense for her that there needed to be a 'letting-go' of the work she had put into her thesis, releasing it to continue in a new way in the wider community.

The space that Clare chose to use for her liturgy was her home, as a place where she felt rooted, and where she had done most of the writing. In the planning session she began to think about the objects and symbols, representing the elements of earth, air, fire and water, that she would use as a focus, to make it a sacred space.

One of the questions we faced in planning the ritual was how to express Clare's feelings of hurt and anger. These were partly related to the ambivalent feelings about academia and the sense of exclusivism and elitism she felt. Clare was also conscious of inequality and injustice, and aware of the privilege and opportunity she had enjoyed, from which others were excluded:

> There's quite a lot of hurt and anger in there, just from — not exactly having to fight the system — but it feels it's been a bit like that. And there's also a sense within that — like I've had the opportunity others haven't had, just because of when and where they were born (Planning session with Clare).

We both felt it was important that these feelings were expressed in the ritual, preferably with the opportunity for other participants to share something of their struggles and anger too. We talked around various ideas before arriving at the idea of tying knots; and it was almost towards the end of the conversation that the symbol of the dreamcatcher emerged.

There has been considerable criticism of the way in which some women's spirituality groups and new age practitioners have taken elements from native American culture and used them in individualistic ways without respect or regard for the political and justice implications. In her work with first nation people, Clare was concerned to be respectful of their culture and traditions, and to avoid the co-optation of others' symbols and stories. For her, the symbolism of the dreamcatcher was one which resonated with both the content and process of her thesis, and was one she could use with integrity and respect.

Other parts of the conversation centred on resources — we chose to use material mostly from the thesis and what we had written ourselves. Clare agreed to look for music for the beginning and end of the ritual, and to play during the making of the dreamcatcher; and she wanted to celebrate with a party at the end!

On the evening I arrived early with friends; Clare had prepared the room, with chairs and cushions around the edge. At the centre was a low table, a bowl of stones and a lit candle. A wooden plate was displayed, and a box full of pieces of ribbon, braid and thread, a small dish of beads, and a pair of large scissors. A large hula-hoop was on the floor, with ribbon wound round it, to form the frame for the dreamcatcher.

Gradually people began to arrive, and I felt a slight nervousness and vulnerability about doing this ritual with my male colleagues present; and also an awareness that there would be people present for whom this kind of ritual would be unfamiliar. I am more used to the relative safety and security of women's groups with a common interest in ritual. There was what seemed quite a long period of waiting for everyone to arrive; and the atmosphere felt a little uncomfortable—people talking quietly or not at all, as if uncertain whether to treat this as a social occasion or a church service.

The ritual began with a welcome from Clare's research supervisor, acknowledging that he was welcoming people to someone else's home for 'a very special moment'. We listened to some music, then joined in opening responses which Clare had written. Clare offered her thanks to those who had contributed to her thesis, naming almost everyone present, and drawing it together in a way that one of the participants later appropriately likened to a web.

Clare read the words of her dedication at the beginning of the thesis, and we moved into the tying of knots in the ribbons. I spoke a few words of introduction; speaking of the cost and ambivalence for Clare in working on the thesis, asking people to think about their own lives, dreams that they sought to make come true, their own struggles against injustice. I invited people to take a ribbon from the box which would be passed round the circle, and tie a knot to represent their own struggles, whether in silence or sharing briefly about what it meant to them. Clare began with words and responses I had written earlier:

> Clare tied a knot for each of these, and then passed the box onto the next person. It moved quite quickly round the first two or three people. Then the first person spoke and shared; and from then on the process flowed freely. After each contribution we responded together:
>
> Great Spirit,
> see our knots of pain
> and catch our tangled dreams (Journal entry, Clare's ritual).

When the box of ribbons had passed around the circle, we began weaving our knotted ribbons onto the dreamcatcher. I explained that we had chosen the dreamcatcher partly for its Native American symbolism of catching the bad dreams, but also for its similarity to a web. Again Clare started us off, soon others joined in, and there was a lifting of spirits, a more playful atmosphere, a lightening, with music playing in the background. This took some time — people thinking about their knots and what they represented, selecting and adding beads. The finished dreamcatcher was beautiful, and I realized that although the knotting and weaving were random, Clare had chosen the colours with care — white for the underlying framework, but lots of blues and purples, some threads of dark red, and a few glittery bits.

When this was complete Clare led us in a prayer she had written for the occasion addressed to 'Dreamcatcher Spirit', and we joined in a poem taken from her thesis. Then there was music while Clare fetched champagne, the group broke into chattering, moving about, and the party began.

When I returned to interview Clare about her ritual and its significance, some of the earlier themes were confirmed, and others emerged, as she reflected on the ritual and compared it with the graduation which she had also attended.

Perhaps what stood out most clearly was the contrast between the ending-of-the-thesis ritual and the graduation ceremony. For Clare, the former was meaningful because it was so clearly personal and related to the work she had been doing in the thesis:

> the ritual was actually significant for me and was centred around the thesis and the thing that had come out of the thesis (Interview, Clare).

The graduation, on the other hand,

> felt like you were on a conveyor belt and you didn't feel very important or very significant (Interview, Clare).

In the different feelings which Clare experienced there was a clear distinction between public and private worlds. The graduation had its part to play in terms of a public recognition and acknowledgement, and was particularly significant for her parents. It also enabled her to connect her own story of academic achievement with that of her mother:

> And I realised that for her [her mother] she was the first woman in her family to get a degree...it meant so much to her even if she didn't understand anything about what I'd written about so I'm very glad I did go to it, even if I didn't feel it was for me at all (Interview, Clare).

The ritual, on the other hand, expressed some of the difficulties and struggles Clare had experienced in a way that could not have been made public:

> For me it's actually about yourself and the people you've journeyed with and what you've achieved...it's actually something quite private. You couldn't have shared the struggle on a stage (Interview, Clare).

An issue which is at the centre of Clare's ritual is her relationship with the academic world. In *Lifting a Ton of Feathers* Paula Caplan (1994) looks at the difficulties and myths confronting women who want to survive in academia, giving practical advice and hints. Rebecca Chopp (1995) sees the presence of women in theological education as a potentially transformative force, contributing the insights and politics of feminist theology. Clare was caught up in this tension, seeking to survive in a patriarchal world on its terms, whilst retaining her own creativity and integrity. Some of her sense of marginalization was perhaps due to the fact of her being a student in an affiliated college—and the first in her college to complete a Ph.D.—but much of it was due to her writing as a feminist, using feminist methodology and ways of working. For Clare her decision to plan a ritual on finishing her thesis was due to her awareness that the secular ceremony of graduation would not adequately reflect her experience or express her feelings:

> I've been trying to think about what a traditional graduation is about. I've got very mixed feelings about that—I can't really see any of the traditional elements that I really want to include, other than gathering of family and friends...I don't really want any elements of handing over certificates or doffing on the head or dressing up (Planning session with Clare).

One of the most important aspects of the ritual for Clare was the symbolic action of tying the knots and weaving them into the dreamcatcher:

> So I think the knotting and people saying what the knots are about or not saying what the knots are about and then weaving them together was very significant—I mean that's the one bit I can actually remember rather than the words that were said or even people that were there (Interview, Clare).

Part of the importance of this symbolic action was that it allowed the naming and expressing of people's struggles and difficulties— not only Clare's own during the writing of the thesis, but those of other participants too—and then the weaving of them, integrating them into a new symbol.

Clare also spoke about the process of planning the ritual together; and how important it was for her that it had been a collaborative process:

> Well, I mean I found it really helpful and we'd worked together before but just to sit down and actually—to sit down and work through it together because my whole way of working is to work in collaboration with other people (Interview, Clare).

Clare spoke of her ritual in terms of recognition and thankfulness for the point she had reached, and as a way of letting go and moving on. But she also felt there was something in the process of ritual that defied verbal explanation:

> the whole question about how do you put into words something that you can't do in words...rituals can actually take on a life of their own...it's not just a head exercise of "let's sit down and write something" —there's much more going on. But again, it's not something you can explain...they're connecting with something outside (Interview, Clare).

Chapter Five

SHAPES AND PATTERNS: WOMEN'S RITUAL MAKING AS TRANSFORMATIVE PRACTICE

Distinct shapes and patterns are emerging in women's rituals, based on their use of sacred space, and their choices of words, images, symbols and symbolic actions. In the construction and making of ritual theo/alogical ideas and concepts are also taking shape and finding expression. This understanding of ritual is very different from that which sees rituals as fixed and formulaic, enacted expressions of established doctrine. Women's rituals do not always fit with traditional definitions of ritual, but are consistent with the practice that some scholars have called 'emerging ritual' or ritualization, and which I prefer to name as 'ritual making'.

Symbol-breaking, Symbol-making

Symbol and symbolic action are widely used in Goddess rituals and feminist liturgy:

> In summary, symbols are things that represent something else and that have the power to evoke memories, feelings and understandings. They are ways of condensing meanings, of permitting different understandings without making difference divisive, and of upholding ambiguity for particular purposes (Caron 1993: 153).

All of the rituals featured here use symbol or symbolic action in some form. Often these take the form of symbolic actions in which all members of the group are invited to participate, bringing their own meanings and understandings in a way that contributes to the multivocality of symbolism. Whilst many symbols endure over time, and so give continuity, the symbols used here are chosen for the particular context, and even familiar symbols are often used in different ways.

In a conscious use of biblical imagery, Alison's redundancy ritual uses thirty silver coins to represent the sense of betrayal and guilt which she feels in relation to her experience at work. These are removed by other participants, who are then invited to light candles for resources of hope and justice for the future. The process of choosing the symbols was important for Alison in helping her to crystallize her intention for the ritual:

> Oddly enough the symbolic action didn't crystallise until the afternoon I was putting it together and I suddenly got the idea of coins and I wanted thirty coins and the idea was that the coins would—the coins would be things that would be out and that I wanted taken away that were bad. And I wanted thirty candles to replace those coins, and those were things that actually only came together...I think it was because once I knew that what I wanted was coins, it simply expressed everything (Interview, Alison).

Rebecca marked her redundancy by using leaves; but the actual ritual actions emerged as four separate actions over a period of some months as she gradually handed over the last responsibilities of her job and embarked on a course of study:

> And you know, because it's autumn, and such a spectacularly beautiful autumn, I've been incredibly aware of the trees, and the leaves letting go or being let go of, and that in a way sums up for me what I need to do—which is let go—and let go and let happen—whatever is going to happen next. So I've focused on leaves as a kind of—you know, a sort of symbol for this ritual and so at the moment I know I'm going to use leaves in some way (Interview, Rebecca).

Jane chose shells as the main symbolic focus for her redundancy ritual, although she also included glass beads and fishes, and candles. In planning, as we discussed various options, she was aware of the impact of symbolism on others, and the importance of simplicity and clarity:

> I think the other thing is that you have to choose symbolism that means something to people and it can be—simple and doesn't require a lot—but it has to mean something to people—it has to be not silly or twee. But also has to be simple enough in that sort of context for people not to be muddled (Interview, Jane).

Runa's re-naming was less structured, but she gathered together a series of objects which symbolized different elements of her connections with her friends, and asked them to do the same; they then exchanged them symbolically with appropriate words:

But I asked each person to bring with them, some thing, some object,
which they felt symbolised for them the quality of their connection
with me, and I said that I would do the same so I, over the days
beforehand, gathered a set of objects, symbols, for me that represented
my own connection with each one of those people and they each
brought one of their own (Interview, Runa).

When Nicola was preparing for her hysterectomy, she chose the
traditional Christian eucharistic symbolism of sharing bread and
wine. However, her interpretation departed from the traditional
in that the bread and wine not only symbolized the body and blood
of Christ, but her own body and blood, in a feminist reclaiming of
women's bodily experience as holy and sacred:

I wanted to make Eucharist again in that context of bringing together
the Eucharist and the reality of my body and blood as they were at that
moment before going into surgery (Interview, Nicola).

When I interviewed Cora she was planning a ritual for her
birthday. It was unstructured, in that she intended to take some
time in solitude and see what emerged. She felt, however, that she
was likely to spend at least part of it outdoors, and that natural
objects would be important in focusing it for her:

I may well find a cave, I will probably find stones, stone circles that
I'm very familiar with, and are a very important part of my connection
to the environment here and I will make gifts to those places and
allow them to help me root my kind of intention, I suppose, my
awareness at this point (Interview, Cora).

The women's rituals in which I have been involved are rich in
symbolism. Although some of them may appear stereotypical and
in danger of becoming clichéd, each woman has chosen the symbolic
objects or actions with care, with relevance to her own situation,
and with an awareness of their significance for others. They carry
the condensation of meaning, the multivocality, and ambiguity
(Kertzer 1998) characteristic of symbols; they mean different things
to different members of the group and take on different layers of
meaning. Lesley Northup (1997) argues that women's use of symbol
is derived either from the natural world or from the activities of
their daily lives, and to a certain extent this is evident here. Alison
uses coins and candles that she happens to have in the house; Jane
uses shells, and glass beads; Cora looks to the countryside around
her home. The dreamcatcher may appear an exception to this, as

something originating in another culture, but it is directly related to the subject of Clare's thesis, and therefore has become a part of her lived experience. Many of the actions too are everyday ones; tying knots, walking around a house, pouring water, even if they are enacted in the more stylized form of ritual. Others are less everyday, but are activities which encourage participation and draw on the creativity of women within the group.

While the use of symbolism is imaginative and creative, there is need for caution. Jane recognizes that it can easily become 'twee' or too cluttered, and whilst in some circles the use of stones and candles for prayer is still radically innovative, in others it has become a caricature of creative prayer. The repetition of familiar symbols and actions is a common feature of ritual, and can give a powerful sense of continuity. But it takes time for symbols to acquire such associations, and in the meantime there is the need for careful consideration of the aptness of a particular action. Susan Ross argues that in postmodern understanding, symbols are equivalent to a language; and like all language, they do not give access to unmediated knowledge, but have to be read and understood within their cultural and social context:

> Although not verbal, symbols do in fact constitute a language, in that they are vehicles of expression, rooted in the body, culture, and history. Symbols themselves participate in a world of meaning, dependent upon cultural and historical context, as does language (Ross 2001: 140).

Marjorie Procter-Smith (1995) urges two notes of caution with regard to the cultural reading of symbols. First, we must be aware that whilst using symbols drawn from women's daily lives and activities can be affirming, it can also perpetuate stereotypical notions of what women's work is—the symbolic use of wool and weaving, rather than nails and hammers, has an ambiguity for women conditioned into stereotyped roles. However, the women's symbols need to be read in the contexts of the rituals, the transitions they mark, and the lived experience of the women. There is a readiness and commitment to challenge stereotypes, whether it is the priestly celebration of Eucharist, the viewing of the world of work as a male preserve, or the refusal to continue to be identified by a man's surname. The symbols and symbolic actions chosen are consistent with the women's resistance of patriarchal tradition. In the particular and contextual way in which they are used, they help the participants to shape their lives in the tension of living in a patriarchal church and society:

> Women experience themselves as liturgical symbol-breakers in the refusal of the uncritical acceptance of traditional symbols and as liturgical symbol-makers of their own. In this feminist symbol-making a very direct and immediate intersection between liturgical symbols and women's lives is evident. The 'ordinary' of women's lives becomes the 'matter' for liturgical symbols (Berger 1999: 127).

Secondly, she argues, we should not use symbols that are derived from the exploitation of nature, or that depend on the exploitation of women's labour, without giving any thought to their origins. It is only when we are fully aware and respectful of the origins of symbolic objects that they can truly be vehicles of prayer.

This is an issue that feminist liturgy, with its ready embrace of symbols from a variety of sources, may yet need to deal with more fully. Many women's liturgies and rituals have a strong sense of social justice and connection with other women: but it is all too easy to take up and use objects and images that have their roots in other cultures, or in our own consumerist capitalism, without due thought to their origins or whether the process of production has exploited others. Clare, in thinking through the symbolism of her ritual, was careful to honour and respect the traditions of the people she had worked with, whilst honouring them in her choice of the dreamcatcher; but whether we choose to buy candles from a cheap supermarket, or consume fairly-traded chocolate, we cannot wholly escape the tensions and ambiguities which our symbols carry with them.

Shaping Sacred Space

The women here not only make conscious use of symbolism within their rituals, but, intentionally or not, their use of space bears symbolic meaning. The majority of the rituals use domestic space. They give various reasons for choosing their homes—for Alison it is partly about the opportunity for intimacy and privacy:

> I always knew it would be here—partly about practicalities of food—but also about intimate space—and space that I know where everything was...It was the back of the house, so it was quite quiet and private (Interview, Alison).

For Jackie, whose ritual marked her renaming, and for Sue, celebrating her sixtieth birthday, their homes are very much bound up with identity, and seem the natural, almost the only possible choice. For Sue, that sense of identity extends outdoors, and includes her creativity:

> Well I think it related to me and my life, you know, I enjoy the garden and I'd done a lot in the garden and it was my creativity in the garden and in the house really. Whereas if I'd had it somewhere else it wouldn't have been me as much really would it? (Interview, Sue).

Jane talks about the importance of welcome and hospitality:

> So it felt like a different kind of use of my home. It felt important to invite people in...felt as if I was saying to people can you come in and share my space psychologically for a couple of hours and spiritually, and make yourself at home as you do that (Interview, Jane).

All of the rituals held in homes finished with a shared meal, either provided by the woman hosting the ritual, or through contributions from the group. For some, this was a regular pattern of their group liturgy; for others the ritual also provided the occasion for a party.

Sharon Parks talks of the importance of creating sacred space through shared meals, and feels that women have a particular wisdom and ability in this:

> We who are women know in our collective memory and practice a wisdom and talent for composing the ritual meal that heals and nourishes and renews the human family, and the range of our hospitality is being extended and beckoned into a deeper vocation (1988: 191).

Whilst this rings some warning bells about female stereotypes and the provision of food, it does also seem to resonate with the experience of these rituals. Offering hospitality and food, whilst not technically part of a ritual, becomes one with it in a blurring of boundaries that works to make the everyday and the domestic sacred. Lisa Isherwood (2007) has pointed to the way in which food has been used as a means of regulation and control of women's bodies, and these women's rituals, in their delight in the provision of food, again challenge patriarchal norms by seeing food and eating as sacred and a blessing.

For Andrea and Louise, whose rituals involved house-blessing, the home is clearly integral to the ritual. A feature of both these rituals is movement through the space, with some appropriate words for each area, and a sense of blessing each part of the home—although in Louise's ritual, the focus is primarily on her new extension:

> So there were different things to say and do at different points of the house, but coming into the back door which I tend to use as my main entrance anyway so there was one sort of ritual at the back door about...asking a blessing on the people who were coming and going through that door and would come and stay hopefully and be part of my life (Interview, Louise).

In Andrea's ritual, her minister, who planned the ritual, provided an appropriate symbolic gift in each room:

> I just remember being really surprised that [name] had got these little presents for me in each room...it was, it was really special, and she'd obviously put a lot of thought into what they were (Interview, Andrea).

I have already noted the possible tension in women's ritual between the desire to be as inclusive as possible, and the need for a safe space. For these rituals, dealing with personal and emotional events in women's lives, the element of safety and a certain degree of privacy is paramount. The setting of boundaries makes it possible for women to make themselves vulnerable in exploring intimate areas of emotion or spirituality. Whilst it would clearly not be true to assert that domestic space is always a safe space for women (some do not have their own homes, for others the home may become a place of violence and abuse) for these women, at this particular point in their lives, the privilege of having a home in which they can be safe, and to which they can invite trusted others, is a gift which makes their rituals possible.

Not all the rituals are in homes, however. Nicola was the only one who chose a religious building, not a church, but a small chapel in the community where she lives. As such, it combines for her both the sacredness of a holy place, but also the intimacy of the domestic:

> And again in that room, you know, to do it in that—it felt very—I can't imagine having done it in a very big, sort of formal, patriarchal church space but there was also something about it was a chapel, albeit in the house, and it was a place where the sacrament was reserved, and there was something about saying it, doing it there (Interview, Nicola).

Interestingly, it is only Cora, from outside the Christian tradition, who speaks of the holiness of church buildings. She senses the pull of a sacred building in a way that no one else mentions:

> And I feel, like churches and so on, which are traditional ritual spaces in our society are very important—I mean they do certainly create a very strong field—even for a non-Christian (Interview, Cora).

For Cora herself, however, it is the connection with nature that is determinative. Although on other occasions she has used her home, and describes an earlier ritual in a sweat lodge, it is the outdoors which beckons her:

> But I—I suppose my path has taken me to look for those places much more in nature and to—like, caves have often provided them, and stone circles and sanctuaries of various sorts that I've found—and places on the earth that I've repeatedly gone to seem to reveal more and more of the sacred—sense of the sacred to me (Interview, Cora).

For many of the women, not only the place was significant, but the arrangement and lay-out of the space. Elizabeth Gray, talking about women creating sacred space in the domestic setting, says:

> Any woman who decides upon the placement of furniture is creating certain space for a certain kind of living. Any woman who chooses color to fill a space with its pervasive and mysterious magic is creating space sacred to the feeling tones of that color (Gray 1988: 100).

Whilst she is talking about the everyday business of housekeeping and decorating, (perhaps in rather idealized terms!) her words reflect something of the care with which women set up their ritual space. For those in the home, the space is almost invariably laid out in as circular a form as possible, usually with chairs and cushions placed round the edges:

> And we cleared the living room, made a great big space, just cushions and chairs and things pushed right out against the side of the room cos I wanted it all to be sort of on floor level you know, we had everyone sat round in a big circle. It was wonderful (Interview, Runa).

Most of the women also created some kind of centrepiece for the room, with cloths and objects carefully chosen for their use in the ritual or their symbolic value. For Clare, this is something she has drawn from her experience of women's liturgy within a group that meets regularly:

> I think the centrepiece is really important—what I like about the women's liturgy group is that we always have something to focus on (Interview, Clare).

In the Goddess tradition, creating sacred space is important and explicit. Each ritual begins with casting a circle, and Runa seems to sense something of this process, as she places a picture of a wolf's head on the door before her ritual:

> It is fascinating now, looking back, because I can see there are lots of elements of ritual that I think probably that were just sort of intuitively appropriate. And now I think "Ooh Yes", because I know I needed to seal the space. Where did that come from? But I just instinctively—I had to have a guardian at the door you know, having this symbolic wolf's head pinned to the outside of my front door to keep—I don't know—negative influences away or something (Interview, Runa).

Cora, who has worked extensively with ritual groups, has a conscious and well-developed sense of creating sacred space:

> I do work with some—drawing boundaries around ritual space in some ways. Like it often feels very important that there are thresholds to ritual space…And I know a lot of traditions have very particular ways of setting up ritual space—for me it's a very intuitive thing. I don't go through a particular speech or invocations necessarily to create it; but I try to find whether it's there or not and if there's something that needs mending before we go on, in the boundaries of the space (Interview, Cora).

For other women, the setting up of sacred space is perhaps more implicit, but it is clearly there in their arrangement of the room, their use of colour, and their choice of symbolic object. Susan Roll (1994) sees the use of the circular form as characteristic of women's ritual, and Lesley Northup (1993; 1997) develops this argument, claiming that the use of the circle (or sometimes, spiral) reflects a horizontal orientation in women's spirituality. Rather than the 'vertical' model of a transcendent God 'up there', women's spirituality, liturgy, and theology stress a relational model characterized by relationality and mutuality. This certainly fits with the ethos and style of the rituals described here, which are participatory, with minimal leadership, and in which all are invited to contribute. The horizontal also stretches out to embrace the mundane, or the natural, or the everyday world—so the ritual space may also be the eating space, the working space, or the playing space.

Feminist theology has resisted the dichotomy between sacred and profane, and so the designation of sacred space within these rituals may seem at first a backward step, a return to patriarchal dualism which negates the holiness of all space, and of the physical, created world. There is a tension here between the desire to claim the world as sacred space, and the need to designate particular times and places as holy. But naming space as sacred for a particular time and purpose is not a denial of the feminist claim that all space is sacred, but a focusing, or condensing, of that claim in an embodied and concrete way. There are boundaries, but they become blurred, so that there is no rigid dualism separating sacred and profane, the holy and the everyday. Rather than all becoming secular, all becomes sacred, and the setting of the boundaries, the arrangement of space, the use of symbolic objects, focuses that sacredness for a particular time and occasion.

Theo/alogy and Spirituality

The women whose rituals I describe come from a diversity of backgrounds, and I did not ask them specifically how they would define their theology or spirituality. What emerges comes out from conversation, from the language they use in written texts within the rituals, and the way they choose and talk about their symbols.

Just as there is no one feminist theology, so in these rituals it is impossible to articulate one set of theological or spiritual beliefs across the rituals. What emerges is the differing ways in which women negotiate their tradition, and allow belief and spirituality to emerge in their ritual making.

Scripture and Tradition

For women within the Christian tradition, there is for many a sense of ambivalence, if not conflict, with church and tradition. Jane expresses this strongly in regard to her redundancy, and for her the conflict is heightened because it is the church that has made her redundant:

> And it hasn't just been emotional — it has been spiritual too. Who was I? Why was I here? What did it all mean? Was there a God? Was there some kind of divine plan?...Most powerfully what does it mean when an institution which claims to represent God tells you that your post is

redundant—I'd not made that connection but it is a powerful message to give anyone. It seemed to bring all sorts of ambivalence I feel about the church to a head (Jane, written script for ritual).

Carol gives a remarkably honest description of her feelings about her faith and call to ministry:

I think God's humour is—and maybe this is true for all of us but I believe it's true for me—that unless I do this weekly preparation for worship and shoved and pushed along with all that you have to do as a Christian minister then I might not even be Christian at all, that I wouldn't—I could now, let the total lot drift...I needn't go to church any more, you know, if I made that decision. Now that's scary actually and I'm quite frightened (Interview, Carol).

She is caught between traditional language and forms, and what she is discovering through feminism; and this emerges when we are planning her ritual:

Uncertain about theology—traditional language doesn't work any more—earlier had said use of 'Lord' rather than 'God' at circle dancing...was difficult (Journal entry, planning session with Carol).

Cora speaks of her sense that until relatively recently, there was little opportunity for the celebration of ritual apart from the church:

I think—there is a sense of a huge absence—I remember, various times in my life, thinking, Oh God, it would be nice to do this in a church—like, birth of a baby, baptism stuff, I've been married twice so it's like, how do you do it? You know, the church gives you that context for a ritual which is quite hard to create outside it. Or was, until the last few years when we've sort of discovered ways (Interview, Cora).

There is, however, a considerable use of Christian themes and traditions within the rituals. Many of the women, however indirectly, make use of biblical themes and passages. Alison uses thirty silver coins in a reference to the story of Judas, and, somewhat to her own surprise, is drawn to the story of Peter to convey the sense of betrayal she has experienced in the workplace:

...and the one that caught my attention was the interpretation of the woman in the courtyard at the trial of Jesus. The phrase is 'she calls him to integrity'—I think it's something like that—and that really caught my attention...I was actually quite surprised how I went for biblical things but that seemed to express very much what I was on about (Interview, Alison).

Jane uses the image of light, and in the candle floating over the water sees echoes of the Genesis creation myth, although she does not consciously make the connection until after the ritual:

> But the light moving over the water has got a very strong biblical resonance—in terms of the first day of creation. I mean, I've only just seen that, I hadn't consciously thought, Oh, Genesis, the light moved on the face of the waters. But there was that in terms of creativity and I think that must have been subconscious for me rather than conscious—it's only just become conscious (Interview, Jane).

Andrea uses a passage from Habakkuk, that for her expressed her hopes and dreams for her house, and something of her sense of the privilege and responsibility of having her own home.

Jackie, in her renaming ritual, draws on a series of poems by Kathy Galloway (1996), using biblical images of exile, desert and home and also chooses the passage from Isaiah which uses the image of names being written on God's palms (Planning session, Jackie).

Nicola's pre-hysterectomy ritual takes the form of a Eucharist, deeply rooted in scripture and church tradition; but talks of her experience with a vivid use of the image of the Ark in the flood:

> Actually a narrative that was extremely pertinent to me all this time was the Genesis legend of the flood and I mean I think I appropriated it in a very personal way but it did feel to me like—it was like all of my known world had been flooded and submerged and I was in the Ark...And there was a period of waiting in the Ark, you know, the flood is over, the waters have stopped falling but we're still—you know, the waters haven't receded, so there was still a long kind of waiting time really (Interview, Nicola).

The women's use of biblical stories and images is often oblique, indirect, rather than explicit. Sometimes passages are read without comment, leaving participants to make the link; at other times the imagery is used (as in the Kathy Galloway poems at Jackie's renaming, or Alison's silver coins) in such a way that only those familiar with scripture stories and images would understand its resonance. There is no traditional preaching or exposition of biblical passages, and they are chosen for their relevance to the women's stories. Janet Wootton, talking of women's use of the Bible in women's preaching, speaks of the way in which, when the Bible is put alongside women's stories, it becomes challenging and subversive:

> Women, like other groups marginalised from power, speak from the chaotic edges of the world known to powerful men. Therefore their worlds and their stories, their use of Scripture tend to overturn the norms and disrupt cosy lives (Wootton 2000: 78).

In addition to biblical narratives, the Christian women use a number of Christian or theological themes, although often deconstructing and reinterpreting them. Alison uses an analogy from *Pilgrim's Progress*, of her burden being rolled away, and the ensuing sense of freedom:

> I have never ever experienced that kind of freedom from a liturgy before or since...It's — the burden does roll down the hill, like Pilgrim's Progress — it really does — and you don't have to go back and pick it up again and stagger on another few miles (Interview, Alison).

Andrea, at her home-blessing, uses words from the Methodist covenant service to express her own strong sense of commitment:

> But it felt very much Andrea's commitment — especially the part from the Methodist covenant service — to hear and see her reading out those words of commitment so clearly and confidently — almost like a taking of vows (Journal entry, Andrea's ritual).

Nicola, facing a major operation, expresses her faith in terms of trust and surrender:

> I wanted to do it as consciously and with as much intention and as much trust — you know, trust in God, trust in the surgeon, trust in the process but knowing as well there's a risk in that...Now in a way going into hospital in and of itself and going into surgery is a surrender but I think I felt for me I wanted and needed to do that very consciously beforehand (Interview, Nicola).

Louise used the word 'redeem' of the process of building an extension to her house, and although she said she probably wasn't using it in the traditional theological sense, went on to give her own interpretation:

> And that's particularly been about how to deal with hurt and anger and which I see being able to deal with hurt and anger in a way which, which leads to a place of freedom. I would say that to me is something about redemption. But in terms of the house situation, I guess maybe I was using the word, maybe, partly in that kind of theological technical way, partly just in terms of more casually, you know, to redeem a situation is to save something good out of it (Interview, Louise).

Jane doesn't use the word redemption, but having begun to talk about forgiveness, amends this to talk in a similar way about transforming the situation:

> "I think I'm still enough of a Christian to want something about forgiveness" — but when I asked who was forgiving whom, she decided that wasn't the right word — maybe more about transforming negatives into positives (Journal entry, planning session with Jane).

She also talks about people making themselves vulnerable, and feels that in a way she can't quite articulate, this also tells us something about God:

> And there was a sense of people that I didn't know very well I felt I knew much better actually having made myself that vulnerable — and they had also made themselves vulnerable to me. And maybe that's about — something about God too but I don't quite know what (Interview, Jane).

Imagery of crucifixion and resurrection appears occasionally, but in relation to the women's stories, rather than the suffering of Christ:

> At the end of her story she asks me to read the poem "Not the last word" from Ann Lewin [1993], which is a very powerful statement about redundancy — ending with an image of crucifixion and no guarantee of resurrection (Journal entry, Jane's ritual).

Marjorie Procter-Smith argues that the centrality of the suffering of Jesus in Christian theology poses a major difficulty for women in relation to prayer. Unless this is reinterpreted, it is very hard to see it as other than a glorification of suffering which reinforces women's suffering. One possible strategy has been to see Christ's suffering in terms of the solidarity of God with those who suffer; but even this, she argues, runs the risk of reinforcing martyrdom and glorifying suffering. Redemption, she argues, needs to be seen in terms of resistance rather than suffering:

> in so far as any of these strategies adopt uncritically the biblical accounts of Jesus or the liturgical interpretation of this life and death, they will finally be unable to resist the patriarchal ordering of sex and gender that includes acceptance and justification of women's suffering, and will not be able to make room for the struggle against suffering (Procter-Smith 1995: 112).

In these rituals women are implicitly (and more explicitly, in Nicola's case) connecting their own sufferings with that of Christ, and so have something of that sense of God's solidarity with them. (Jane talks about coming to a sense of a God who 'empathises'). They do not talk explicitly of resistance, but they do omit or refuse traditional interpretations of Christ's death as in any way substitutionary, and express their hope in terms of transformation rather than resurrection. Nonetheless underlying this is a hope that the presence of God/dess can be life-giving in painful situations, and in this there is something of resistance. This is not expressed verbally, but is symbolized powerfully in Clare's ritual, where the dreamcatcher becomes a beautiful creation, that still incorporates our knots of pain:

> And I say, "but it [the dreamcatcher] wouldn't be mere decoration—a reminder, pain linked with creativity, like birth; and weaving it in is an act of faith, of hope in spite of it all" and A adds "And the champagne corks at the bottom would say, 'Yes, it is!'" And I realise, later, that this is not only the symbolism of creation and birth, but also, in a way, of death and resurrection (Journal entry, Clare's ritual).

Many of the women in these rituals are working with biblical stories and theological images that are part of their heritage, often so familiar that they can be alluded to rather than expounded. Christian imagery has resonances for them with the churches in which they have been nurtured, with past worship and liturgy, and the theology in which they have been trained. At the same time they are negotiating the tradition in their own way, mining its resources to tell their own stories and speak to their own experience. They are exercising, whether consciously or not, what Marjorie Procter-Smith (1990: 53) calls 'liturgical anamnesis'. She sees this as a two-fold process, in which liturgy both reclaims traditional texts, and also reconstructs them in ways that enable us to remember women's experience and oppression, to honour experiences and rituals of women's bodies, and to name God as female. Just as Elisabeth Schussler Fiorenza has argued for a 'historical imagination' (1983) which reconstructs the lives of biblical women, so we need 'liturgical imagination' which can enable us to celebrate the immanence of God in our lives:

> By its nature, the liturgy is interpretive and imaginative, since it directs our attention to a reality which goes beyond everyday reality. This process must now be employed in the service of a feminist reconstruction of our common liturgical memory (1990: 54).

Whilst it is not always made explicit, we can see something of this process at work in these rituals—sometimes subconsciously, but often conscious and intentional.

Language and Concepts for God/dess

There are a variety of names and images used for God in the rituals and in women's interviews. Louise simply uses the term God throughout her ritual; Jane tends to talk of God in the interview, although on one occasion she uses God/Goddess. The opening responses of her ritual, and the prayer for the lighting of the candle, address God as spirit of truth, of love, and of life, and ask for the gifts of wisdom, healing, and creativity.

Clare considers various possibilities 'Partly thanksgiving to God, Goddess, spirit whatever we choose to go with' before settling on Spirit or great Spirit. She often uses this in conjunction with other attributes of God which, whilst they need not be female, tend to have associations with feminist theology: Spirit of Wisdom, Dreamcatcher Spirit (Clare, written script for ritual). Wisdom language also features in one of the prayers in Carol's ritual, in the response 'Praise to Wisdom, the Holy Friend of all Creation'.

Andrea's house-blessing mainly uses 'God' but includes a prayer from Jean Gaskin (1995: 91) which addresses God as 'our Mother', 'our Father' and 'our Companion'; and ends with the evocative blessing:

> May the wild beauty of God,
> may the indwelling peace of God,
> May the surprising mystery of God
> inhabit this new home. Amen.

In Jackie's renaming I chose to use the term God and 'the holy name of God', (as I felt Goddess-language would be alienating to some of the participants) but deliberately used the female pronoun in the blessing at the end:

> May God, whose name is holy,
> write our names upon her palms;
> and hold us in love and wisdom
> until she brings us home. Amen. (Written script for Jackie's ritual).

Although not directly an attribute of God, Jackie and one of the participants in the ritual were particularly struck by the phrase 'Daughter and Friend of God':

> But for somebody who wasn't quite into feminism in the same way that we are to be so struck by the meaning for me — and for her as well — of daughter and friend of God — again in retrospect, made it equally, well even more powerful, so I did find that difficult to say (Interview, Jackie).

There is a strong sense of creation imagery in Clare's ritual, with a prayer that begins by addressing the Creator, and then continues to address various elements of creation, such as the elements, the forests and rocks, the sun, moon and stars, and animals and birds. This is sustained in other elements of her ritual, and is an important theme for her. Although less explicit in other rituals, the image of God as creator/creating occurs frequently; and creation or nature imagery is particularly strong for Cora.

There are also many references which talk in more general terms about spirituality, or our spiritual journey, without naming a transcendent divine being:

> There seems to me to be a number of us around in the world at the moment — at least in the kind of world I live in — who are keen to sort of own our own spirituality and create our own spiritual paths and to me ritual is a very important part of that (Planning session with Rebecca).

Jane speaks of the diversity of belief within her own group, in which although different names and images for God may be used, there is a certain commonality of feminist belief:

> Something about the collective — that although that group represents quite a spectrum of beliefs... — there is enough commonality in terms of belief that's not about how we describe the divine but about the properties of God/Goddess (Interview, Jane).

There is some use of the term Goddess, but mostly from the women outside the Christian tradition.

Cora speaks of the Goddess in terms of a holistic connectedness with the whole of creation:

> And that for me is totally what the Goddess is about; the Goddess is for me about embracing the whole, you know, it's not about for men, for women, for this group or that or people or animals — it's like completely the overarching principle of wholeness (Interview, Cora).

She uses the myth of the Goddess Inanna as an image for her own experience of menopause:

> The other thing that's been very much around for me in coming up to this present ritual has been the idea of the descent myths and I've been rereading the myth of Inanna and how she lets go of all her regalia as she descends into the depths (Interview, Cora).

Runa says that she had no particular religious belief when she first performed her ritual, but now would see it in terms of the Goddess:

> now I say it's the Goddess, it's this deep creative process that runs through life, that's what I think of as Goddess, the great spiritual process that we're all part of — at that time I wouldn't have seen it like that (Interview, Runa).

Surprisingly, there is little explicitly female language for God in these rituals; but what is absent, consistently throughout, is any use of male imagery. There are no references to God as Father, King, or Lord. Although there are some references to Gospel narratives and hence to Jesus, there are no prayers addressed to Jesus, although occasionally to Christ; and frequent references to the Spirit. The traditional Trinitarian formula, if it is used at all, is rendered as 'Creator, Redeemer and Spirit'.

These rituals have definitely moved away from male language about God to use inclusive terms; most of the terms used for addressing God can be understood as either male or female. In Marjorie Procter-Smith's view (1990) this is insufficient to be liberating for women; because we are so used to hearing male God-language, gender-neutral terms such as Creator and Spirit may still be heard as male. I am not convinced, however, that this is the case in these rituals. Feminist theology has made out a strong case for seeing the Spirit as female, and developing the imagery of Proverbs 8 has given a foundation for seeing Wisdom as a female image of divinity. For many of the Christian women in this ritual, there is sufficient familiarity with these arguments for these terms to have female connotations. The predominance of Wisdom and Creation imagery (both strong in feminist spirituality), the sense of an immanent God, and of mutuality rather than hierarchy (the preference for language of friendship and partnership rather than that of lordship and submission) help to develop a context in which that God may be seen as female. Jane's use on a couple of occasions of the term God/Goddess, and the use of female pronouns in the blessing in Jackie's liturgy, suggests the possibility that God is imaged in female terms, whichever term is used. Equally it is impossible to be certain of this; and, like symbols, 'God-language' has a certain multivocality or ambiguity about it that allows it to be interpreted in different ways by the hearers. Probably the most that we can say, then, is that the Christian women in these rituals at least are open to the possibility of seeing God in female terms; for others, such as Cora and Runa, the femaleness of Goddess is much more explicit. Charlotte Caron claims:

> Use of "goddess" is an act of ideological resistance, an act of affirmation for and of women, an act that increases the capacity of women to be self-determining in the world (1993: 105).

For most of the women, their resistance is neither so strong nor so explicit; nevertheless, they are beginning to use new language and imagery for the divine that allows them to see and name themselves as 'daughters and friends of God'.

Defining and Interpreting Ritual

There are clear patterns emerging in these rituals, in relation to symbol, space, and belief; but it is important also to look at them from the perspective of some traditional definitions and interpretations of ritual.

Ritual is a difficult word to define, with a range of differing meanings and understandings, both in conversational usage and in academic scholarship. Many traditional definitions of ritual see it as fixed and formulaic; for example, the article on ritual by Zuesse in *The Encyclopaedia of Religion* says:

> For our purposes, we shall understand as 'ritual' those conscious and voluntary, repetitious and stylised symbolic bodily actions that are centred on cosmic structures and/or sacred presences (1993: 405).

In my own Free Church tradition, ritual is often used pejoratively, frequently in conjunction with the word 'empty', to denote an activity that is devoid of the sincerity of true belief, a mechanical performing of actions. Others use it as a word to describe habitual actions, often performed without conscious thought or intention—like the 'ritual' of brushing teeth, or locking the house at night. Whilst I have used the term ritual as the most inclusive term to describe these events, I am not sure that it is always the term the women themselves would have chosen. Whilst some would be comfortable with it, some from within the Christian tradition might well prefer the term liturgy; others might use ceremony. I want to reflect on these women's rituals, liturgies or ceremonies in the context of current ritual theory, to see what parallels can be drawn, and where distinctions need to be made.

Much ritual theory is grounded in Emile Durkheim's (1976 [1915]) view which sees rites as secondary to religious belief. He puts forward a theory of religion which sees it as a totality of rites and beliefs. In a dualistic understanding of the world as divided into sacred and profane, beliefs are attempts to represent the nature of the sacred realm, while rites are more like rules of conduct which must be followed in the presence of the sacred. Belief is a system of thought, or opinion; ritual is a mode of action which expresses or communicates belief. The belief is primary: 'It is possible to define the rite only after we have defined the belief' (Durkheim 1976: 36) and this remains the case even when the belief system in which the rite originated has all but disappeared, and only the folk-lore or observance of the ritual remains. Even though belief is primary, the ritual plays an important part in helping to maintain the cohesiveness of social structure, and its fixed form and repetitious performance is the means of ensuring continuity and stability.

Clifford Geertz develops an understanding of religion which is based on its role in the transmission of culture. He defines religion as:

> (1) a system of symbols which acts to (2) establish powerful, pervasive, and long-lasting moods and motivations in men by (3) formulating conceptions of a general order of existence and (4) clothing these conceptions with such an aura of factuality that the moods and motivations seem uniquely realistic (1973: 90).

Within a religious system, symbols act powerfully to convey or induce moods and feelings, in such a way that human experience is seen and interpreted within a world view that gives shape and order to the chaos and ambiguity of human living. The use of symbols takes the order and form of the rite which helps to give a sense of the order and shape of the world:

> It is in some sort of ceremonial form — even if that form is hardly more than the recitation of a myth, the consultation of an oracle, or the

decoration of a grave — that the moods and motivations which sacred symbols induce in men and the general concepts of the order of existence which they formulate for men meet and reinforce one another (1973: 112).

In this way the enactment of a ritual reinforces the authority of religious belief, giving symbolic and embodied form to a world view, and a sense of cosmic order. In many definitions, unvarying repetition is one of the defining characteristics of ritual. Stanley Tambiah, for example, defines ritual as:

> a culturally constructed system of symbolic communication. It is constituted of patterned and ordered sequences of words and acts, often expressed in multiple media, whose content and arrangement are characterized in varying degrees by formality (conventionality), stereotyping (rigidity), condensation (fusion), and redundancy (repetition) (Tambiah 1985: 128).

He does not, however, follow Durkheim's insistence that belief is primary, and places more emphasis on the action and performance of ritual as communicating and constructing a sense of meaning, social stability, and belief in an ordered cosmos:

> Moreover, when beliefs are taken to be prior to ritual action, the latter is considered as derivative and secondary, and is ignored or undervalued in its own right as a medium for transmitting meanings, constructing social reality, or, for that matter, creating and bringing to life the cosmological scheme itself (Tambiah 1985: 129).

It is the repeated performance of ritual in its fixed form that gives it its effectiveness, and although rites may be modified and revised, this revision itself is dependent upon a limited number of formats, and continues to rely heavily on repetition. It is the stereotypical and repetitive nature of ritual that gives it its power as an intense and heightened power of communication:

> Religious ritual may be defined, for the purposes of this paper, as the prescribed performance of conventionalized acts manifestly directed toward the involvement of nonempirical or supernatural agencies in the affairs of the actors (Rappaport 1979: 28).

Ritual enactments or performances have two aspects: the canonical, the prescribed values, words and actions which are laid down; and the indexical, those values and elements which relate to the immediate context and situation. There is therefore, in Roy Rappaport's understanding of ritual, some attention to the individual state of mind of participants; but the ritual, rather than expressing feeling, is a vehicle for enabling the participants to conform to social norms:

> He has, so to speak, signalled to himself that he has imposed a simple yes-no decision upon whatever ambivalence, fear and doubt he may have been experiencing. There is nothing for him to do now but to bring his private processes into accord with the new public status that follows from his ritual act (Rappaport 1979: 185).

Ritual is a social activity prescribed for the participants, not something which they have devised or which necessarily reflects or expresses their feelings:

> I take ritual to be a form or structure, defining it as the performance of more or less invariant sequences of formal acts and utterances not encoded by the performers (Rappaport 1979: 175).

The idea of ritual as repetitive and unvarying emerges in a number of different contexts. David Kertzer, in talking of rituals in relation to power, adopts the standard definition in 'defining ritual as symbolic behavior that is socially structured and repetitive' (Kertzer 1988: 9). Although he concedes that individuals may create new rituals, they continue to draw on existing symbols, and more usually, participants engage in rituals which they have had no hand in creating. The repetition of rituals over time gives continuity and a sense of linking the present participants with past and future. Pamela Cooper-White talks of the power and efficacy of ritual in therapy, and stresses the power of symbolic action, but again sees repetition as key to this:

> I would propose a working definition of ritual as any act which symbolically carries conscious or unconscious meaning and is repeated over a given period of time (1998–99: 69).

There is therefore a considerable body of thought which sees the power of ritual as residing in its fixed, prescribed form — the use of symbols and symbolic actions which are repeated unchangingly over time, and the enactment or performance of which construct or reinforce beliefs, values, or social relations.

But the women's rituals that I have described do not fit this pattern. They are contextual — each one is unique to its own situation, and although they may use written resources, prayers, or poems from elsewhere, each is crafted to fit the particular woman's experience and situation. They do use symbols and symbolic action, and there are certainly some symbols which occur more frequently than others in women's rituals and liturgies; but there is no one symbol or format which can be seen as universal or enduring over time—they are located in particular enactments and contexts. There are no 'canonical' elements—whilst there are resources available, there is no prescribed order or format; and where traditional resources are chosen, they are used eclectically, because they are seen as relevant to the individual woman's experience, situation, or state of mind. There are theological references, and implicit belief here, but no sense of a clear body of doctrine which must be incorporated or expressed in the ritual for it to be valid. According to this set of definitions, women's ritual is no such thing—it may be creative, artistic or enjoyable, but does not fit neatly into this understanding of ritual.

Ritual Making as Strategic Practice

There are, however, other understandings of ritual which provide a more helpful framework for looking at these women's rituals. Catherine Bell examines the ritual theory of scholars such as Durkheim, Geertz, Tambiah and Rappaport, and argues that in their thinking about ritual they set up a duality, of belief and ritual, or thought and action, which they then use ritual to resolve; so that ritual is both one half of a binary opposition, but also the means of trying to integrate the two. Such dualism, she argues, is never neutral—there is an implicit assumption that thought and belief are primary, which therefore fails to take ritual seriously as a practice on its own terms. To a certain extent, performance theory[1] (such as that of Tambiah and Rappaport) seeks to overcome this by focusing on the performance or enactment of ritual as social practice, but introduces a third dualism—that of the actors who perform the ritual, and the theorist who observes and analyses:

> Most simply, we might say, ritual is to the symbols it dramatizes as action is to thought; on a second level, ritual integrates thought and action; and on a third level, a focus on ritual performance interprets *our* thoughts and *their* action (Bell 1992: 32 Author's italics).

---

1. I return to performance theory in chapter eight, with an emphasis on performance as embodied activity, rather than an event which is observed.

Bell argues that we should look at ritual as a social practice, one in which certain actions are differentiated and set apart by the actors themselves, a process which she calls 'ritualization'. Ritual participants construct certain actions, times or places as sacred, and mark them off from everyday living:

> With this approach in mind, I will use the term ritualization to draw attention to the way in which certain social activities strategically distinguish themselves in relation to other actions. In a very preliminary sense, ritualization is a way of acting that is designed and orchestrated to distinguish and privilege what is being done in comparison to other, usually more quotidian, activities. As such, ritualization is a matter of various culturally specific strategies for setting some activities off from others, for creating and privileging a qualitative distinction between the "sacred" and the "profane", and for ascribing such distinctions to realities thought to transcend the powers of human actors (Bell 1992: 74).

In doing so, they may make use of certain strategies, such as formality or repetition, but these are not essential characteristics of ritual. A Catholic mass, for example, might be celebrated with great formality and repetition; or it might be an informal folk mass in someone's kitchen; but in either case, it is differentiated from the everyday act of sharing a meal, and thus becomes a ritual practice:

> Yet if ritual is interpreted in terms of practice, it becomes clear that formality, fixity and repetition are not intrinsic qualities of rituals so much as they are a frequent, but not universal strategy for producing ritual acts (Bell 1992: 92).

Looking at ritual as social practice, Bell argues, shows that it shares four features with other forms of practice. First, human activity is situational—it derives from, and in turn shapes, a particular context. This means that, however much ritual uses techniques of fixity and repetition, the way of designating ritual is always provisional, dependent upon cultural and social location and circumstance. Second, practice is strategic—it has a certain expediency and manipulation about it, designed to achieve certain ends. However, third, there is a 'misrecognition' involved—there is not a conscious awareness of the strategies being used. This is not a deliberate mystification of ritual, building up a sense of mystery, or inexplicable esoteric practices. Rather, it refers to the way in which ritual participants attribute their activities to the revelation, command or activities of divine or transcendent powers, without recognizing them as their own construction. Fourth, ritual as social practice shows 'redemptive hegemony' — it both reflects and also reinforces or resists the social and power relationships in which it is embedded.

Bell's thinking gives a useful framework for looking at these women's rituals as social practice. They are certainly contextual and situational — each participant has constructed and shaped her own ritual in relation to her particular context and experience. They are also strategic — they are a way in which women have chosen to negotiate, manage or interpret the changes and transitions in their lives. They are embedded in a social context of patriarchal society and religion, and as such are both shaped by, and resist, patterns of power and domination. However, Bell's concept of 'misrecognition' does raise some questions in this context:

> Ritualization does not see how it actively creates place, force, event, and tradition, how it redefines or generates the circumstances to which it is responding. It does not see how its own actions reorder and reinterpret the circumstances so as to afford the sense of a fit among the main spheres of experience — body, community, and cosmos (Bell 1992: 109).

Whilst Bell's argument may be true in some cases, in the rituals I have studied women show a conscious intention to create or set apart a time or a space, a careful choice of symbol and symbolic action, and an awareness of their agency in the process. While they use images of deity and spirituality, and talk of divine power or energy at work, the women are quite clear that the ritual actions are their own constructions, rather than something that is revealed or given. Whilst for some ritual participants there may be the kind of 'not seeing' that Bell describes, the act of creating and enacting one's own ritual suggests a conscious intention and agency. For these women, ritual is a chosen strategy, and they are aware of the processes involved in that choice.

The understanding of ritual as a constructed and creative practice is found in other contemporary thinking. One of the major writers in this area is Ronald Grimes, who is a key figure in the relatively new but growing discipline of ritual studies. He argues for the inadequacy of many traditional rites, and sees the need for construction of new rituals that are consistent with contemporary experience. He defines ritual as '*sequences of ordinary action rendered special by virtue of their condensation, elevation or stylization'* (Grimes 2000: 70–71; author's italics). In this understanding, the intention of the participants is key. Not all repeated action can be classed as ritual, but only that which is in some way made special by the way it is understood and performed. In ritual, there is a tension between the traditional and the innovative, and rites are constantly under revision:

> Every tradition is marked by a perennial tension between those who would keep things the same (and thus connected to sacred origins) and those who would update them (thus making them relevant to participants...Rites are always in the process of being forgotten and reinvented, exported and adapted, conserved and reimagined (Grimes 2000: 190–91).

This is not to say that all ritual invention is creative or imaginative; it can fall into stereotyped patterns, or be oppressive in its effect. There is need therefore for ritual criticism, analogous to literary criticism. This is not an easy process, however, as rituals and those who perform them tend to be resistant; and the right to criticize needs to be related to participation and respect:

> Rites, like myths and dreams, resist criticism or, if you prefer, people resist having their rites, myths and dreams subject to criticism. The right to engage in it at all is probably either bought with membership and participation or directly dependent upon the richness of one's observation and interpretations (Grimes 2000: 291).

Grimes makes a distinction between rites, which he sees as the finished product, and ritualizing, the process of creating rites, which is much more fluid, and less prone to support the status quo (Grimes 2000). Others have followed his work in stressing the creative potential of ritual.

For many people the ritual of the church has become disconnected with their lived experience (Anderson and Foley 2001). Yet in spite of the disconnected, fragmented society in which we live, the need for some kind of ritual and ceremony which can provide meaningful interpretation persists. Women's making of ritual is set in the broader context of a postmodern desire for ritual which expresses and speaks to contemporary experience.

Tom Driver (1998) argues that ritual and ritualized behaviour is universal—found in animals as well as throughout human culture. In contemporary Western society and church, however, 'ritual boredom' is prevalent, and rites need to be both liberated from dullness and irrelevance, and liberating for the participants as a form of praxis working towards freedom and justice. Ritual needs both a 'confessional' mode, in which individual stories and experiences are shared, and a sense of identity formed; and an ethical mode, which looks beyond itself to the shaping of communal values and the celebration of ethical acts. He builds on Rappaport's work in understanding the function of ritual in creating a sense of order, but feels that Rappaport places too much emphasis on invariance in this — rituals do change and need adaptation; and part of their transformative power lies in their ability to create community.

Lesley Northup (1997) begins not with traditional definitions of ritual, but with her observation and analysis of the liturgies and rituals enacted by groups of women in a variety of settings. She also chooses the term 'ritualizing' to convey the sense of fluidity, process and dynamism in the women's liturgical and ritual practices she describes. Like Grimes, she sees the process of construction as one which is acknowledged and intentional. Women's rituals include reflexivity, the ability to reflect on and critique the ritual action, and there is therefore a need to develop the discipline of 'ritual criticism' (Northup 1993).

The rituals I have studied have much in common with what Northup and Grimes call 'ritualizing', although I find this a somewhat clumsy term, and prefer to talk about making, creating or enacting ritual.

Each ritual is unique, specifically created for the occasion, and although they may contain published resources or symbols that have been used before, they are particular and contextual in their application, and do not draw on fixed or canonical forms. Driver and Grimes both speak of creative ritual taking place amongst marginalized groups, and in some instances the rituals here emerge in resistance to an established form. Clare, for example, creates her own ritual to mark the completion of her thesis because of her dissatisfaction with traditional graduation:

> Yes, and I think those are the things that are marked by Latin and gowns and silly hats — those are the things I don't want — so it's trying to finding things to replace the traditional things that say what I do want it to be about (Planning session with Clare).

Nicola's celebration of the Eucharist before her hysterectomy is in part a protest against patriarchal religion and its denial of the power of the human, especially female, body:

> Although in a way the primary thing was about getting me prepared for my hysterectomy at another level I was actually thinking—well, I probably wasn't thinking this but something about the Eucharist— even the bloody Eucharist is controlled and contained by these men but actually the irony is that so often it's so unbodily, isn't it? (Interview, Nicola).

Women's ritual-making does not start from pre-conceived beliefs and religious convictions, as in Durkheim's understanding. The account of theology and spirituality in women's ritual-making given above shows not clearly defined belief and creeds, but diversity, and the emergence of theology and spirituality within the ritual action. Teresa Berger reinterprets the traditional concept of 'lex orandi, lex credendi' ('the law of praying, the law of believing). Traditionally, she argues, this has been seen in dualistic terms, suggesting an opposition of the devotional non-scholarly experience of prayer (primarily the sphere of women) and the academic liturgical reflection (predominantly done by men). Reclaiming this, she argues that the contemporary experience of women in liturgy and ritual-making makes liturgy into a crucial site for interpreting and constructing faith and theology in a way that emphasizes women's power:

> The importance of liturgy as a site of struggle over what shapes Christian women's lives cannot be over-emphasized. For the Christian tradition in which liturgical authority seemed to be the prerogative of a male priesthood, or more recently, a caste of (mostly male) liturgical experts, the fact that women themselves now actively construct and interpret their liturgical world is a primary mode of claiming power. To put it differently, women today have rendered visible the liturgy as a crucial site for what, arguably it has always been: the negotiation between faith and women's lives (Berger 2001: 73).

She is clearly speaking from a Christian (Catholic) perspective, but for women speaking outside the Christian tradition, a similar process is operating. Their ritual making is both expressing, but also constructing and giving shape to their understanding of spirituality:

> But I would say that that is the specialness of ritual that it does consciously raise spiritual intent. It's very important to tune in,

spiritually if you like, and align myself with the planet and have myself as part of that kind of divine flow if you like of existence so I suppose ritualizing something, issues, helps to really, you know, hone that spiritual intent (Interview, Rebecca).

So the women's ritual making portrayed here is, in Bell's terms, a strategic practice that women choose to negotiate the changes and transitions in their lives. It makes creative use of symbol and space to interpret and construct not only experience, but theo/alogy and spirituality. It is contextual and strategic—it aims not only to express an existing reality, but to change and make a difference to their context.

And as I said at the beginning, ritual is very important, so I expect it to make a difference. Some issues I can talk about 'till the cows come home, but if I actually engage in that kind of ritual, that pivotal, I expect it to be different as a result of it (Planning session with Rebecca).

Women's ritual making is an intentional and consciously-chosen act. It has transformative potential and power, shaping women's lives, actions, and—whatever name they use—their encounter with the sacred.

Case Study Three

SHELLS AND FISH — JANE'S STORY

Jane had been made redundant as a result of structural re-organization. Although the period of re-organization had caused her some stress, there was much about the job that she loved; and in addition to the inevitable economic and practical consequences, the loss of work had a far-reaching impact on her sense of identity and creativity.

She decided that she would like to lead the women's group to which she belonged in a ritual marking her redundancy. When she first spoke to me about it, she was looking for new work, but felt the need of some kind of completion, and hoped that it would 'settle' some things for her at a personal level.

She felt it would be helpful to involve me in the planning, and so a few days before the ritual was due to be held she visited me for lunch and to talk through her ideas. She had done a lot of the thinking in advance, and I felt I contributed very little, except to act as a sounding-board for her. She started off by listing the feelings she had been through during the last few months; inevitably negative feelings of pain, loss and grief. At this stage, she expressed less anger than I would have expected; although later it came through clearly in her ritual and the subsequent interview.

When I asked her what she wanted out of the ritual, she said (half-jokingly) 'A job!' and then talked more generally about 'being in charge', in contrast to the feelings of helplessness evoked by redundancy. She talked about how much of her identity, her relationships and her creativity had been tied up with her job and the professional and social networks it involved.

As we focused on how this might be expressed, she had a number of possibilities in mind for symbols or symbolic actions. The one to which Jane kept coming back was the use of shells to symbolize what her work meant to her, and her feeling that in losing her paid work she had lost something of the protective shell which her sense of identity gave her. After further discussion, she focused on the idea of putting shells in water to let go of negative experiences and feelings. She talked about how she wanted to end – 'with a bowl of water, with shells at the bottom, with a floating candle on top, and for us all to light candles for wishes' (planning session with Jane).

Visualizing the end of the ritual seemed to give her clarity about the structure; we decided that what was missing was something to represent a positive affirmation of skills and qualities. We decided to use glass beads for this, placed in the water along with the shells, so that negatives and positives would be transformed together by the light of a candle floating in the bowl. Jane went away with a clear structure in mind, and the tasks of writing her story and a prayer for lighting the candle, and choosing some music. She telephoned me later that evening to say she had written out her story to read at the beginning – she thought perhaps it was 'too long and dramatic – but it had been very cathartic to write it' (Journal entry, Jane's ritual).

The ritual itself was held on the Sunday evening after we met, at Jane's home. The room was arranged with cushions and chairs, and Jane's small table in the centre, with a bowl of water, some candles, some shells and a dish of glass beads and fish. There was laughter and joking as people arrived and settled in. Jane welcomed people and introduced the evening, acknowledging some apprehension about her feelings, and receiving reassurance from the group. After some music and opening responses, Jane read her story, which echoed some of the feelings she had described to me earlier, and powerfully captured some of the tensions and ambivalences around her experience of work and redundancy.

In the story she introduced the image of the shell which she had decided to use as a symbol later on in the ritual:

> This has felt like a painful stripping of an outer shell which had protected me as the animal inside in lots of ways. So I have used shells as one symbol of what we might either have to let go or even want to let go about work – be it paid or unpaid (Written script for Jane's ritual).

She asked me to read a poem written by Ann Lewin (1993) about redundancy, using the image of crucifixion. Then she passed around a bowl of shells, inviting us each to take one (or more) to symbolize letting go of negative aspects or roles in relation to work, paid or unpaid, in order to be more ourselves.

In turn we placed our shells into the bowl of water, sharing our feelings verbally if we chose to. Most people did so, with a variety of meanings — policies or practices at work which they found difficult; feelings of vulnerability within the church's culture of vocation; frustrations with work or colleagues; experiences of bullying; colleagues being made redundant. Some did not take up the theme of work directly, but talked of loss of identity in other ways, relating to family or the break-up of relationships. At the end Jane added more shells of her own — 'for letting go of shame — because it isn't her fault; resentment — because it isn't their fault' (Journal entry, Jane's ritual). Then she passed around the glass beads, along with some glass fish which she had happened to find, for people to share the positive aspects of creativity in their present situations. The mood became quieter and more expansive, as people expressed feelings of being able to make a difference, of status at work, of the freedom of working for themselves. For one woman the fish itself was significant, speaking of a fluidity to swim through the water, and in and out of the shells. Jane herself spoke of reaffirming her creativity, and the importance of the sense of belonging which her friendships gave her. When we had all added our beads and fish to the bowl with the shells, we joined in the prayer which Jane had written, as she lit a candle and floated it on top of the water. The remaining candles spread around the table were lit as we offered our hopes and prayers for ourselves and others; and we finished by singing a version of the Celtic blessing 'Deep peace of the running wave to you':

> the bowl looks beautiful with its mixture of shells and glass beads, some nesting within the shells, the small glass fishes, and the candle floating on top — surrounded by ten tea lights round the edge of the table — and it reminds me of my sense during the planning session, that it was when she said how she wanted to end up, that the whole thing came together. A very simple ritual, few scripted words, but a lot of powerful sharing, a very clear shape to it (Journal entry, Jane's ritual).

I returned about seven weeks later to interview Jane about her ritual. She had gone into her office for a leaving function and felt she had been able to say her goodbyes, privately and publicly, as honestly and well as she could. She had been successful in obtaining a new post which would build on her experience and develop it. She felt the ritual had helped her to move on in a number of ways, making a formal ending to her previous work, and preparing for a new beginning.

The presence of others and the opportunity to express her feelings in a slightly more public setting than previously had helped her to let go of much of her pain, and anger. But this went beyond others listening to her—it was their own sharing and acknowledgement which was powerful for her:

> cos the process of letting go actually involved other people acknowledging what was there as well as my just splurging on in a vacuum (Interview, Jane).

As well as supporting her in her vulnerability, members of the group shared their own experiences, pain and anger, hopes and insights, and this had added another dimension for her. The ritual itself was a significant point in her whole process of moving through the painful transition of redundancy, particularly because it had enabled her to take some control in what had felt a helpless situation. For her this was:

> Probably the most significant point in the process. Because it was also about taking charge of what was going on in a way that was more fundamental than I'd done before (Interview, Jane).

Jane was aware that although at one level she was in charge, at another level, as people added their own meanings and understandings, the process was out of her hands:

> And although I had structured it in terms of being in charge of what was going to happen and where we were going to end up, I hadn't structured it in terms of what the content would be. And I think, again, I think there's something about structuring a process and enabling other people to fill in the content that is quite powerful (Interview, Jane).

The symbolism of the candle and the transforming of negatives into positives had worked for her:

> And I think halfway through the liturgy...I lit a floating candle and everyone else said the prayer, I think, about transforming the good and the bad, and changing...the negatives to positives. And I think that's what happened for me psychologically (Interview, Jane).

She was aware that she had planned the symbolism carefully, trying to keep it simple and uncluttered, and focusing on the goal:

I chose—well, it was partly because I knew where I wanted to end up, so there was a kind of goal about the symbolism. I chose the water because the water always symbolised transforming and flowing and cleansing. I chose the shells because of what they represented about letting things go and the negatives. And I think you helped to choose the beads and then fishes came in by accident because I hadn't realised I had fishes and beads in together, in that bowl. But it felt important that there was something that initially had been positive and initially had been negative (Interview, Jane).

She found it hard to put into words exactly how that process had worked, but saw it as a reshaping, psychologically and spiritually:

There may be also something about the power of subconscious in that when you see in our process—that when you see that—an extremely attractive decoration has been made out of all this mess and the lights in the dark look extremely helpful and attractive and beautiful—there's something about the beauty of that—that gives you hope (Interview, Jane).

The ritual is one part of a process of letting go, gathering strength, moving on, and finding a new beginning, which has created a sense of empowerment for Jane:

To be honest, I didn't believe in a God who cared very much that I had been made redundant, or who was actually prepared to do anything about it—before I did that ritual. By the end of the ritual I did have a sense of a God/Goddess who did care that I had been made redundant and was willing to empower me to do more about it (Interview, Jane).

Chapter Six

RE-(W)RITING THE SELF: NARRATIVE, IDENTITY AND AGENCY

As women told me about their rituals, I found that they were also telling me elements of their life-stories. They described events that led up to and surrounded their rituals, recounting losses, relationships and events which were central for them at the time. They began to put into words their hopes and intentions for the future. In so doing they were engaging in a process of making sense of their experiences, constructing their meaning, expressed and shaped by the words, images and symbols which they used.

Ritual shares some of the features of narrative and can function in similar ways in enabling participants to retell or re-enact and interpret aspects of their lives and experiences. Some of the work that has been done on the narrative construction of identity can help us see how ritual, whilst not technically a story, is used by the women (sometimes consciously and intentionally, sometimes less overtly) to construct their own experience, identity, and theology.

With the development of post-modernism has come a deconstruction of notions of 'the essential self' which can be discovered and expressed. Ideas of the rational, thinking Cartesian self are replaced by notions of a 'self' which is fragmentary, fluid, and shifting, negotiated and constructed through a variety of social and cultural influences. 'Identity' is not a fixed core, but assumed or enacted according to the context and circumstances, and to a certain extent at least, determined by gender, race and social location.

Such a notion of the self raises questions about ideas of autonomy and agency. For feminists, just beginning to discover a sense of self and self-worth, the questions are particularly acute. As Michelle Crossley rather wryly remarks:

> The need to maintain an element of individuality, agency and autonomy, and not simply to "die" into the fragmentary, disordered condition characterised by post-modern theorists is particularly

important from a feminist perspective. This is because feminism is partly about enabling women to "discover" the independence and autonomy that comes from experiencing the kind of self post-modernists are in the business of deconstructing. As many women have never experienced such a self in the first place, it is unlikely that they will be as willing to give it up as the post-modern acolytes (2000: 39).

In order to be able to talk about a self that has some kind of sense of coherence, continuity, and agency within the fragmentation of postmodernism, there is a turn to the idea of narrative, found across a number of disciplines — social sciences, philosophy, psychology and theology. In the absence of a defined, unchanging 'core self', the self is the life about which a story can be told.

Narrative and the Construction of the Self

The use of narrative is attractive in a post-modern world-view for a number of reasons. Hinchman & Hinchman (2001) argue that it enables an emphasis on human agency and the potential to shape our worlds; it allows for a plurality of stories, which can complement or challenge one another, over against a body of authoritative 'objective' knowledge; and it allows for further exploration and understanding of social worlds.

Alisdair MacIntyre uses the concept of the unity of self in narrative as a basis for his ethical thinking arguing for:

a concept of a self whose unity resides in the unity of a narrative which links birth to life to death as narrative beginning to middle to end (MacIntyre 1989: 91).

Human actions are only intelligible as part of a story, and we learn to interpret them from the stories we hear from others, from childhood onwards. The story provides a framework in which actions are located in time, motivation explained and understood, and which point to a future intention.

While many theorists draw their examples of narrative from literary texts or the therapeutic setting, Ochs and Capps look to the emergence of narrative and story-telling in everyday life. With detailed analysis of conversation, they show how stories and narrative emerge in social interactions to interpret and give shape to experience. This is not an easy process, as the desire to be real and authentic does not always lend itself to coherence; narratives do not emerge neatly plotted and fully-formed, but struggling to find shape in the process of communicating experience. The act of telling a story is a 'sense-making process' (Ochs and Capps 2001: 15) rather than the displaying of a finished, polished product:

> All narrative exhibits tension between the desire to construct an over-arching storyline that ties events together in a seamless explanatory framework and the desire to capture the complexities of the events experienced, including haphazard details, uncertainties, and conflicting sensibilities amongst protagonists (Ochs and Capps 2001: 4).

The theme of the construction of identity through narrative has been particularly developed in the writings of the French philosopher, Paul Ricoeur. Whilst Ricoeur's theories of narrative have their roots in literary texts, he argues that life and literary narrative have many parallels; the literary texts enable us to see more clearly what is happening in the reality of lives as they are lived and experienced. What Ricoeur calls the 'pre-narrative quality of human experience' enables us to speak of life as an incipient story, and thus of life as *'an activity and a desire in search of a narrative'* (Ricoeur 1991: 434). He argues that human experience itself has a narrative quality – it can only be understood and given shape in the form of a narrative that explains and makes connections (Ricoeur 1995; 1994). There is a constant interplay between experience, the stories we tell, and the selves we are constructing; our narrative imposes a structure on the open-endedness of experience, but that experience is constantly being revised, as we construct our interpretation of our lives (our selves):

> This open-endedness places us in a situation where we can bring ourselves together narratively only by superimposing in some way a configuration with a beginning, a middle and an ending. But at the same time, we are always in the process of revising the text, the narrative of our lives (Ricoeur 1995: 309).

This is not to argue that the narrative is a fully-formed, polished text; social practices, whilst not explicitly narrative in their form, nevertheless have a narrative quality about them:

> This is not to say that practices as such contain ready-made narrative scenarios, but their organisation gives them a pre-narrative quality which in the past I placed under the heading of *mimesis* (Ricoeur 1994: 157).

Ricoeur describes the process of constructing the story as enplotment. The story takes shape as we recount life-experiences and events, whether we are agents, or the objects of others' actions. As we tell the story, we attribute, whether explicitly or implicitly, motives and causes, and so establish a chain of 'who did what and how' (Ricoeur 1994: 146). From the retelling of actions emerges a sense of character, or identity. We can never, of course, tell the complete story of our own lives—the story of our birth, and even more so, our conception, is hidden from memory, and the ending of our life-story, in death, is unknown to us.

Ricoeur does not argue for complete autonomy or agency in constructing our life-stories—what happens in our lives is not totally within our control—but narrative enables us to engage in the process of making sense of our experiences. In that sense we are not the authors, or initiators, of our own life-stories, but we are co-authors, in that the telling of the story enables us to interpret and give meaning to the events, circumstances and relationships through which we live:

> By narrating a life of which I am not the author as to existence, I make myself the coauthor as to its meaning (Ricoeur 1994: 162).

As the story is told, so a sense of self or identity emerges from it:

> The narrative constructs the identity of the character, what can be called his or her narrative identity, in constructing that of the story told. It is the identity of the story that makes the identity of the character (Ricoeur 1994: 147–48).

Ricoeur uses the terms 'idem' and 'ipse' to expand his notion of self, and its identity and continuity through change and time. The self is not the same (idem) in terms of a fixed, unchanging, essential form; rather, it is dynamic, fluid, but finds its continuity, is still the same self (ipse) through the continuity of the story which it tells. In this way Ricoeur attempts to hold together the notion of a continuing identity or self with the notion of change and meaningful action:

> This dilemma disappears if we substitute for identity understood as being the same (idem), identity understood in the sense of oneself as self-same [soi-meme] (ipse). The difference between idem and ipse is nothing more than the difference between a substantial or formal identity and a narrative identity (Ricoeur 1990: 246).

For feminists, Ricoeur offers an understanding of narrative as a way of constructing identity which can break through the impasse of the rejection of the essential, rationalist self, and the lack of autonomy and agency which this brings. Lois McNay argues that Ricoeur's concept of narrative provides a way through between essentialism and determinism, offering a possibility of agency and autonomy that still allows for an element of construction of self and experience:

> The idea of narrative shares the poststructural emphasis on the constructed nature of identity; there is nothing inevitable or fixed about the types of narrative coherence that may emerge from the flux of events. Yet, at the same time, the centrality of narrative to a sense of self suggests that there are powerful constraints or limits to the ways in which identity may be changed (McNay 2000: 80).

She argues that narrative has been widely used by feminist thinkers, but in two very different ways. Some talk of a culturally-determined metanarrative, imposed on the lives of women, a patriarchal narrative which constrains choices or limits; others privilege individual stories as authentic experience, in a view which is in danger of falling into the naivety of failing to recognize the interpretive character of even the most basic narrative. Ricoeur's analysis of identity as constructed through time helps to overcome this dichotomy, allowing for both structural determinism and autonomy as an individual constructs her life-story:

> As the privileged medium through which the inherent temporality of being is expressed, narrative simultaneously gives shape to identity and is the means through which selfhood is expressed. In other words, narrative is regarded not as determining but as generative of a form of self-identity which itself is neither freely willed nor externally imposed. This idea of the narrative dimensions of subject formation offers a fuller account of the creative and autonomous aspects of agency (McNay 2000: 85).

Such an understanding helps to explain the existence and persistence of social practices which go against prevailing cultural norms, such as the aspects of women's experience which contradict the dominant cultural narrative of romantic, heterosexual love and marriage. Whilst these narratives may be central in institutional practices and norms, the existence of counter cultural practices points to the existence and resistance of alternative stories.

Ricoeur's view of narrative also allows for temporal discontinuity in women's experience. McNay argues that women's understanding of time has often been characterized as cyclical over against a masculine idea of time as linear and progressive. This is an over-simplification, however, which does not take account of the complexities of women's lives, in which their time consists of an interweaving of different kinds of professional, domestic and relational strands, each demanding different uses of and concepts of time. Ricoeur's concept of narrative allows women to see their identity shifting and changing through time, whilst still retaining some sense of continuity of the person:

> Narrative is the mode through which individuals attempt to integrate the non-synchronous and often conflictual elements of their lives and experiences (McNay 2000: 113).

Whilst McNay sees many strengths in Ricoeur's work, arguing that narrative offers a middle way between the essential, autonomous self on the one hand and the fragmented self of postmodern plurality on the other, she argues that he does not pay sufficient attention to questions of power, and that this analysis needs to be incorporated into his work. Whilst his thinking is open to the possibility of this, he does not include a detailed analysis of the way in which ideological narratives operate. A feminist understanding acknowledges that although dominant narratives shape the way in which individual stories are told, contesting stories of marginalized groups continue to emerge and survive. While some writers, for example Maria Pia Lara (1998: 8), go too far in privileging these as more authentic accounts of experience, their persistence points to the role they play in helping to form and maintain the identity of such groups. Narrative therefore has a part to play in constructing a sense of the self within individuals and communities, in a way that moves from individual identity into a political arena. Women and other marginalized groups in telling stories of their identity are exercising agency over against prevailing cultural norms:

> Culturally sanctioned narratives are central to the imposition of hegemonic identities and the emergence of new or contesting forms inevitably highlights the relations of power that underlie the production of narrative discourse (McNay 2000: 114).

Ritual and Narrative

Just as narrative can play a part in the construction of self and identity through the telling of a story, so the making of ritual serves some of the same functions. As with narrative, ritual can be seen as a sense-making process, a way of giving shape and meaning to the particular experiences and transitions that are the focus of the ritual activity.

It is not that these rituals include fully-framed coherent narratives. Lesley Northup (1997) lists a number of different ways in which women's ritualizing includes narrative — autobiography, storytelling and myth, the use of sacred texts (whether biblical or from the 'canon' of feminist writers), and reflexivity or reflecting on the process of ritual itself. The autobiographical sharing of personal stories, similar to the process in consciousness-raising groups, is a common characteristic of women's liturgy and ritual.

In the rituals I have described here there is relatively little reference to the stories of other women, whether biblical or from other sources. Where rituals use biblical texts they tend to allude to them verbally or symbolically, rather than reading or retelling scriptural stories. The primary use of narrative is in sharing stories of a personal and autobiographical nature, and usually in a fragmented or allusive way.

Writers on ritual frequently see a connection between ritual and story. For Anderson and Foley ritual and story belong together. Both are means by which we interpret our world and try to make sense of our experience. They are similar in the ways in which they enable us to make and express meaning, and ritual provides the opportunity for the expression of our stories:

> it is nonetheless true that our search for meaning is a search for an appropriate narrative for life. In this quest, ritualization becomes indispensable, for it provides time, space, symbols and bodily enactment for disclosing, entering and interpreting the many stories that comprise our individual and communal narration and give shape and meaning to our lives (Anderson and Foley 2001: 27).

Writers and practitioners in the field of psychotherapy also speak of the importance of enactment. Pamela Cooper-White (1998–99) uses this term for the non-verbal cues and communications in therapy and argues that an enactment may be a ritual action, such as prayer, which occurs in the therapeutic context. She sees ritual as a necessary stage towards the verbalization of a story that is necessary for effective healing:

> In cases where there is severe trauma stemming from preverbal stages of development, it is crucial, in fact, to help the patient move from inchoate and vague memories of unmetabolised experience through symbolization and finally verbalization in the form of an organising narrative (1998–99: 70).

Family therapists have been using ritual or ritual enactments since the early 1970s (Giblin 1998–99), seeing it as a vital means of helping clients to make sense of the contradictions and tensions of experience, and find healing. Giblin sees one of the major functions of ritual in family therapy as the formation and shaping of identity; but another major function is to offer space for storytelling and listening to stories. Stories and rituals need to be integrated in order for there to be an effective sense of creating meaning; and part of the therapist's task is to help make that connection:

> Therapists often encounter ritual disconnected from story and meaning, or story in search of ritual. In both cases, the therapeutic task is to evoke and/or listen to vital stories and connect them with meaningful ritual (Giblin 1998–99: 98).

In both these approaches ritual and story (or narrative) are closely integrated, and seen as existing together; but they are still separate entities, and I am left with the feeling that ritual is seen as expressing—perhaps in a dramatic or colourful way—a story that could (or needs to be) told in words.

But writers such as Bell, Driver, and Grimes see ritual not as something expressing something else—action expressing belief, or symbols expressing a story—but as a social activity meaningful in itself. Ritual, particularly the kind of ritualizing that is creative and invented (Grimes 1993), is a social process and a strategy (Bell 1992), which demands our attention and interpretation for itself. Ricoeur speaks of meaningful action which can be studied as one would a text. In his thinking, social practices and actions can be studied and observed in ways that are parallel to the study of written texts. Like written texts, they 'fix' action in a particular time and location; they have their own autonomy, in that we can never fully distinguish our own actions and their consequences from those of others; they have a relevance and importance beyond the immediate; and they lead to an indefinite number of future possibilities:

My claim is that action itself, action as meaningful, may become an object of science, without losing its character of meaningfulness, through a kind of objectification similar to the fixation which occurs in writing (Ricoeur 1971: 538).

Ritual making, therefore, is a meaningful action, a social process, which does not simply use or express a story, but is itself a story — albeit one that is provisional and, at least partially, non-verbal. In ritual, in its symbols, its negotiated, shared meanings, its fragments of autobiography, is an emerging story which has meaning for the primary actor who has created and performed the ritual, but also has multilevelled layers of meaning for other participants too.

In the process of constructing their rituals, participants begin to shape their experience in words, and so in the planning stages, we see the beginning of what Ricoeur describes as enplotment. They describe what has happened, ascribe motives to themselves or others, talk about possible causes of events, or the feelings that have led them to the point of transition. Similarly, as they look back and reflect on the rituals, they identify significant turning points and developments within the story. The shape of the ritual has a beginning, a middle, and an end, and so their experiences of change or transition, with all their sense of chaos or opportunity, begin to fit into a narrative framework. Their rituals are not giving expression to a narrative that is already plotted, but their stories form and take shape in the process of planning, enacting and reflecting on the rituals they have created. Jane was the only woman who chose to tell her own story in a deliberate way at the beginning of her ritual, and her story of redundancy begins to take a new form as she is able to let go of negative feelings and transform them into positives.

Jackie deliberately chose not to tell her story, but it was important to her that others knew it; and the pain and hurt she had experienced was alluded to symbolically as she burnt papers and sealed objects in the box.

In Ricoeur's terminology, in ritual the women are becoming co-authors of their own lives. They do not determine what has happened, but they are using ritual as a strategy to give sense and meaning to life-events, to actively shape their own response. In the process, a construction of self or identity is emerging for each of them.

The rituals also show some of the temporality of narrative. In dealing with transition and change, there is inevitably a very clear location in time. Often this is reflected in the ritual itself, with a shape or structure that refers back to past events and hurt, roots itself in the present moment, and then looks forward to future hopes and intentions. So for Alison, she begins with reference to the past hurt and betrayal, which is symbolically taken away in the form of silver coins, before she can look for resources for the future. Carol's ritual looks back over the past ten years, names the struggle and uncertainty of the present, and then moves into hopes for an-as-yet unknown future.

There is too an open-endedness about the future in many of the rituals — there are hopes and intentions, but no certainty. As in narrative, ritual has a future-oriented dimension. Ricoeur points out that the narrative of a human life is not ended until death; there is a sense therefore in which the story is never complete, but always open to future possibilities. The 'present' of the ritual contains hopes, expectations and anticipations of the future; thus in constructing a narrative we are 'co-authoring' not only past and present, but to a certain extent the future too.

When Jane was planning her ritual, I asked her what she wanted from it, and she replied half-jokingly, 'A job!' A week after the ritual she was interviewed for and appointed to a new post. She is understandably cautious in speaking about cause-and-effect, but nonetheless sees a connection between the enactment of the ritual and the subsequent unfolding of events:

> And I am perfectly sure that the positiveness of that experience was actually what carried me through in the interview a week later...But I wasn't altogether surprised in terms of the sense of empowerment — the psychological sense of empowerment — and possibly spiritual sense of empowerment as well (Interview, Jane).

There is therefore a sense, however ill-defined, that although ritual is a point in an ongoing process, there is something in it that shapes the way in which that process continues to unfold. The ritual process is not only marking a shift in identity that has already taken place — it has a part to play in shaping the way in which identity will continue to be constructed as subsequent life events and relationships unfold.

Similarly Clare, planning her thesis ritual, is conscious of the need to move on, but unsure where that will take her:

> There's also an element of moving on—moving on, making a space
> for other things, for myself and family, and maybe things will, things
> still carrying on from the thesis—but moving on from the written,
> back into church and community (Planning session with Clare).

Louise and Andrea, in their house-blessings, have hopes and
intentions as to how the space will be used, but cannot know for
sure how their plans will work out. Runa, particularly, sees her
change of name and the ritual marking it as a process that is only
just beginning:

> And the Runa koan—well—unfolding itself all over the place. And
> that's wonderful, I think it is magic, and I think that's what rituals do,
> they unleash a process which can go anywhere for years and years in
> advance. It's like sowing a seed—who knows what's going to spring
> up if you're receptive to it, because it's not all under—it's not all about
> control, you know, there's this unconscious aspect, or deeper spiritual
> aspect—limitless, really, in its potential (Interview, Runa).

So these rituals are not so much telling a story, nor are they
expressing a story that is already written. Rather, the process of
planning, performing and reflecting on the ritual is a process in
which the story begins to emerge—it is *poesis*, a making, of a story.

Identity and Agency in Women's Ritual Making

In many of the rituals, identity is a key theme. For Jane, redundancy
reveals the way her identity was tied up with her work and the
network of relationships that went with it. With the loss of her
work, she has lost the 'shell' which gave her identity, leaving her
feeling vulnerable and exposed. The ritual was a particular point in
a process of losing a sense of identity and beginning to find a new
one in other ways:

> I've done more than I would usually do with my parish church actually
> and I've found that my identity is less caught up with a role and more
> caught up with who I am myself (Interview, Jane).

It is particularly clear in Jackie's and Runa's renaming rituals,
where 'who they are' is very much at the heart of the ritual.

Runa's ritual, as we saw earlier, begins with her realization that
she wishes to publish something about her past experience, without
her family being identified. On the other hand, speaking out about
her abuse is important to her, so she does not wish to remain

anonymous. Rather than write under a pseudonym, she chose to take a new name; so in one sense her identity was not the same (*idem*); but there was a continuity of selfhood (*ipse*) between the person who had these experiences and the person writing about them:

> And I had this real dilemma about that because I really wanted to own my own experience and to stand up and speak out about it and it seemed really important for me that I could speak my truth and be identified with it...it was sort of within the cover of a name my family wouldn't recognise but if it became my real name there wasn't a separation between Runa the writer and Runa who lives her life and everyone could know (Interview, Runa).

Jackie too recognizes the discontinuity involved in taking a new name, as she realizes that people will not necessarily connect her new name with work that she has published previously; nevertheless the taking of a new name has become a significant act of liberation in enabling her to move on into a new identity:

> Any new publication will come under my new name and again not make that connection—all that sort of questioning in relation to the future. But I still think the future for me is, it is about freedom—it's freedom to be connected with whatever I have chosen, my identity (Planning session with Jackie).

Other rituals touch on identity in different ways. Rebecca is conscious not only of losing her identity through the loss of her job, but also of creating a new identity as she moves into a new phase of her life:

> I'm feeling amused at myself, if I stand up in a strange pulpit or meet people for the first time, I'm aware of that feeling of, "Oh, who shall I be? How shall I describe myself? Shall I be a ministry student? Shall I just be me?" (Planning session with Rebecca).

In some rituals, the sense of identity is less explicit, but still present. For Carol, her sense of identity is tied up with her sense of calling, and Clare is trying to tie together the different strands of what it means to be a minister, an academic, and an active presence in her local community. Cora talks about her passage into the menopause as learning to trust and assume a new identity as an elder and crone:

> It's more like—something like eldership, and like letting go of preconceptions of what eldership is and really seeing if I can get to a

deep level of trust that whatever I am, you know, I am an elder now, somehow. And I remember when we did the ritual last year, the sweat lodge ceremony, we were all women who were somewhere around the menopause and we talked a lot about being baby crones and not really knowing how to do it. And it feels like—I still don't know how to do it but I'm actually—yeah, it feels like time to grow into it, to embrace it, to accept that cloak somehow (Interview, Cora).

For Sue, the question of identity is less problematic, but she is still aware that retirement on her 60th birthday brings a change in identity and role, and expresses this in a poem using the image of a river flowing into the sea:

And then the theme of identity is there. I've got "where is identity in these wider waters?" And then I thought of all the things that women are—sisters and aunts—being a sister or aunt was never available, and neither was mother or grandmother you see...And then there was sort of the work, and dare I relinquish those adult roles...(Interview, Sue).

However the women define or speak about identity, what comes through very clearly is their sense of agency and empowerment in carrying out a ritual.

The theme of 'taking charge' occurs several times in Jane's reflections on her ritual, and is clearly significant in giving her some sense of her own agency in the feelings of powerlessness and helplessness which being made redundant had engendered in her.

Runa, too, sees her ritual as enabling her to take on a sense of agency and empowerment in relation to her environment:

So in one sense it's hard to say I had a new sense of self dating from the ritual but I'm convinced that it did really help. I think one of the things it did was to enhance my sense of power over my life (Interview, Runa).

I have already described how Jackie saw the taking of a new name and identity as a liberating act; she also talks of it in terms of moving from being passive to active, claiming her agency and power:

I had taken the action. It was a positive thing that I had done, when all the things that led up to the breakdown of the marriage and the divorce I was very passive. I was taking an active stand to make the break and reclaim myself (Interview, Jackie).

For these women, whether their identity is linked to their work, their home, or the names by which they are known, the experience of transition brings challenges that cause them to look again at who they are, how they see themselves, and how they present themselves to others. They do not have a naïve sense of the 'essential self' which they express in ritual, but consciously engage in ritual as one strategy (often amongst others) for negotiating the transition and beginning the process of rethinking or reconstructing identity. In so far as they create rituals for themselves, or take a large share in providing ideas and symbols for them, they are exercising agency at times when they are potentially vulnerable, under pressure, or even overwhelmed by the changes in their life-circumstances and the powerful emotions which accompany them. They are attempting to make sense of who they are, and making their own stories through the symbolism and performance of ritual in a way which is liberating and empowering.

Shared Stories

The creation of identity through narrative and story-making, although it has strong resonances with the individual sense of self, is not purely about the individual. The notion of the self constructed through story does not place the narrator alone in a garret, writing her story in quiet reflection and solitude. The stories that shape self are told, interpreted, retold and negotiated in a process of interaction with others. Stories are shared, and in that sharing, the self is negotiated and constructed. Ricoeur (1995) talks of how we are all part of one another's stories, and MacIntyre argues this makes us accountable to one another and so becomes the basis for ethics (1989).

The interweaving of stories, in a web of human connections, is a strong theme in the writing of Hannah Arendt. There is no such thing as an individual story in isolation, because one story affects and is affected by others. There is therefore a social dimension to all human storytelling. She speaks of story not so much in terms of individual construction of the self, but as the basis for action in the world, and as the prerequisite of any understanding of politics or the public sphere:

> The realm of human affairs, strictly speaking, consists of the web of human relationships, which exists whenever men [sic] live together. The disclosure of the 'web' through speech, and the setting of a new beginning through action, always fall into an existing web where

their immediate consequences can be felt. Together they start a new
process which eventually emerges as the unique life story of the
newcomer, affecting uniquely the life stories of all those with whom
he comes into contact (Arendt 1998: 183–84).

Even the most private emotions and experiences take on a
different level of reality when they are communicated to, and heard
by, others. Speech and communication are a form of action, or praxis,
which enable human beings to take their place in the world and
shape the course of events. These are seen most clearly in
storytelling, and other forms of artistic expression which — although
Arendt does not use the term — could surely include the creative
use of images, symbol and drama in ritual:

> Compared with the reality which comes from being seen and heard,
> even the greatest forces of intimate life — the passions of the heart, the
> thoughts of the mind, the delights of the senses — lead an uncertain,
> shadowy kind of existence unless and until they are transformed,
> deprivatized and deindividualized, as it were, into a shape to fit them
> for public appearance. The most current of such transformations occurs
> in storytelling and generally in artistic transpositions of individual
> experiences (Arendt 1998: 50).

For her the capacity to speak of the continuity of history and
politics depends on the ability to tell individual life-stories:

> That every individual life between birth and death can eventually be
> told as a story with beginning and end is the pre-political and
> prehistorical condition of history, the great story without beginning
> and end (Arendt 1998: 184).

The feminist philosopher Adriana Cavarero builds on Arendt's
insistence on the shared nature of stories to develop the social and
political dimensions of identity. Philosophical language and abstract
rationality are insufficient in answer to the question 'who am I?'
Rather, that question is answered in the process of storytelling,
through the 'narratable self'. The 'narratable self', she argues, should
not be reified as the product of narrative; rather the narratable self
is formed in a process of storytelling that requires an other to hear
the story and reflect it back to the teller, enabling her to recognize
her self in her own story. Any sense of personal identity requires
an 'other' — either to hear the story in the first place, or to tell it
back to the actor:

> For her [Arendt], it follows from the fact that the category of personal identity postulates an other as necessary. Even before another can render tangible the identity of someone by telling him/her his/her story, many others have indeed been spectators of the constitutive exposure of the very same identity to their gaze (Cavarero 2000: 20).

The need for the other to tell our own story back to us is typified by birth—we cannot tell the story of our own birth, but rely on having it told to us by others:

> The tale of our own beginning, the story of our birth, nevertheless can only come to the existent in the form of a narration told by others. The beginning of the narratable self and the beginning of her own story are always a tale told by others (Cavarero 2000: 39).

It is not the finished product of the story that creates identity, but the process of wanting to tell, which has its origins in memory. Cavarero argues that women in particular are drawn to storytelling. Their exclusion from public spheres, and the denial or suppression of their capacity for abstract knowledge has given them a preference for the particular, the located, the contextual. So storytelling is embedded in women's everyday lives as a feature of their relationality:

> In the kitchen, on the train, in the hospitals, sitting with a pizza or a drink—women are usually the ones who tell life-stories (2000: 53–54).

The political space of conciousness-raising groups, in which stories are more intentionally shared and heard, is an extension of an everyday practice of storytelling familiar to many women.

Cavarero, like Ricoeur and Arendt, stresses the importance of storytelling. Although most of her examples are taken from literary texts, she recognizes the activity of storytelling as an everyday aspect of women's lives. This process, this impulse to tell and to hear one's own story, creates the 'narratable self' — the continuous, coherent self about which a story can be told.

Arendt's work and her image of the web is further developed in the writings of Seyla Benhabib. She argues that the death of the subject in postmodernism is not helpful to feminism. She wrestles with the tension between the situatedness of women's lives, and the demand for a sense of autonomy and agency. However much we are dependent on culturally-available or dominant narratives, there needs to be a sense of authorship of our lives:

These narratives are deeply coloured and structured by the codes of expectable and understandable biographies and identities in our cultures. We can concede all that, but nevertheless we must still argue that we are not merely extensions of our histories, that vis-a-vis our own stories we are in the position of author and character at once. The situated and gendered subject is heteronomously determined but still strives toward autonomy (Benhabib 1992: 214).

She argues that the self gains its coherence from a unity of narrative, when the story is told from the point of view of both teller and listener. To hear the story from only the others' perspective is to make the subject into a victim, defined by others' terms; but for the story to be told only by an individual can fall into narcissism and isolation. This integration, of individual agency and an acknowledgement of the participation of and interrelationship with others she describes as an integration of autonomy and solidarity, or justice and care:

A coherent sense of self is attained with the successful integration of autonomy and solidarity, or with the right mix of justice and care. Justice and autonomy alone cannot sustain and nourish that web of narratives in which human beings sense of self unfolds; but solidarity and care alone cannot raise the self to the level not only of being the subject but also the author of a coherent life-story (Benhabib 1992: 198).

In most of the rituals I have looked at, there has been a communal element—rituals have taken place with a group of friends or family members, and this sharing of stories emerges clearly. One woman may enact her story, but others tell theirs too—and meanings are multilayered and enriched, taking on new forms as women share. For Jane, the presence of others made the ritual an interactive process, in which the basic structure she had provided was filled out with the layers of meaning and various concerns that others brought. Again, her own story was added to and changed as others shared theirs:

So there was a richness—and when people articulated that there was a richness about that symbolism...and the thing took on a new life because of the people who were there (Interview, Jane).

Runa expresses most clearly her awareness that her identity is relationally constructed, and says of her ritual:

I felt like it was weaving a sort of web of connectedness in which I was taking on this new name, but also that I was in a sense constructing myself very symbolically because each person represented a slightly different aspect of me in the world, my way of being (Interview, Runa).

In her ritual, her connection with others is symbolized by the objects they have brought, and this is part of the process of constructing who she is. It is her relationship with others that helps her to construct her identity; her connection with each of the people she has invited represented different aspects of her self:

But I asked each person to bring with them something, some object, which they felt symbolised for them the quality of their connection with me, and I said that I would do the same so I, over the days beforehand, gathered a set of objects, symbols, for me that represented my own connection with each one of those people, and they each brought one of their own (Interview, Runa).

In Jackie's renaming, she felt that having others make the letters of her name would help consolidate her sense of identity in a creative but very concrete way:

So what I thought is, if they did that on small pieces of card then we could actually put them together to create the surname and I could write my first name...it's concrete action and would help to consolidate within me the identity of the name (Planning session with Jackie).

Clare expressed a sense of interconnecting stories as she talked about why she wanted others to participate in her ritual:

so it was about where other people are at as well and that I'm not just journeying on my own but I'm journeying alongside, with, interconnecting with other people who've got their own journeys and their own difficulties and moments of celebration (Interview, Clare).

When she expresses her sense of thanks and appreciation, she includes everyone in a way that one of the participants compares to a web:

Clare then speaks her thanks — this is unscripted and she names everyone...and their contribution to the thesis...The way she draws everyone in together in her thanks is lovely; later, A likens it to a web (Journal entry, Clare's ritual).

For the women in these rituals parts of their own stories and their sense of their own identities, are reflected back to them, even if obliquely, in the insights and stories of others. There is a strong sense for them that other people are part of their stories, that the others bring their stories too, and that the whole is not simply totalling up of experience, but a process of negotiating meanings and interpretations in a multi-layered making of meanings. They are not only the co-authors of their own stories; they are inviting others to share in the process of forming a story so that the group becomes co-author of the narrative that is taking shape in ritual. Their identity or sense of self is not formed in a vacuum, but is taking shape in the symbolic making of stories in the interactive, intersubjective process of the ritual.

Political Stories

As McNay, Cavarero and Benhabib assert, to talk about shared stories and the public realm immediately raises political questions. For feminists, public space is not a neutral, objective arena, but one of dominant and competing narratives. The stories which women tell are both shaped by, and resist, the wider cultural and political narratives in which they are embedded.

Plummer (1995: 17) looks at sexual stories as *'social actions embedded in social worlds'*. He examines stories of rape and abuse, gay and lesbian coming-out stories, and stories of recovery based on 12-step programmes, and argues that for each category of story, there needs to be a social world which can both receive and hear the stories, and which in turn gives shape to them. Stories are produced and received at four levels: the personal, the situational, the organizational, and the cultural-historical. Meanings are not fixed, but emerge, change, and are shaped as part of an interactive political process as they enter public discourse:

> The private pains increasingly become public ones; the personal sufferings become collective participations; the pathological languages turn to political ones. Stories of private, pathological pain have become stories of public, political participation (Plummer 1995: 109–10).

One of the functions of ritual as a strategy, according to Catherine Bell (1992), is to negotiate power relations. In some rituals this is to confirm and support the status quo, but it is also to challenge the current hegemony with different patterns of power and interconnectedness.

Jane, Alison and Rebecca express a sense of loss and bereavement in redundancy which originates in a culture that places a high value on the work ethic, with the status and sense of identity that accompanies paid employment, as well as the Christian culture and language of vocation. For Jane, her ritual is a way of claiming empowerment for herself in the face of the patriarchal structures and context that have brought about her redundancy:

> I think one of the interesting things about redundancy is how far people take responsibility for a process that is actually not of their making, and they retroflect stuff that actually is stuff that's about the institution (Interview, Jane).

For her, the sense of power is important—she needs to be 'in charge' of the ritual in contrast to the sense of powerlessness and helplessness she felt in the patriarchal world of work and church. True, this is primarily a personal sense of power and authority, but it is one she sees herself taking into the more public arena in the job to which she has just been appointed:

> and I thought, this is the—the next job I do is going to be much more authoritative than I've been before, much more managerial, and I thought yes I'm ready to do that. So there's also something about having much more confidence in myself (Interview, Jane).

Jackie's renaming is in defiance of the prevalent heterosexual narrative of marriage, which insists that a woman take her husband's name:

> And it's also a statement "I am what I am", and that whole business of taking on someone else's name fills me with anger and horror. I cannot do this any longer, why people do it—but we all did it, we all do it, and I don't see any reason for it at all (Planning session with Jackie).

She is well aware that, although conventions are changing, what she is doing is a challenge to the prevailing culture which defines a married woman's identity in relation to that of her husband:

> but you still occasionally get phone calls you know, can I speak to the householder, meaning the man, and it is something about nobody having any kind of other claim on me at all (Interview, Jackie).

Runa's story could not have been told, nor her ritual enacted, without the context of a culture of recognition and willingness to hear, and work therapeutically with, women's stories of abuse, as in Plummer's emphasis on the social context of stories. In choosing her new name she is consciously rejecting the name and label that have been given her by her biological family and society:

> I can define myself, name myself, and that I don't somehow need to carry with me the definition of me my family had placed upon me — symbolised by the name they'd given me (Interview, Runa).

She recognizes and has to deal with the social and legal implications of changing her name which follow her ritual, but it is the ritual itself which remains important as an expression of her own agency and power.

These women are aware that their lives and experiences have been shaped by a wider political, patriarchal context, and are consciously shaping their stories and rituals in ways that enable them to reclaim the power of naming and interpreting. Their use of ritual as a strategy is a political act of subversion and resistance, which enables them to claim some agency in making their own stories.

Stories Which Can't Be Told

It has almost become an axiom, both in therapy and theology, that telling one's story is therapeutic, liberating and empowering. But Antze and Lambek question this assumption:

> there is nothing liberating in narrative per se. Merely to transfer the story from embodied symptoms to words is not necessarily either to interpret it or to exorcise it (1996: xix).

It may be that there are stories which are too painful to be told; Elaine Scarry talks of the way in which physical pain fragments and destroys language:

> Physical pain does not simply resist language but actively destroys it, bringing about an immediate reversion to a state anterior to language, to the sounds and cries a human being makes before language is learned (1985: 4).

Arthur Frank, in talking of the different categories of narrative of illness, includes what he calls chaos narratives. The chaos of illness can only be related from a safe distance, when it is possible to step outside and reflect — it cannot be told as it is being lived through:

> The teller of chaos stories is pre-eminently the wounded storyteller, but those who are truly living the chaos cannot tell in words. To turn

the chaos into a verbal story is to have some reflective grasp on it. The
chaos that can be told in story is already taking place at a distance and
is being reflected on retrospectively...Lived chaos makes reflection,
and consequently storytelling, impossible (1995: 98).

For survivors of the traumas of childhood abuse, who experience
memory loss and disassociation, the telling of the story in words
may become impossible:

There is no narrative of trauma then, no memory—only speaking in
signs (Kirmayer 1996: 175).

In instances such as these, it is futile or oppressive to insist on, or
even look for, a coherent narrative. To do so may be to invite a
kind of premature closure, a 'cheap grace' which glosses over the
pain, for the sake of finding a story that can be seen as liberating.
Dominick LaCapra, working amongst holocaust survivors, stresses
the ethical importance for interviewers of avoiding any minimizing
of the trauma:

Also dubious is a response...that circumvents, denies, or represses the
trauma that called it into existence, for example, through unqualified
objectification, formal analysis, or harmonizing, indeed redemptive
narrative through which one derives from the suffering of others
something career-enhancing, "spiritually" uplifting, or identity-
forming for oneself or one's group (LaCapra 2001: 98–99).

Whatever the motive, for a hearer to seek to impose a narrative
framework on another person's pain or trauma may be a
continuation of abuse. Sometimes, as Heather Walton writes in
relation to chaplains and pastoral carers, silence is the only
appropriate response:

However those who have worked closely with those in pain or grief
would probably be the first to admit that for some people there may
be no comfort to be found in storytelling. Some simply do not find a
narrative that can be made to fit the appalling circumstances that
confront them (H. Walton 2002: 3).

She argues that rather than words, what is needed is 'poesis'—
metaphors, symbols and images that are less clear-cut and cerebral
than coherent narrative:

What is needed is not narrative but poesis; images, symbols and
metaphors that carry the pain of trauma without committing the
blasphemy of trying to represent, comprehend or reconcile the horror
in story form (H. Walton 2002: 4).

There are important warnings here about the assumption that telling one's story is both necessary and sufficient for healing. It does not always bring liberation or empowerment to tell a story; sometimes it can reinforce shame or humiliation, or perpetuate the identity of a victim. Sometimes the retelling is not the person's own, but takes a shape or form that they feel others want to hear. Plummer (1995) has shown how certain genres of stories develop according to the social and political context in which they are heard. And sometimes the retelling is imposed, as a carer or even researcher seeks to impose order and interpretation on an experience that continues to feel disordered and chaotic for the sufferer. There may well be times when the story can only be told indirectly through allusion, symbol, metaphor and embodied action. There may be times when even this piecing together of fragments of story is inadequate, and silence is the only fitting response.

Although for some ritual enactment is seen as a stage on the way to verbalization, there may be those for whom the process of moving from embodied action to words is not an option — the depth of trauma that they have experienced can only be expressed through the language of the body. Whether this is through bodily symptoms, the infliction of self-harm, or ritual actions, the body is the only vehicle which allows them to express or process their pain. Clearly the women in my study, in creating and reflecting on their rituals, were able to verbalize their experience, although the rituals they performed often touched on emotions in a more powerful, less conscious way. But it may be that for others the process of creating ritual demands too much conscious verbalization; and bodily actions, or the performance of established ritual, may enable them to find a language without words which conveys their trauma.

But there are some who would argue that we should not give up on the idea of story altogether — that even in the fragmented sharing, a story is beginning to emerge. Frank, having spoken about chaos narratives which can only be told in retrospect, goes on to talk about what he calls testimony narratives, and the importance of sharing a story that bears witness to suffering and pain that would otherwise remain hidden and unrecognized. There is still pain that cannot be told, but the testimony of a witness to that pain brings to our awareness both the limits of words and the silence:

> The more that is told, the more we are made conscious of remaining on the edge of a silence (Frank 1995: 138).

What is crucial here is that the story is heard and received—it is not the construction of the narrative that is redemptive, but the bearing witness to another human being.

Kirmayer, having spoken of the difficulties for some abuse survivors of remembering and sharing their stories, goes on to contrast this with the telling of stories of Holocaust survivors. He suggests that there is a social explanation for the difference, in that holocaust survivors, after an initial silence and denial, encountered a context in which their stories could be received and endorsed by others. Their experience is one of solidarity and validation in remembering; whilst for many abuse survivors the context of retelling is one of shame, in which social and familial bonds are broken by the recounting of their experiences:

> There is a crucial distinction between the social space in which the trauma occurred and the contemporary space in which it is (or is not) recalled. In the case of the disassociative disorder patient and the Holocaust victim, the difference is between a public space of solidarity and a private space of shame (Kirmayer 1996: 189).

Michael Jackson, too, out of his work amongst refugees, speaks of the stories that cannot be told, writing in incomplete sentences that in themselves convey the brokenness and inadequacy of language:

> Every place of violence and social suffering becomes, for a time, a place of silence. Deserted villages. Unmarked graves. Stunned survivors, whom words fail. Words are a travesty, for words cannot bring back what has been lost (Jackson 2002: 132).

He goes on to argue, however, that in this silence, the emerging of stories is an imperative—not because the individual is empowered by telling his or her own story, but because the very act of beginning to tell a story, however fragmented, is a reaching-out in an attempt to form a social bond with another. In this way stories are an attempt to overcome the fragmentation and isolation of trauma and violence to form bonds of common humanity:

> Stories are redemptive, then, not because they preserve or represent the truth of any individual life but because they offer the perennial possibility that one see oneself as, and discover oneself through, another, despite the the barriers of space, time and difference (Jackson 2002: 250).

He recognizes, however, that questions of whose story is told and heard are political questions; and that the telling of stories is incomplete without accompanying action to bring about justice. Stories are a way of beginning to move from the personal, private and isolated, into the social and political realms.

Shoshana Felman and Dori Laub from their work with survivors of the Holocaust, talk about the impossibility of bearing witness to the trauma of the event. There is both an 'imperative to tell' (Felman and Laub 1992: 78) and 'the impossibility of telling' (1992: 79). Although the story is too painful and hidden to be articulated, it is important that in some way there is a witness—someone who can listen to the testimony, and, eventually, enable the survivor to reintegrate his/her own story as part of life:

> The testimony is, therefore, the process by which the narrator (the survivor) reclaims his position as a witness; reconstitutes the internal "thou", and thus the possibility of a witness or a listener inside himself.

In my experience, repossessing one's life story through giving testimony is itself a form of action, of change, which one has to actually pass through, in order to continue and complete the process of survival after liberation (Felman and Laub 1992: 85).

This testimony is not a coherent narrative, with enplotment and character; but emerges in fragments of memory that cannot be constrained into a coherent shape and structure:

> As a relation to events, testimony seems to be composed of bits and pieces of a memory that has been overwhelmed by occurrences that have not settled into understanding or remembrance, acts that cannot be construed as knowledge nor assimilated into full cognition, events in excess of our frame of reference...(Felman and Laub 1992: 5).

In looking at the rituals of the women I have worked with, I hesitate to draw too much from work with survivors of the holocaust, refugees, or victims of abuse. Whatever painful and turbulent experiences they have been through, at the point of planning the ritual none of the women I interviewed were subject to unspeakable trauma. The changes they are dealing with are not extreme, 'limit' experiences, but the kind of changes and transitions that many women encounter. But there is a strong confessional, or giving of testimony element to the rituals—a sense that this is what I have experienced or am going through—and a wish for others to witness and acknowledge this. Whilst a number of them talk about others as witnesses, Jackie expresses it in a biblical image:

> but the very fact that it has been witnessed — I don't know whether this is almost Hebrews 12, isn't it, with the cloud of witnesses and the importance of them sharing that act at a very significant stage of what is a spiritual journey (Interview, Jackie).

Conversations with those who plan and construct rituals for others have talked about their role partly in terms of 'bearing witness'. For Elizabeth Baxter, working at Holy Rood House, her role is that of a witness to pain that is often not put into words, but displayed in symbolic action, ritual or artwork.

> The community will act as witness to the story and the storyteller, who may indeed have lost all sense of feeling, and for whom beauty and love are reproaches to their place of pain (Baxter 2007: 24).

Because I was working with women who have created their own rituals, they are fluent and articulate about their experiences. It may well be that in order to create one's own ritual, there already needs to be a certain degree of coming to terms with the experience. Nevertheless the rituals I have studied do not tell a story in a coherent and direct way, but have some of the fragmentation and indirect story-telling of what Heather Walton calls 'poesis'. There is something of the confessional testimony about them; they are bearing witness to their experiences and reaching out in the hope that others will hear; and the story, rather than being told and interpreted, is formed and made in the process.

The one exception in the rituals I have studied is Carol's. Whilst we held a conversation in which she described her feelings and contributed ideas, because of the pressure she felt under she deliberately chose to leave the actual planning of the ritual to me, and did not want to know beforehand what would happen. There was therefore in her ritual less conscious agency, and interestingly, in the subsequent interview, less awareness of what had taken place. What did register with her, however, was the affect and atmosphere of the event, which she describes in terms that come closer to an experience of 'liminality' than any of the other rituals.

> But actually there's that sort of significant sort of — bit like the picture as I drew it there — I used to love doing this in geography — meanderings like in a river and what do you call — you know when it

suddenly begins to get cut off...the oxbow — that's it — so it's sort of life, a ritual, then life carries on again (Interview, Carol).

Perhaps it is when someone is literally 'lost for words' as a result of pain or trauma that existing rituals with the familiarity of repetition and past association come into their own.

Like narrative, ritual helps to construct and form identity; it is an interactive, social process which involves others in that construction, and in doing so at least begins to negotiate power relations. It has an open-endedness to the future, and in its performance or enactment begins to shape the way in which identity or the self continues to be constructed. The participants are dealing with painful or life-changing personal events, and beginning to bring them into a more public realm, negotiating their meaning and finding their own ways of giving voice to their stories over against the prevailing discourse.

Ritual is perhaps less formed than narrative (certainly less so than narrative texts); it is more symbolic, allusive, inchoate; but it is serving some of the same function in enabling participants to make some sense of life-events and transitions, enabling them to make and shape their lives into story.

A Feminist Theological/Thealogical Perspective

Ritual can be seen, like narrative, as attempting to find a way of talking about the self in a postmodern framework. When ideas of the essential unity of the self finding its place in a grand story (a metanarrative) of humanity and divinity are no longer tenable, the construction of the self negotiated from individual and shared stories provides a way of allowing us still to talk about the self and human agency in coherent terms.

This use of narrative has been addressed by a number of theologians. In canonical narrative theology (Graham, Walton and Ward 2005) the emphasis has not been so much on human stories and narratives, as on the narrative qualities of theological texts and confessional documents. Ricoeur argues that the foundational documents of faith are not metaphysical statements of doctrine, but 'narratives, prophecies, legislative texts, proverbs and wisdom sayings, hymns, prayers and liturgical formulas' (Ricoeur 1995; [1974]: 37). Johann Metz (1989; [1973]) argues that rather than narrative being dismissed as a 'pre-critical' form of theology we need to see narratives as the form in which salvation-history is communicated.

Although it is an attempt to respond to postmodernism, narrative theology has not completely abandoned the notion of a metanarrative. Stanley Hauerwas and William Willimon (1989: 53) talk of a God who is 'taking the disconnected elements of our lives and pulling them together into a coherent story that means something' and Anderson and Foley (2001: 7) talk of ritual as the place where the human story meets the divine (by which they mean the Christian) story. It is this meeting and connecting of divine and human stories that is potentially transformative.

In feminist thought generally, and in feminist theology, there has been a rather different emphasis. Here the importance of narrative is in women telling their own stories — constructive narrative theology (Graham, Walton and Ward 2005). Phrases such as Nelle Morton's 'hearing into speech', and giving women a voice, speak of the need for women's experiences to be listened to attentively and taken seriously. Consciousness-raising groups were a common feature of the feminist movement, and in women's liturgy a commonly-used piece by Edwina Gately (1995: 73) begins: 'We told our stories — That's all'.

Underlying this is an assumption that for a woman, telling her story is empowering and enabling in itself. But feminists have moved from this to recognize more of the process of interpretation and construction that takes place in such storytelling. Stevi Jackson writes:

> I will argue that telling stories can never communicate "raw experience." Narratives entail processes of representation, interpretation, and reconstruction (1998: 48-49).

The place of story in feminist theology is indebted to narrative theology, but it uses story in a distinct way. There is less desire to place human stories within the context of the divine (patriarchal) narrative, and more of a search for theological meaning in the stories themselves. This is also true of women's rituals and story, as Northup argues:

> Thus, although women's ritualizing may seem comfortably ensconced in the narrative theology camp, it has clear affinities — especially in its stress on particularity, difference, and performance, with post-modern cultural and literary theory (1997: 83).

Whilst narrative theology may have much to offer feminists seeking to find a way of recovering agency, it is nonetheless founded on a patriarchal narrative. For a theology which gives voice and meaning to women's experience, women's storytelling is a pre-requisite:

> If it is true that we are storied people, that we discover the meaning of our lives in our narratives, then for women's lives to become truly authentic, they need to first create their own narrative history (Say 1990: 111).

Some writers have looked at this in relation to pastoral care. Riet Bons-Storm (1996) looks at women's self-narratives in pastoral care and counselling, and shows how the stories women tell about their lives are shaped by dominant socio-cultural and psychological narratives. There is a need for carers or listeners to move beyond patriarchal expectations and to give women space to develop and tell their own stories. Christie Cozad Neuger (2000) too, talks of dominant cultural narratives as harmful, and argues that the constructed nature of these must be exposed and challenged. At the same time, alternative stories and narratives which resist cultural norms need to be encouraged and nurtured.

For narrative to empower women, it needs to enable them to develop a sense of 'narrative agency'. Rebecca Chopp argues that Christian narratives have often been used to silence women's own voices, and theological education for women is partly a process of creating their own stories in solidarity with others, and in relation to the Christian tradition:

> The notion of narrativity as a fundamental practice of feminist theological education allows us a multiperspectival way to understand how women and men intentionally create their lives in relation to their culture, their bodies, their individual experiences, and their Christian communities (Chopp 1995: 31).

She argues that there are four processes or 'base points' involved in this. First is the naming of women's experiences, which have often been invisible in Christian theological thinking; and women's novels and poetry have been an important resource in this. Feminist theologians have recognized however that it is not possible or legitimate to talk of women's experience as if this were a universal norm, and so the second part of the process is a recognition and privileging of contextuality and difference. Thirdly, for women to develop narrative agency there needs to be a reconstruction of Christian tradition and the dominant symbols that are used; and finally the development of a moral or ethical framework.

Nicola Slee, in her research, found that narrative was one of the primary ways in which women described their faith development, enabling them to 'claim a narrative agency' which 'challenges and subverts standard or traditional cultural narratives' (2004a: 70).

For many feminist theologians, then, women's storytelling and ritualizing is in Elaine Graham's terms (2002) a disclosive practice — not a human story placed in conversation with the divine, but a human process that carries within it revelations and signs of divine presence and activity.

This has some resonances with the rituals I have described here. As I argued in an earlier chapter, few of the rituals assume or use a divine metanarrative as a framework. There are certainly allusions and references to the Judaeo-Christian story, but Jane, in talking about her ritual, expresses a diversity of belief that is not unusual in women's ritual or spirituality groups:

> Something about the collective — that although that group represents quite a spectrum of beliefs — probably isn't — there is enough commonality in terms of belief that's not about how we describe the divine but about the properties of God/Goddess...And there's a commonality about the feminist thing, about reclaiming the dark actually. Because part of that was about me reclaiming the dark and transforming the dark — and about the reclaiming and the transformation and the change (Interview, Jane).

Others, like Runa, work with a less-clearly defined belief in Goddess as divine, creative energy:

> now I say it's the Goddess, it's this deep creative process that runs through life, that's what I think of as Goddess, the great spiritual process that we're all part of — (Interview, Runa)

But in the rituals themselves these ideas are not fully or consciously expressed; they are implicit and inchoate, still taking shape in the process of choosing and enacting symbolism, of exchanging fragments of story. These rituals do not (only) express previously-held beliefs; they help to form and shape those beliefs as part of the construction of self. Jackie talks about how her own spirituality and belief became clearer in the process of planning her ritual:

> I think that's something else I wanted to say about the preparation as
> well—I think after the first session you helped me to articulate the
> spiritual side much more clearly than I had. It was always there—but
> I wasn't naming it to myself or to you clearly at first (Interview, Jackie).

Just as feminists are beginning to realize that we cannot talk of 'women's experience' as if it is raw, unmediated, but rather something constructed in the telling and negotiated within social processes, so beliefs about God/Goddess are not a pre-existent framework, but are emerging, shaped and formed by the story-making and symbolic enactment of the ritual process.

Mary Fulkerson traces theories of the deconstruction of self, and argues their relevance for feminist theology. The concept of humanity made in the image of God is one which can provide a useful theological framework, but can still be used in a manner that suggests a dualistic opposition of male and female. What is needed, she argues, is the need for feminists to develop stories of the outside and of God which challenge patriarchal hegemony:

> A good feminist theological story will be an incomplete story of a
> God-loved creation, a creation for which the only requisite features of
> imaging God are finitude and dependence (1997: 114)

Narrative theology speaks of a divine story—a story that is clearly plotted and provides a coherent framework to make sense of human lives. Early feminist theology, with its emphasis on women's stories and their power to convey and express divine truth, could be said to suggest a storytelling God—a God present and revealed in women's stories. But that still presupposes a divine telling, a giving of an already-formed story, albeit one that has been hidden or buried by patriarchal religion. I prefer to speak of a storymaking God/Goddess—one who co-creates our stories with us, shaping our selves, identities and experiences through the fragmented stories, the multi-layered symbolism, and the embodied action of the ritualizing process.

Case Study Four

THE NAME THAT'S YET TO BE — JACKIE'S STORY

Jackie is a friend who had experienced a painful marriage and divorce. She had initially retained her married name, for the sake of continuity for her children, but as they grew older decided she wanted to change her last name, and asked me to work with her in planning a ritual or ceremony to mark this.

Our first meeting took place some months before the ritual. Jackie invited me for a meal, and we talked informally about her ideas. She talked about needing to let go of the pain of the past, but also of a sense of celebration — of singleness, friendship, creativity, spirituality, connectedness with the environment. She had already decided on her new name, choosing her grandmother's maiden name so that, although she only knew a little about her, there was some sense of family history and continuity. She felt that the ritual needed to include some form of writing or making her name, and wanted this to involve others in some way, because their support and friendship had been so important to her in her journey. We thought of biblical passages and imagery — Jackie wanted to use the verse from Isaiah 49 which speaks of names written on God's palms, and to use imagery of water in some way.

We met again a couple of months later, and by this time Jackie's ideas had become much clearer. She had chosen the date of the ritual to coincide with her wedding anniversary, and had arranged to sign the legal documents shortly beforehand. She had also begun to think through the various people who would have to be notified, and begun to recognize the public and irrevocable nature of the step she was taking:

> I think it's also that I've realised in doing the legal stuff and in thinking about, this will be my identity for next year and my name for next year I've realised the enormity of it and what I'm doing...I've made the decision, I've signed all the documents. This is about going public and there's no going back (Planning session with Jackie).

We talked about symbolizing letting go of the past by burning, possibly a copy of her marriage certificate or photographs, but Jackie was also clear that she wanted to keep some things for her children. We discussed placing them in a box, which we would all help her to seal. She had found a poem, *Exodus Experience*, by Kathy Galloway (1996) which used the themes of home, exile, desert, and promised land. She had also worked out a process in which each member of the group could make one letter of her first and last names, so that we could then put them together. She felt this and the burning needed to be done in her back room, because of space, and as we talked the idea of using the movement from one to the other emerged, giving us a symbolic 'threshold' moment before we moved into declaring her new identity in the front room, which she described as 'my haven, my sanctuary' (planning session with Jackie). By the end of the evening we felt a shape had emerged, and I agreed to go away and put together a liturgy, including some writing of my own, whilst Jackie worked on the practicalities of finding a box, and the card and materials for creating her name.

Shortly before the ritual we met again to go through what I had written, giving Jackie the opportunity to make alterations, and to go through the use of space and practicalities about who would bring what.

I arrived about half an hour before the ritual was due to begin. Some friends were already there, others arrived and we joined in drinks and chat until everyone was present. Jackie began by welcoming everybody more formally, going around the circle introducing us to one another, and saying something about each person and their significance to her—sometimes humorous, but always affirming and with a serious element. She lit some candles around the fireplace and we had a few moments of quiet before some opening responses invoking the name of God, and our intention in sharing in the ritual.

We used extracts of *Exodus Experience* interspersed through the evening, and read by different members of the group. The first part used the image of home as sanctuary, and then went on to talk about home as violent, ending with 'This does not feel like sanctuary':

> Very poignant, especially knowing something of [the reader's] story —
> and Jackie had been very definite, in an intuitive kind of way, about
> who should read which piece (Journal entry, Jackie's ritual).

Jackie wanted to symbolize letting-go of the past, without going into details of the story. She set light to papers and photos torn up ready to burn in the grate; and we helped her put other items (including her wedding dress) which would not burn easily into a bin liner, which she then asked two of the group to throw into the garden ready to go to the tip later on:

> Various people put things in, then [names] take her at her word, and literally, with a one-two-three, throw the bag through the (open!) door halfway down the lawn (Journal entry, Jackie's ritual).

We placed the items Jackie had decided to pass on to her children in a beautiful box which she had bought, and then all tied it with string in order to seal it:

> This actually took a long time, as the thread was quite fiddly to work with, and everyone did it individually, taking their time over it...but it did serve to symbolise all of us helping Jackie to let go of and seal off the past—something perhaps none of us can do alone and unaided (Journal entry, Jackie's ritual).

A short prayer for God's help in letting go concluded that section of the ritual, and we moved on with a further extract from the poem, on exile and desert, and the miracle of survival, ending with the line: 'A new sense of identity is founded'. Jackie talked about her new name, and why she had chosen it. She then gave each of us a piece of card, and we began making the letters of her name, using boxes of craft materials brought by one of the group members:

> This works out just as we'd hoped—fun, playful, a bit chaotic at first, putting tables out and getting [name]'s boxes unpacked. People delighted with the bits and pieces, finding different things to use, some enjoying the messiness of finger paints, others with glue, and one person consulting a dictionary to find words beginning with her letter (Journal entry, Jackie's ritual).

When we'd finished we placed the letters in order on a large sheet of card, each person saying something about Jackie and what she meant to them, often expressed in the way they had formed or decorated the letters.

We moved into the hallway for readings from Isa. 43: 1–7 and Isa. 49: 13–18, and another extract from the poem, ending with the image of the wilderness blossoming with flowers. Jackie stepped into the front room, followed by the rest of us; she placed the card with her new name in the fireplace and stood by it. Together we read a declaration of her three names, including her new surname, and she echoed the last few lines of it:

> Having been looking through this I'm just reminded that one of the most powerful things I felt which was...where everyone had said we know you as [her new name]. And then I spoke my bit and the reality of that was I think probably one of the most powerful moments, and the recognition that I was actually able with the strength of my friends around me, who had said these words, to claim my new name (Interview, Jackie).

There was a pause, tense with emotion, and then we moved on to expressing our hopes for Jackie and for others. First we passed round a jug for each person to pour water on to glass beads, expressing their own hopes and wishes, and then lit candles to float on the water for each section of a prayer I had written, seeking to express what Jackie's new name might mean for her. We closed with the hymn I had written for the occasion, and a blessing, and the evening continued with a party.

When I returned to interview Jackie a month later, there were several elements that stood out for her. She spoke first of all of the support of her friends. She had invited people who had shared different parts of her journey with her, and was touched by the affirmation that they gave her:

> I think the first bit there were so many people here who had walked with me on the journey and I was really overwhelmed by the fact they cared enough to come from quite significant distances...and really genuinely wanted to be here because they understood the significance for me as well (Interview, Jackie).

For Jackie, some of the words of the ritual took on a new meaning because of the people who read them, and the experience and interpretation they shared:

> For though it had meaning for me they were also making it meaningful for themselves because again they knew the story, and as you know, I deliberately chose a particular part for particular people to say and they were all aware I think of the resonances of the things that they knew—and that made it again—it made a kind of personal link with each person who was saying the words, and therefore made the words more meaningful (Interview, Jackie).

One particular contribution was striking—during the party two of Jackie's friends offered to take the bin bag we had thrown into the garden, put it in the car, and take it to the tip, so that Jackie would not need to take it back herself. This made the symbolism of throwing away and letting go very concrete, and was very powerful for Jackie:

> But the other thing that took me completely by surprise was having bagged up my wedding dress…they had sensed how important it was actually throwing it into the garden and then not wanting to take it into the house; but taking it round the side passage and then offering to take it themselves and I never needed to see it or touch it or do anything else with it again (Interview, Jackie).

She also remarked how enjoyable the evening had been; although a serious occasion, the making of the letters of her name had been playful and fun:

> The sheer enjoyment of being together and the way that particularly with the making of the letters, everybody, it took so long, and everyone was just enjoying it (Interview, Jackie).

Another important dimension of the ritual for her was the move from one room into the other. Something which began for practical reasons of space became one of the most significant moments of the ritual for her:

> but there were other parts of it in which the atmosphere took me by surprise because they were so powerful—particularly I think the movement…from the back room into the front room and the significance of that—very very powerful…The physical movement mirrored the emotional and spiritual movement away from the past into, you know, I was claiming my identity, my future (Interview, Jackie).

We discussed the relationship of the renaming ceremony to the legal process of taking a new name. Shortly before the ritual Jackie had visited a solicitor with a friend to make a statutory declaration of her new name, and that legal document was on display in her front room. For Jackie, both were significant, but it was the ritual that she saw as the public commitment, which supported and sustained her in claiming her new identity:

> It had a kind of public dimension in it. Other times, when you change your name, it's very public, say at a marriage, it was a public declaration rather than just doing it in the privacy of a solicitor's office…which as I've said, was also much more powerful than I'd anticipated. It was making it public (Interview, Jackie).

For Jackie, the legal act and the ritual combined to enable her finally to be released from a painful association with her ex-husband, to affirm a continuity with all that she valued in terms of friendship and creativity, and to shape her own identity in the future:

> because I now have no connection with him, no dependence not even my name, and what we did was in a sense creating or affirming that independence, that new identity, so it was sealing the break—again the legality was more the signing the document in the solicitor's— sealing that but in a much more profound way. It's about what goes in the depths of the psyche and the spirit (Interview, Jackie).

Chapter Seven

PRIVATE OR PUBLIC?

The Communal Dimension of Women's Ritual Making

Almost all of the rituals in this study are conducted in the presence of other people, often other women, but sometimes in mixed groups. Some are with ongoing groups meeting regularly, others with people gathered for the specific occasion. The two exceptions are Cora and Rebecca. Cora, when I interviewed her, was planning a ritual for her birthday which would be solitary; but this was unusual for her, and she also talked about more communal rituals she had experienced. Of Rebecca's four ritual occasions relating to her redundancy, one was shared with one other friend, two with groups of people, and for the final one she was alone.

Much of the literature on women's liturgy and ritual stresses its collaborative or communal dimension. Usually, however, this is seen in terms of planning being a shared process, and writers such as Susan Roll (1998) and Diann Neu (1993a, 1993b) argue that collaborative planning and leadership are essential characteristics of feminist liturgy. In these rituals, however, the planning is usually done by the person whose transition it is, perhaps working with one other person. However, in most instances the role of other people is crucial, and its significance is articulated by the women in a number of different ways.

The roles played by others in accompanying the women working through transition are a crucial part of the process, and shape the ways in which these rituals broaden out from the individual to the communal. Through the involvement of others, these personal rituals move from the private to the public realm, touching on the wider social dimensions of women's lives.

Safety and Support

Some of the women interviewed were—and are—part of groups that meet regularly for some kind of sharing, liturgy or ritual. For Louise, holding her own ritual as part of the group's ongoing programme seemed a natural thing to do, although she was concerned to widen the theme of the evening so that it had relevance to others too:

> And I was, still am, was at that point, part of a kind of experimental alternative liturgy group and when it came to be my turn to do the liturgy I thought, well, let's do something around house-blessing but blessing of people as well so that it wasn't just a liturgy that was personal to me; but it was going to be something that people would support me in but actually there would be something in it for them as well because I felt that's kind of part of the ethos of the group really (Interview, Louise).

Jane, too, invited her regular group to share in the ritual she planned about her redundancy:

> I wanted it integrated into something bigger than just something to grieve or mourn about my experience. And some of those people who I like but I don't know particularly well I wouldn't have felt easy about just saying, "Would you like to come round one evening", if it hadn't been part of that ongoing framework (Interview, Jane).

Most of the women, however, specifically invited those whom they wished to come. So, for Clare, it was important to have people who had shared some of the experiences of the past few years with her, and contributed in some way to the completion of her thesis:

> I think the real thing was gathering—sort of people who've been significant to the actual thesis—people that knew something about it and about me—and had journeyed with me (Interview, Clare).

For Jackie, an important element in having people who had shared some of the journey was that she did not need to go into long explanations or retell painful parts of the story:

> Yes and the fact that they were people with whom I have been able to be vulnerable at all stages over the last five or six years—it couldn't just be anybody—not like a wedding where you know, you gather all and sundry but people who had the sensitivity to be there for me in all sorts of ways, to be able simply to rejoice because they knew—it didn't have to be articulated, but they knew—where it was coming from (Interview, Jackie).

First and foremost, when the women reflect on their rituals they talk of others offering support. This was partly an acknowledgement of support that others had offered in the past, but also a recognition that their actual presence was important. The nature of the support offered was expressed in different ways. For Alison, it was about trusting people and being able to be vulnerable with them:

> It was also about people that I wouldn't have minded talking to about the bad bits—the bits that I felt ashamed of and bad about—people I didn't mind sharing that with, who would be able to handle it (Interview, Alison).

For Jane, it was important that she could be angry without being judged, and this gave her a sense of safety within the group:

> And I think once that part of the ritual was over and my anger had been heard and accepted I didn't need to go on doing it...I've now found the places where it's safe to do anger...and I'm not going to be judged (Interview, Jane).

For Louise, the sense of safety and vulnerability had grown as the group has shared and developed trust over the years:

> I mean, it is a group whose very essence is about enabling the various members to work through things but with other people if they want to and to do that in all sorts of different ways...So the group were an obvious group to do the ritual with, but because they were a group with whom I can be out and who share at quite deep levels all sorts of stuff (Interview, Louise).

In addition to a sense of trust and vulnerability, which gives safety within the group, women talk about the positive aspects of friendship, creativity and enjoyment. Carol expresses her appreciation of the creativity and friendship she finds within the group and the liturgy:

> There's a warmth, a comfortableness about the names of the people whose work is included in it which I enjoy...And that was lovely you know, I mean just the abundance of the creativity of the people who were there, who are my friends (Interview, Carol).

Not many of the participants explicitly state the support that they receive through the prayers of others, but for both Jane and Nicola that is an important element:

> I was very supported all through but I think there was something about wanting to ask a couple of people to be with me in the place of

prayer—to support me in that way very overtly. I knew people were praying for me but I actually wanted a couple of people to be alongside me as I—I think I did see it as a sort of gesture of surrender and that is a kind of scary thing to do isn't it? (Interview, Nicola).

For some of the participants, the sense of safety is increased by the knowledge that others in the group share common beliefs, or are familiar with ritual. For Alison, as well as having people who have shared her journey, it is important that they have some understanding of what she is trying to do with ritual:

But the other element was people who were comfortable with ritual— it wouldn't have been good to have somebody there who was ill at ease at that. Two things basically—people who understood about ritual, and people I trusted to know things about me (Interview, Alison).

Louise, whose ritual takes place as part of the ongoing life of a group, recognizes the importance of their openness and willingness to engage in something other than conventional liturgy:

They are the kind of group who would go along with stuff that wouldn't be seen as usual church ritual. They—I mean, it is a group whose very essence is about enabling the various members to work through things but with other people if they want to and to do that in all sorts of different ways (Interview, Louise).

But this was not the case for all the participants. Some had invited those who were not accustomed to ritual or liturgy, but whose presence was nonetheless important in terms of the support and friendship they had offered. So, for Clare, inviting her childminder, whose work had enabled her to complete the thesis, was significant; and although she had been anxious about how some of her guests would react, felt all had gained from the event:

There were a few people who would never have been to something like that before and I think they—quite enjoyed it even though it was something they were not familiar with. I think it made an impression. I think there were certain people I'd invited who wouldn't really have had any kind of understanding of what rituals were for or about on a sort of intellectual level but I think they felt honoured sort of to be invited (Interview, Clare).

Andrea, too, expressed some hesitation about some of her friends who had no church background, or did not share her Christian beliefs; nevertheless there was a sense that part of her intention in carrying out a house-blessing rather than having a house-warming

party was to make a clear statement about her beliefs and her hopes
for her new home:

> I suppose it was also because some of it felt quite exposing, in a way,
> because some of them didn't really know that side of me, my
> beliefs...But at the same time it felt important for people to know that
> so I suppose that was one reason (Interview, Andrea).

So although for the most part women have invited friends who
will share or at least understand their intentions, and have some
familiarity with the ritual process, this is not always the case; the
primary motivation seems to be the quality and depth of
relationship. There is a strong sense of safe community, in which
women going through life-changing events are held and supported
by friends whom they trust, with whom they can relax, laugh and
be vulnerable. Even those whose rituals were not celebrated in a
group setting say that this is unusual for them — usually other people
would be involved in some way or another.

Ritual is often seen as having the function of providing support
and building community; Elaine Ramshaw (1987) in writing of ritual
and pastoral care, sees one of the main functions of ritual as bonding
community, and Cynthia Eller (1993) sees ritual as the 'glue' that
holds together the groups of the women's spirituality movement.
However, many of these women do not see building community as
a function of their rituals; rather, the community of friendship and
shared experience is the ground out of which the ritual springs.
The sharing in ritual may strengthen existing bonds or create new
ones; but that is secondary; what is primary is the sense of
relatedness and connection which makes the ritual gathering
possible in the first place. The women gain a sense of safety and
solidarity, which they find empowering. Ada Maria Isasi-Diaz,
writing about the place of *mujerista* liturgies in the liberation struggle
sees the ritual space as an important element in providing women
with the confidence and sense of power that they need for their
struggle:

> Here, in the safe space provided by this ritual, they had no need to
> pretend, for they were with others who accepted them even without
> full understanding. Here in this safe space many recovered their voices,
> voices silenced by the marginality that we suffer as Hispanics, and
> especially as Hispanic women (Isasi-Diaz 1995: 107).

Witness and Acknowledgement

Another word which women use of the other participants in their rituals is witness; there is a sense that the transitions they are making and the emotions they are experiencing need to be witnessed and acknowledged. Rebecca, who sees it as quite possible to carry out ritual actions alone, still sees something 'special' in the sharing within a group:

> And it's so special doing it, you know, to have someone—to have someone as a witness—and have somebody kind of sharing themselves too (Planning session with Rebecca).

Andrea, too sees it as important to make a public commitment in terms of her Christian faith and her hopes for her new home:

> But yeah, I suppose I did think of them as witnesses...I don't really know if I can put that into words but it was really important to have other people there (Interview, Andrea).

Several of the women talk about the importance of having experience and feelings acknowledged, in a semi-public setting that seems to go beyond simple conversation with friends. For Sue, whose work as a therapist was conducted in a relatively private sphere, it seemed important to have the ending of that work acknowledged:

> No, I'd have just finished, wouldn't I? And nobody would have known, in a sense, you know what I mean?...So it was like I wanted it to be registered really, you know, to finish...Well, I think it was my acknowledgement really but I think, I mean, I think drawing the other people in (Interview, Sue).

Jane talked of how sharing her feelings within the ritual felt different and more public than sharing with friends:

> Because one thing that the liturgy did was to—settle or acknowledge—acknowledge, I think—a lot of very negative feelings that I had about being made redundant and to give me permission to acknowledge them and to have other people who were prepared to listen to my doing so. And on the whole I hadn't done that publicly—I'd done it privately with various individuals but I'd not done it publicly (Interview, Jane).

Runa makes the point that since a name is public, used by others, their acknowledgement of a new name is essential:

> So it was very much about my community acknowledging that this change had taken place in order for it to be real...so that I could

experience myself as Runa I needed everybody to start calling me
that. So they had to be there to say yes, we acknowledge and accept
that this is who you are. So I'm sure it came out of all of that as well
(Interview, Runa).

There seems to be a strong element of what Tom Driver (1998)
describes as 'confessional', in which participants declare something
of their own identity and truth, in these rituals — women are
describing and interpreting the transitions in their lives in a way
that seeks to be honest and authentic for them. It is important for
them that this process is heard and acknowledged, and that
acknowledgement is part of the sense of affirmation which they
receive from the rituals.

Shared Meanings

Participants in the rituals are not passive witnesses or observers,
however attentive or supportive. They have an active part to play,
and bring their own meanings and agenda to the event, in a way
that shapes and transforms it. Sometimes this is through doing
something on behalf of the participants, as in the disposal of Jackie's
wedding dress. It also comes through in Alison's ritual, when she
asks her friends to remove the silver coins representing betrayal,
and replace them with candles signifying strength or resources.
She is very clear that this is something she cannot do for herself,
but needs the energy and support of the group to accomplish her
intentions:

the coins were laid out, and what I wanted to happen was for my
friends to take them away, one by one because it wasn't something I
felt able to do for myself. I suppose it's like — the nearest thing I can
say confession and absolution — that was being done for me, someone
else was carrying it away and I didn't have to carry it any longer...And
again it was really important people did that for me (Interview,
Alison).

For many there was a sense that others in the ritual brought
their own concerns, hopes, sadness or joys; and that whatever the
theme, others could relate to it in some way from their own
experience and events of their own lives:

people then participating in the ritual but not centring it around me so
it was about where other people are at as well. And that I'm not just
journeying on my own, but I'm journeying alongside, with,

interconnecting with other people who've got their own journeys and
their own difficulties and moments of celebration (Interview, Clare).

As people brought their own concerns and interpretations, the
meaning of the event changed; there was an intersubjective process
of constructing meaning which added different layers to the
symbols, words, and actions of the ritual. Jane recognized this
explicitly when I asked her how she saw the role of other
participants:

> Emotional support. Appropriate sharing of experience. Broadening of
> the symbolism. Broadening of interpretation. Producing a kind of
> collective — no, no, not a collective — a multi-layered way of looking
> at things which in fact when people are doing that sort of thing they
> do (Interview, Jane).

For a number of reasons, then, the collectivity of ritual is
experienced by the participants as empowering. Their own
experience of transition is, through symbol and ritual enactment,
interpreted in a wider context which is energising and empowering.

Cora spoke of the inclusive and collective sense of prayer during
a previous menopause ritual which she had experienced in a women's
sweat lodge:

> I think my most strongest memory of that ritual was — really interesting
> now — the round of prayers in the sweat lodge that was for the collective
> was incredibly focused in a way that just bowled me over...and I've
> never had quite such a sense that each women's prayer for the collective
> seemed to be like a part of the whole, like a segment of the orange, so
> that when we'd all spoken it was as if we'd covered every single area
> of praying for the collective and this world really (Interview, Cora).

It is clear that for some of the women this is seen not just as a
social phenomenon, but as a spiritual experience of connectedness
and divine power. Jane uses the image of the web (common in
women's spirituality) for the sense of being upheld through prayer
during her experience of redundancy:

> And I think I'd been aware that that had been quite an upholding kind
> of experience even though I'd been quite despairing sometimes — that
> somehow I hadn't cracked, or reached the complete bottom because
> there was something going on rather like a spider's web of concern that
> I was aware of that stopped my giving up altogether (Interview, Jane).

Rebecca sees the power of women meeting together and
celebrating ritual collectively as an experience of divinity:

> And really some of the most powerful experiences of my life have
> been in large groups of women engaging in ritual activities, so I think
> that spiritually we do feed from each other, you know, in that idea of
> channelling the divine you know, we have more power when we act
> collectively so it is important (Planning session with Rebecca).

In their different and individual voices women testify to the
collective power of ritual. However personal and individual the
transition, in almost all instances there is a sense of support, energy
and empowerment in sharing the experience with others, and
together creating meaning through symbol, action and word.

The sense of mutuality and relationality which we see here is a
key concept in feminist thought. Neuger (1999) argues for the need
to hold together the uniqueness of each woman's experience, and
the embedding of women's stories in their social context. The former
alone can lead to fragmentation, and the inability to reach a shared
narrative; the latter can make it difficult for women to break free
from gender stereotypes and prescribed roles and definitions. She
argues for a 'historicist alternative' which:

> offers a way to talk about women's lives, but women's lives within
> particular contexts and circumstances. It allows a shared narrative that
> may lead to shared meanings, identities and political analyses, but it
> does so recognising that the shared narrative is partial and evolving
> over time (1999: 128).

In ritual, with its social and collective dimension, one woman's
particular life-story or transition is explored and interpreted, but
within the shared narratives and experiences of others. Shared ritual
provides a context for meaning-making which acknowledges the
social embeddedness of women's lives, their connectedness with
one another and the wider world, and adds layers of interpretation
to the individual's unique story. It is experienced by the women in
this study as a dimension that is supportive, strengthening and
empowering, and enables them to catch glimpses of what they name
as divine.

The Collective Dimension of Ritual

Most definitions of ritual see it as a social practice, usually taking
place in a collective or public setting. Often this is seen in functional
terms, so that one of the roles of ritual is seen as reinforcing authority

and supporting social cohesion. Durkheim, for example, writes of religious beliefs and practices:

> That is why we can rest assured in advance that the practices of the cult, whatever they may be, are something more than movements without importance and gestures without efficacy. By the mere fact that their apparent function is to strengthen the bonds attaching the believer to his god, they at the same time really strengthen the bonds attaching the individual to the society of which he is a member, since the god is only a figurative expression of the society (1976: 226).

Rappaport sees ritual as:

> *the* basic social act. I will argue, in fact, that social contract, morality, the concept of the sacred, the notion of the divine, and even a paradigm of creation are intrinsic to ritual's structure (1979: 174).

There are others, however, for whom the social and political nature of ritual need not necessarily be conservative. David Kertzer, for example, does not see ritual as necessarily making for social cohesion. Whilst ritual may be used to legitimate authority and reinforce the status quo, it can also be used as a weapon in the political struggle by less dominant groups:

> rituals are far more than means of communicating the result of political struggles that take place in other arenas. Rituals have their own power and are themselves an important field of political struggle (1988: 104).

The power of ritual for oppressed groups lies in their collectivity. They can help give an oppressed group a sense of new identity, provide a focus for loyalty and action, and draw others in:

> If rites can be powerful weapons of the elite, they also represent one of the most potent weapons of the powerless. Lacking the formal organization and the material resources that help perpetuate the role of the elite, the politically deprived need a means of defining a new collectivity. This collectivity, created though rituals and symbols, not only provides people with an identity different from that encouraged by the elite, but also serves as a means to recruit others to their side (1988: 180–81).

Catherine Bell includes a discussion on the theory of power within ritual. She argues that the process of ritualization is an intentional social act, which can be used as a strategy to negotiate power relations. The objectifying of ideas and symbols, and embodied action can create and construct social realities:

> Within the intricacies of this objectification and embodiment lies the
> ability of ritualization to create social bodies in the image of
> relationships of power, social bodies that are those very relationships
> of power. If it is at all accurate to say that ritualization controls—by
> modeling, defining, molding, and so on—it is this type of control that
> must be understood (1992: 207).

Whilst these may perpetuate existing patterns, it is also possible
for ritual to appropriate, negotiate, or even subvert existing patterns
of domination in a 'redemptive hegemony' which is potentially
transformative. Power should not be seen as a reified entity, the
possession of one group, but rather in Foucauldian terms, as an
interacting web of relationships, in which power is constantly
negotiated and renegotiated. It is possible, therefore, for individuals,
whilst participating in ritual practices which may be imposed by a
dominant group, to negotiate and appropriate them on their own
terms. Whilst Bell does not deal specifically with the process of
ritual making, as opposed to participation in established rites, her
understanding of ritual as a strategic social practice which can
negotiate, rather than simply express, power relationships, opens
up the way for an understanding of ritual making as a potential
force for change.

Private or Public?

While the social and collective dimension is clearly perceived as
significant and empowering for the women participating in these
rituals, the private and personal nature of the events raises questions
about their wider relevance. Feminists, such as Diann Neu, Janet
Walton and Marjorie Procter-Smith, all link feminist liturgy and
ritual with a concern for social justice; however, these rituals are
not focusing on themes that are public, social issues but on personal
events in women's lives. It could be argued that their private
domestic nature makes them irrelevant, simply the activity of a
small clique. Grimes points out that whilst traditionally ritual has
been seen as social and collective, contemporary Western ritual has
a much more individualistic tone, focusing on self-expression and
the individual's bodily existence.

> Much contemporary ritualizing is focused on the body and articulated
> using the rhetoric of the self. This focus and rhetoric gives emergent
> ritual a distinctively individualistic ethos that sets it in opposition to

the standard scholarly view of ritual as a group-oriented phenomenon that is essentially collective and necessarily social (Grimes 1993: 10).

The rituals that I have studied are individualistic and personal, and sometimes intentionally and deliberately private. Nicola says of her pre-hysterectomy ritual:

> So I had a feeling that I needed to do something and it felt very much because of the intimate nature of the hysterectomy it didn't feel like it would be something to do massively publicly. I mean, it wasn't something that I would take to my local church actually (Interview, Nicola).

Carol, marking ten years of ministry, is conscious of the difference between a public act of worship and her celebration with a small group. She feels the need of this in giving her a sense of safety and freedom, but also expresses some anxiety about the danger of becoming a 'clique':

> It was a gathering around me, us, of significant people instead of all comers who might like to come which is different isn't it?...So I have got a little bit of uncertainty about it from the point of view of, how intimate and personal do you keep this thing?...But yes, not wanting to be cliquey about celebrating something which has actually been quite a public living out of something. On the other hand, needing that space, needing that for me—I'm not sure about that (Interview, Carol).

In some ways, women's ritual making seems to be far from the traditional understanding of collective ritual. The rituals here are taking place in small groups, often in domestic space, and dealing with individual and deeply personal emotions. They do, however, have elements which touch on what are usually considered public or social issues. Those which relate to redundancy speak clearly to the public realm of work, rather than to the private, domestic sphere. The changing of one's name is a very public process, with practical, legal and financial implications. The ending of a thesis confers academic status and is publicly marked by graduation. In all these instances, the women concerned discuss the relationship of public and private in relation to their rituals.

In speaking of her redundancy, Jane clearly recognizes the wider structural implications of the world of work. It has impinged on her life in an immediate and personal way, but redundancy is a wider social issue that affects many others:

> So when you're made redundant you are caught up by something
> that's structurally much bigger than you as an individual. It's not an
> individual experience that happens (Interview, Jane).

For Jackie and Runa, changing their names meant a semi-public
process of legal requirements and notifying various bodies. For
Jackie the legal aspect was the private occasion, the signing of a
statutory declaration in a solicitor's office, accompanied by one
friend; whereas the ritual, although held in her home and with a
small group, was the more public occasion. Both the legal signing
and the ritual were necessary, but for Jackie, as with Clare, it was
her own ritual which held the greater meaning and significance
for her:

> I mean, they both made it legitimate in different ways...So the kind of
> legal side was just something I had to accept and was just glad to do...it
> was a kind of external thing but it was a necessary foundation. It did
> legitimate what we then did although the real thing for me was
> something that had no kind of legality at all. But that was the most
> significant thing that we did on that night (Interview, Jackie).

Runa expresses similar feelings with regard to her renaming:

> And that was important too, that I had the legal bit of it too. And then
> of course there followed months and months of writing to all these
> organisations, banks and bills and people and getting it all done...That
> was important but in a sense it was just crossing "t"s and dotting "i"s.
> The main thing was the ritual (Interview, Runa).

For Clare, the ritual she holds in her own home is private,
personal, and much more meaningful than the public event of
graduation. She does, however, attend her graduation, and
recognizes its importance to others—in particular, to her family
and her supervisor:

> So yes, I think going to both, having both, the ritual and the graduation,
> I think they did very different functions. Bit like a wedding—it's a
> question of who is it for? Is it for the people getting married or is it for
> all the family and friends? And I think the first ritual was for me and
> the second ritual was very much for other people (Interview, Clare).

In other rituals the public implications are less obvious, but still
present. Sue and Cora's rituals both concern ageing, and Cora's
comments on the honouring of older women challenge social and
conventional stereotypes which are often negative:

Maybe 20 or so others who were under 50 made a circle round us and were dancing round us and honoured us, and we just sat soaking it up and it was, Oh, incredible!...and it was just one of those moments that I thought, this is how the world could be, maybe should be (Interview, Cora).

The home has typically been seen as a private sphere, but for Louise and Andrea, their homes are places of openness and hospitality, and there is a clear intention to make the space available and accessible to others. Andrea expresses something of that tension between home as private space and hospitality as she talks about her reasons for doing the ritual:

I wanted people to know about why I was doing it. So I wanted it to have the aspect of kind of salvation but also questioning cos I suppose I also felt a bit uneasy about buying a flat. I mean, I had owned a house before but I felt the same uneasiness then as well, so I wanted it to include aspects of that questioning, sort of why have I bought it and what is it for? What could it be used for? What do I hope it will be? It feels like creativity and welcoming, but also a place of solitude and retreat, so I definitely wanted those two aspects of it (Interview, Andrea).

The medical treatment of women's bodies is far from being a private issue, and in preparing for her operation Nicola became aware of advice and literature in the secular sphere. In publishing the prayer-poem (Slee 2004b) she used in what was essentially a private and intimate ritual she has in a sense reached out beyond the personal to the public realm.

Although they are personal and in some senses private events, the rituals do not simply reflect the social realities which women experience, but attempt to interpret and construct them in alternative ways. They are implicitly redefining the boundaries of what is private and what is public, confronting the dualism that marginalizes women's experience of work, or that renders invisible the social dimensions of ageing and attitudes to women's bodies. There is a conscious attempt to negotiate the social and public realities which form the context for women's lives. The feminist insistence that 'the personal is political' and the work of some feminist theorists argue for a redefinition of private and public that would reinforce the argument that these rituals have wider public and social implications.

For Hannah Arendt, to engage in speech and action of any kind is to be in relationship with others, part of a complex human web in which all actions are interrelated, and each affects the other. In this understanding, the most personal or intimate feelings or pain move into a different realm when they are given expression in word or action—they become part of the common life of humanity. The only way to be truly private is to be entirely deprived of speech or action:

> To live an entirely private life means above all to be deprived of the reality that comes from being seen and heard by others, to be deprived of an "objective" relationship with them that comes from being related to and separated from them through the intermediary of a common world of things, to be deprived of the possibility of achieving something more permanent than life itself (1998: 58).

In this way, to speak or act in any way is to be in interaction with other human beings, and therefore part of public life. These women's rituals, therefore, are public in the sense that they take private pain and personal experiences of transition into the realm of speech and action; they become part of the 'web'—itself a popular image in women's spirituality—that makes up our common life.

Arendt's view seems to abolish almost entirely the distinction between public and private. Iris Marion Young draws on her work, but attempts to preserve the distinction, although redefining it. She claims that the distinction between private and public has often been seen in hierarchical terms, parallel to the dualisms of feminine and masculine, feeling and reason. Whilst she still allows for a distinction between private and public, she is insistent that they should not be seen as totally different realms:

> This manner of formulating the concepts of public and private, which is inspired by feminist confrontations with traditional public theory, does not deny their distinction. It does deny, however, a social division between public and private spheres, each with different kinds of institutions, activities, and human attributes (1990: 120)

She argues that privacy has generally been seen as excluding people or issues from the public realm. In this sense, it is, as Arendt has argued, about a deprivation. Young, however, argues that privacy should be seen as that part of an individual's life which he or she has the right to keep private, to exclude others from. She names two key principles: first, that nothing should be forced into privacy by others, and second, that no social institution or practice should be excluded from public debate.

Feminist thinking and activism has broken down the hierarchical dualism between public and private, bringing into public awareness and debate issues and practices previously consigned to the private realm, and therefore marginalized or made invisible:

> The feminist slogan "the personal is political" expresses the principle that no social practices or activities should be excluded as improper subjects for public discussion, expression, or collective choice. The contemporary women's movement has made public issues out of many practices claimed to be too trivial or private for public discussion: the meaning of pronouns, domestic violence against women, the practice of men's opening doors for women, the sexual assault of women and children, the sexual division of housework, and so on (1990: 120–21).

Many of these women's rituals are engaged in the same kind of process, taking experiences, feelings or events that are often regarded as private, and by their words or symbolic actions, speaking into the wider arena of human social affairs.

There has been considerable interest in recent years in developing public theology:

> a theology, talk about God, which claims to point to publicly accessible truth, to contribute to public discussion by witnessing to a truth which is relevant to what is going on in the world and to the pressing issues facing people and societies today (Forrester 2000: 127).

It is a theology which aims to speak in terms of faith and Gospel in a public world and society that is plural, fragmented and globalized, taking the agenda of the 'public square' seriously, but drawing out issues that need to be addressed. Its aim to make Christian faith and theology relevant and accessible in a secular and postmodern society is laudable; but what is considered 'public' requires close scrutiny if it is not to fall into the hierarchical dualism which Young critiques. It is easy to categorize what happens in home or family, or the discourse which stereotypes women's bodies and ageing, as private, and thereby exclude it from public debate and theology. Young's argument, however, maintains that whilst individuals have the right to privacy, to exclude the realities of their lives from public concern is a denial and a deprivation. Public theology needs to acknowledge the dualism of private and public in the past, and expand the boundaries of what is public in response to feminist critique.

In making their rituals, the women here are engaging in what Bell calls 'strategic practice'. They are negotiating the tension between private and public in two ways. First, in Arendt's terms, they are inserting their lives into the public world of human word and action; by articulating their experience in word and symbol they are engaged in action that is public, that changes and has effects in the wider world of human living. Second, the collective nature of their ritual making in relation to experiences and settings normally considered private or domestic begins to break down the dualism between public and private.

Ritual not only reflects social reality but constructs it, not only creating an alternative reality amongst the participants but effecting change in the wider social order. Ritual is a form of discourse, and as such shapes consciousness and can maintain or challenge power relations. Lesley Northup argues that women's ritualizing is a power for change. Where ritual is in the hands of dominant groups (as is the case with much public and collective ritual), the very fact that women are gathering and shaping their own rituals independently of institutional religion constitutes a challenge to the status quo:

> Women worshiping together enact a social drama whose purpose, at least subliminally, is precisely to disrupt, demystify, delegitimate and deconstruct both some institutional religious forces and the social structures they create and fortify. Although these essentially political goals might not be consciously deployed, the mere fact that women gather separately to engage in ritualized behavior is a disruptive statement (1997: 91).

For others, the very fact that women are creating rituals for their own lives and experiences is overturning the traditional public/ private dichotomy:

> The very presence of ritualizing women in the public sphere is itself an overturning of the traditional division of public and private, the public having been the sphere of men and the private the sphere of women (Larson-Miller 1998: 70).

Marjorie Procter-Smith sees liturgy and political action as inseparably linked; and whilst she perhaps expands the definition of worship too far, she makes an important point in seeing women's worship as part of their political work:

It remains for the feminist liturgical movement...to claim liturgy as the political work of women within a political democratic model of church. It is essential, moreover, that this political work of women include the acts traditionally associated with liturgy and worship as well as claim the religious power of acts not traditionally associated with worship. Acts of prayer, invocation, petition, lament and imprecation must be seen as political acts, while organizing, petitioning, protesting, voting and collaborating must be seen as acts of worship (2003: 506–507).

The women whose rituals I have written about here do not make explicit claims for their rituals as political actions; but however much they value personal and private safe space, there is an awareness of wider social implications. For many years the private has been seen as the domestic, female sphere; whilst the public sphere of work and politics belongs to men. This is another dichotomy or boundary that is being blurred in these rituals, which take private intimate events and declare them publicly; and challenge the public conventions and assumptions in a personal, authentic reshaping of symbols. They have already begun the process which Marjorie Procter-Smith advocates:

An essential place to begin is the development of strategies that overcome the public/private dichotomy that assigns the private sphere to women and thus to women's ritualizing practices (Procter-Smith 2003: 511).

Case Study Five

THIS IS MY BODY: NICOLA'S STORY

Unlike the other stories of rituals I have included, I was not present at Nicola's, nor did I share in the planning. I had known Nicola for some years through feminist theology networks, and when I spoke about my research at a conference, she offered to be interviewed about a ritual she had enacted just before her hysterectomy. Her ritual emerged from a prayer-poem, *This Woman's Body*, which she wrote and subsequently published (Slee 2004) and so my telling of her story is based both upon her interview and her written text.

Nicola's ritual took place shortly before her hysterectomy. She had gone through a long period of loss — of job, income, and home:

> It happened to come at a time when there was just a whole lot of other loss really — it feels like it was a time of immense kind of tearing down and stripping (Interview, Nicola).

Whilst waiting for the operation Nicola had plenty of time for reflection, and began to think about how she could mark the event and her sense of loss in a spiritual way. She found little in the way of resources to speak to her situation:

> And I needed to mark it in some kind of liturgical way, and I needed to find — again one of the things I thought was really interesting, hysterectomy is one of the most common operations there is. And I could find plenty of self-help books, you know, what would happen when I went into hospital...but I could find virtually nothing on women — maybe it is there but I just couldn't find it — but I searched for women writing about hysterectomy again from a more spiritual perspective (Interview, Nicola).

But she did come across a sermon 'This is my body' (Lunn 1994) in *Silence in Heaven* which spoke of hospitalization and the loss of blood in relation to Christ's words 'this is my body, this is my blood'. This sparked her off in writing her own piece, 'This Woman's Body'.

> Quite a long piece — again with this repeated refrain 'this is my body, this is my blood' and very much taking those words and wanting to say, 'This is my woman's body, this is my blood' (Interview, Nicola).

Out of the writing of the piece, a ritual emerged. Nicola felt a strong sense that the piece needed to be spoken aloud, shared with other women who were supporting her at the time.

> I think there was something about wanting to ask a couple of people to be with me in the place of prayer, to support me in that way very overtly (Interview, Nicola).

She was very clear that there was a significant difference between the writing of the piece and hearing it spoken:

> Why does the naming of something make a difference? But it makes a profound difference — it kind of puts you into a different relation to the reality, doesn't it? And again, it's that hearing yourself say something, of seeing something performed (Interview, Nicola).

She was equally clear that this should not be a public occasion, but needed to be a quiet and intimate gathering. As she was living at the time in a Catholic community, she used the room there which served as a quiet room or chapel for community prayers. It therefore had the sense both of being at home, but also sacred space, with a simple altar and the presence of the reserved sacrament. The Eucharist had always been an important part of Nicola's liturgical practice, and she was clear that this would be the central symbolism of her ritual.

> I wanted to make eucharist again in that context of bringing together the Eucharist and the reality of my body and blood as they were at that moment before going into surgery. So again there was something about, yeah, wanting to make a eucharistic ritual which again is more than — so I suppose there is something about wanting to evoke, claim, very overtly Christ's presence in my womb, in my blood. (Interview, Nicola).

On the day, Nicola made a centerpiece around the simple altar in the chapel, using crimson cloths to symbolize women's blood, with candles and flowers, and invited two close friends to join her. There was a period of silence, and some quiet music, and then she read the poem she had written, with her friends joining in the repeated refrain, 'This is my body, this is my blood'. They shared bread and wine together, and then ended with a bodily blessing written by

Diann Neu, in which they used scented water to bless each part of their bodies, including a blessing of Nicola's womb:

> including bless my womb and bless its resting…I laid hands on my womb and the rest and security you have given to me—and sent it to a time of rest in readiness for death. And then…yeah, like saying goodbye to my womb and that's how we ended (Interview, Nicola).

Nicola's ritual took place shortly before her operation, and for her it was very much part of the whole process of loss, of pruning, and of stripping away in which the ritual itself was the turning point. Throughout the process she experienced a strong sense of peace and of being held, even through the loss and the fear.

> There were times of terror when all this was being stripped away but I think I also had a sense of profound holding and peace—sorry, such cliché, but I did! (Interview, Nicola).

As she spoke of the period after the operation, and her recovery, she used the image of the Ark—a sense that all her familiar world was submerged, and she was adrift with the few possessions that were left, waiting to reach a safe shore. And although there was a period of waiting and recovery, she had a strong sense of something new beginning, and a new energy to take up the threads of a changed life:

> You know, the waters haven't receded, so there was still a long kind of waiting time really, but there was a beginning of sort of, this thing of moving into new time and moving towards new land, new world (Interview, Nicola).

Nicola's ritual is deeply rooted in her own embodied experience. She begins from her bodily experience of bleeding, which for her is intimately connected with her gender and her sexuality:

> But there was also very specific stuff about no longer bleeding. And lots of women said to me, "Oh, lucky you, you know, you'll never have to have another period". And I actually felt that as a loss. And again, I couldn't exactly explain to you but it seemed quite connected—well it's obvious—it seemed quite connected to my whole being—you know, sexual and gendered being—once you're bleeding (Interview, Nicola).

She is aware of the feminist theology which has critiqued patriarchal dualism and reclaimed the holiness of women's bodies, but now this is immediate and personal for her:

> You know, this has been seen as taboo, you know, defiled and not to be in a holy place. And of course I knew all that theology and that was part of it but it had suddenly become extremely immediate and it wasn't just about something general in feminist theology — it was about what it proclaimed, saying something about my body and blood (Interview, Nicola).

The Eucharist which has always been part of her spiritual practice is celebrated not in its patriarchal form, but in an act of resistance which reclaims the messy realities and pain of women's bodily existence.

> And it's so often divorced from real bodies and the messiness and the pain and it's done up there by men in priestly garb so I think I was also trying to claim Eucharist and say, you know the Eucharist really should be about this (Interview, Nicola).

The piece which she wrote and used in the ritual celebrates her own bodily experience:

> If I look again at the piece that I wrote, it was almost like a retrospective of my whole life. It starts with a woman's body — you know, of knowledge and wisdom...this woman's body of mine which had never been named or known or held as sacred in church (Interview, Nicola).

It goes on beyond her personal experience to recognize the particularity of other women's experience, that she has not known: and so extends beyond the personal and individual to protest at the oppression and violence that has been done to women's bodies:

> There is so much this woman's body of mine
> has never known:
>> the abuse of violation
>> the degradation of poverty
>> the despoliation of conquest or invasion
>> the mutilation of war and pillage and rape (Slee 2004b: 91).

Her text explicitly makes the connection between her woman's body and the body and blood of Christ, making sacred her own bodily experience:

> So I will speak again my body's bounty
> I will name my body's knowledge
> I will praise my body's courage
> I will eat of her flesh
> I will drink of her blood
> I will receive at her hands
>> of the life-giving death and the death-dealing life.

And I will know her as sacred
    and honoured
    and highly-favoured
    and chosen
    and God-taken, blessed, broken and offered,
for
This is my body, this is my blood (Slee 2004b: 92).

Chapter Eight

PERFORMING THE BODY: RITUAL, SACRAMENT AND EMBODIED THEOLOGY

We have already seen how the women's rituals are a way of enabling the participants to become co-authors of their own stories, developing agency and shaping narrative and theology. Because the rituals are communal events, the stories are told, shared and interwoven with others. But in ritual, the stories are not only told, but enacted—albeit in symbolic and stylized form, the narrative takes shape in action. It is not only told, but performed. Kristin Langellier (2003) recognizes the pervasiveness of personal narrative in conversation, and in more public events, but argues that the performance of narrative, whether in public events, or in ritual, situates it in a particular context that makes the identity and agency of the storyteller more concrete and embodied:

> But performance and performativity open a pathway through the celebratory and suspicious terrain of personal narrative...a way that is embodied, material, situated and critical (2003: 447–48).

Embodied Action

Ritual is primarily about action. Although there may be set words within a ritual (for example, the vows and declarations at a marriage service or the words of the committal at a funeral), primarily when we think of ritual we think about actions (the water sprinkled on a baby's forehead, or the eating and drinking of bread and wine at a Eucharist). Ritual is about action, embodied, symbolic, and usually performed according to a set formula or script in the presence of others.

The rituals that women are creating and inventing for themselves are rich in embodied action. Northup (1997) lists a number of actions which she finds to be common in women's ritualizing—naming, healing, smudging, dancing, chanting, narrative, reverencing the ancestors, using natural and domestic objects as symbols, and eating. She also includes reflexivity, arguing that self-conscious reflection on the ritual is an integral part of the process. In addition, many women's rituals focus on bodily themes such as ageing, birth, menstruation and menopause.

All of these rituals use some form of embodied action—such as making a dreamcatcher, burning papers and photographs, moving around a house, lighting candles, placing shells in water, and sharing bread and wine. Some of the rituals here relate specifically to bodily themes—Nicola's Eucharist before her hysterectomy, Cora's marking of the menopause, Sue's celebration of her sixtieth birthday. To understand why embodied action is so crucial to these rituals we turn to ideas of performativity in ritual theory and the theoretical framework offered by theories on construction of gender and feminist theologies of embodiment.

Ritual Performance

Theories of performativity in ritual draw on Austin's work on performative speech-acts. J.L. Austin coined the term performative utterances to describe those sayings, or speech-acts, which accomplish acts in the process of speaking—for example, 'I declare you husband and wife' or 'I name this ship'—which do what they say they do. In these instances the saying of the words forms the main part of the action taking place. They do not describe an action, nor give expression to feelings, nor issue a command—rather they accomplish an action in the moment of saying the words:

> I propose to call it a performative sentence, or a performative utterance, or, for short, "a performative"...The name is derived, of course, from "perform", the usual verb with the noun "action": it indicates that the issuing of the utterance is the performing of an action—it is not normally thought of as just saying something (Austin 1976: 6).

Such statements are neither true nor false—but they do depend on the acceptance of certain conventions and circumstances to be effective. They may depend on the authority or status of the person uttering them (such as the officiating minister, priest or registrar) or the establishing of the right conditions (a prescribed place, time, or form of words). Such requirements of status or condition are socially determined; but provided that agreed procedures are adhered to, they guarantee the effectiveness of performative utterance (Austin 1976).

This thinking underlies the understanding of ritual as performative — as action which actually accomplishes what it describes or symbolically enacts — that does what it says it does. The anthropologist, Roy Rappaport, sees ritual as affecting and regulating events in the external world. He draws on his fieldwork amongst the Tsembaya peoples to argue that their ritual cycles have actual effects in the material world, with regard to the environment and relationships with neighbouring tribes. Whilst this is not recognized as the purpose of the ritual by the actors, it nevertheless has concrete effects in the material world. There are certain aspects to ritual which Rappaport sees as key in this process. First, he argues that ritual is not simply a means of communication — it is, and has to be, a performance:

> performance is not merely a way to express something, but is itself an aspect of that which it is expressing (Rappaport 1979: 177).

There are two elements to the performance — one is what he calls 'indexical', indicating the current emotional or psychological state of the performers; the other is 'canonical' — the unvarying, formal, eternal aspect which is embedded in the ritual form. This formal character helps to ensure that the correct conventions and forms are observed in order for the performance to be effective:

> The formality of liturgical orders helps to ensure that whatever performatives they may incorporate are performed by authorized people with respect to eligible persons or entities under proper circumstances in accordance with proper procedures. Moreover, the formality of ritual makes very clear and explicit what it is that is being done...Ritual, this is to say, not only ensures the correctness of the performative enactment, it also makes the performatives it carries explicit, and it generally makes them weighty as well (Rappaport 1979: 190).

The set form of the ritual establishes order and moves beyond the private feelings and intentions to the public enactment. Particular beliefs or feelings on the part of the actors are not necessary — what is important is an acceptance of the form of the ritual and the conventions of observance and authority which underlie it.

Pattern and form are seen as key elements in establishing the performativity of ritual (Tambiah 1985). If ritual is seen as founded on faith in cosmological and eternal realities then there has to be a fixed unvarying form. There are three elements or aspects to the ritual – there is the actual doing of the action, a staged performance, and an indication of the values and feelings communicated through a coded simulation. The performance of ritual does not depend on the private feelings and emotions of the participants – rather, by enacting those feelings in the public realm, it creates a social distance from them in its conventionalized and stylized form.

Bodily action and the physical techniques at the heart of ritual are seen as instrumental in constructing social reality (Crossley 2004):

> What many rituals manifest, however, particularly public and social rituals, is an understanding of the social world to which the agent belongs, that is, of its values, beliefs, distinctions, social positions, and hierarchies. Furthermore, at the same time, they constitute the practical know-how necessary for the reproduction of that social world (Crossley 2004: 38).

Ritual may therefore be used by the powerful to reinforce their dominance, using the bodily processes and techniques of ritual to create an intersubjective state of mind which the participants 'misrecognise' as worship:

> Ritual can involve an imaginative intentionality, effecting a 'magical' transformation of situation...Through the power of ritual as an imaginative act, make-believe misrecognised as worship, they bring their God into existence for themselves (Crossley 2004: 44).

The repetition of ritual helps to create a cultural memory (Buckland 1995) which helps to define and shape the identity of a community:

> Rituals characteristically employ a rhetoric of fixity and stasis, especially under the sign of the repetition of the past through which a community, or a powerful minority within the community, manages its identity and negotiates transitions. This amounts to the creation and organisation – the management – of a "cultural memory" (Buckland 1995: 55).

Gender roles are one element of such a cultural identity, and Diane Bell illustrates this through her study of ritual in Aboriginal society. In a culture where male and female roles are strongly segregated, women's rituals have a particular work to do in maintaining gender roles and social cohesion. They do not simply express the reality that exists, but help to shape and maintain it:

> To the extent that women's rituals endure and encode crucial aspects
> of gender relations and therefore of aboriginal culture, women and
> their rituals contribute most significantly to the continuity of aboriginal
> structures in a colonial frontier society (Bell 1996: 47).

There is therefore a strand of argument which sees the performative power of ritual in its frequent repetition of bodily actions, practices, and techniques, creating a reality which is seen by the participants not as their own social construction, but an external (usually divine or transcendent) reality.

However, there are others who argue that rites do not necessarily have to be fixed and invariable in order to be performative. Although there may be a fixed script or liturgy, the context of the enactment, the moods and feelings of the actors, and the reactions of any spectators means that the performance itself is not fully determined, but fluid, unique and unrepeatable (Brown 2003). The script is necessary, but in the performance of it a creative tension is set up between what is prescribed and what actually happens in the immediacy of the ritual:

> In this way, no script can ever fully encapsulate a performance; rather,
> a performance represents a creative tension between the "what should
> be" of the script and the "what happens" of the actual performance. To
> speak of performance is not merely to be concerned with the intricate
> form of the event as envisaged by the script, but also, to explore the
> unscripted dimensions of the activity. One might say perhaps that a
> performance is *scripted action in action* (Brown 2003: 5).

Whilst for many scholars, the formality and fixity of religious ritual gives it its performative power, for others this leads to a questioning of its contemporary relevance and continuing value. Nathan Mitchell sees a suspicion of traditional ritual in contemporary society, but argues that such an analysis fails to take account of the growth of what he calls 'emerging ritual', in both secular life and in religion. He sees such ritual as emerging often amongst marginalized groups, and cites the way in which 'Gay Pride Parades' function as vehicles for social change:

> The public nature of these processions not only unites participants—
> bringing them "out of the closet"—but embodies and promotes their
> struggle for civil rights (Mitchell 1995: 125).

He goes on to give a detailed analysis of the ritual dimensions of the Twelve-Step Programme followed within Alcoholics Anonymous, and concludes:

> The most creative ritual resources appear to be emerging among families (where rites bond members in ways blood cannot) and among persons marginalized by illness and/or intense social antipathy (e.g., alcoholics; persons with AIDS) (1995: 128).

Ronald Grimes is one of the scholars who has argued most strongly for the reinvention and creation of new rites. He argues that many of our rites of passage in modern Western society need reinvention, and in some cases (for example, initiation into adulthood) no appropriate rites exist at all. Unlike fixed and established ritual, however, 'invented' rites do not carry social support or the weight of tradition; instead they are often created by groups on the margins of society, using one-off metaphors and symbols:

> Unlike rites, ritualizing does not typically garner broad social support; it seems too innovative, dangerously creative, and insufficiently traditional. So deliberate ritualizing happens in the margins and is alternatively stigmatized and romanticized (Grimes 2000: 29).

Rituals must be local and specific to the situation, but equally open to learn from the past, from other cultures, and from a process of self-evaluation and criticism. They work with imagination and metaphor, and although they may create new images, over time these images too, with repeated use, practice and performance will go deeper and become inscribed on bodies and minds of participants. For Grimes, the process of creating and enacting ritual is not simply expressive of meaning, but is both performative, and in the case of rites of passage, transformative:

> To enact any kind of rite is to perform, but to enact a rite of passage is to transform (Grimes 2000: 7).

For many, religious ritual no longer has this transformative power, and Tom Driver has a concern to transform and liberate rites in the context of Christian worship. He argues that Christian liturgy and ritual has often been seen as text, rather than performance, and that we need to recover and explore the performative dimension:

> let us start by recalling that human lives are shaped not only, not even principally, by the ideas we have in our minds, but even more by the actions we perform with our bodies (Driver 1998: 79).

If this is true of our lives, then it needs to be reflected in our rituals. We need to pay attention not just to what is said, but what is done and enacted in ritual. Ritual does not simply express what we think or feel; it shapes the way we see the world and our subsequent action.

> Rites of passage are performed not simply to *mark* transitions, but to effect them (Driver 1998: 93).

In this process there are four different aspects to any performance. One is the theatrical, the way in which something is communicated and displayed to others, often through the setting, the symbols used, the multimedia dimension. Another is the confessional, the element of ritual which includes the telling of someone's own story, their truth and identity as they see it. Third, there is the ethical, the concern that the ritual will have for wider society and the external world. And there is ritual itself—for Driver argues that not every performance is ritual—only that which seeks to encounter and engage with transcendent powers in some way:

> A ritual is an efficacious performance that invokes the presence and action of powers which, without the ritual, would not be present or active at that time and place, or would be so in a different way (Driver 1998: 97).

In the enactment of a ritual all these dimensions need to be present, although some may predominate more than others.

There is therefore considerable agreement about the performative character of ritual. It is a social act, a practice which is embodied in symbol and action, and which has concrete effects in the material world. Some, however, such as Rappaport and Tambiah, see ritual accomplishing this through its fixed, formal character; others, such as Grimes and Driver, see the process of creating and inventing ritual (ritualization) as a process which enables a restructuring of personal vision and social relations. I have already argued that contemporary women's rituals are much closer to the latter way of thinking. They are not fixed and invariable, although there are common patterns emerging and symbols repeated over time. Neither do they receive wide social sanction or public acknowledgement—

most are enacted in private, domestic space without official recognition from church or any other institution. Often they are looking at transitions that are invisible in public or liturgical discourse.

We can take this a stage further however, and examine, if ritual has an effect in the material world, how that can be defined and described. For Tambiah and Rappaport, ritual works in a primarily conservative fashion—it serves the function of reinforcing and maintaining the status quo. Whilst its practitioners may not see or recognize this, understanding ritual in terms of its engagement with divine or otherworldly powers, what it in fact achieves is to maintain social norms or an ecological balance. Because ritual is encoded in canonical form, with unvarying patterns and processes, it establishes order and gives legitimacy to the way of life and understanding which it symbolizes:

> The unfalsifiable supported by the undeniable yields the unquestionable, which transforms the dubious, the arbitrary, and the conventional into the correct, the necessary, and the natural. This structure is, I would suggest, the foundation upon which the human way of life stands, and it is realized in ritual (Rappaport 1979: 217).

For some writers, however, this function of ritual, whilst recognized, can be oppressive. Grimes is adamant that, far from being 'unquestionable', ritual demands reflection and critique:

> Rites may become not only irrelevant but oppressive. In the wrong hands, they can be tools for oppression as surely as they can be instruments of healing. During moments of passage, people are peculiarly vulnerable—not only open to the transformative power of ritual but also open to ceremonial manipulation. Since rites of passage have been employed to mystify the sources of power and therefore to control others, we cannot assume they are above critique, even when they appear sacrosanct (Grimes 2000: 293).

However, because rituals are so powerful, because they are not simply expressive of meaning, but also performative, they can also construct alternative visions and new meanings.

Driver similarly sees the potential for rites to be oppressive or liberating; and one of the main concerns of his book is to argue that rites of passage and the sacraments within the Christian tradition should be both liberated *from* dryness or irrelevance, and liberating *for* the participants:

One of the ways in which ritual, religion and liberative action are alike is that they all construct alternative worlds, nourishing themselves with imaginative visions (Driver 1998: 80).

If ritual and religious practices construct, rather than express, belief then a greater focus on practice can lead to increased understanding. Amy Hollywood argues that philosophy of religion has often focused on belief rather than religious practice, whereas for religious believers, the latter is more often at the forefront of their lived experience:

Rituals, like bodily practices, do not carry symbolic meanings, but instead *do* things. They create certain kinds of subjects, dispositions, moods, emotions, and desires. Put in another way, they are like performative speech acts, for that to which they refer is constituted through the action itself (Hollywood 2004: 58).

However, if beliefs and convictions can be learned and constructed through ritual, then potentially they can also be changed or transformed by it:

Even if we begin to recognise the learned nature of many of our most deeply embedded dispositions and beliefs, new practices that enable a re-formation of the self will be required for their transformation (Hollywood 2004: 66).

It is this power of ritual performance to subvert, reconstruct and transform that is at the heart of women's ritualizing.

Ladelle McWhorter analyses her own participation in a commitment ceremony with her same-sex partner in her exploration of ritual. She uses Foucault's work on ritual as a technology of power (Foucault 1979) and begins with a suspicion that same-sex commitment ceremonies, although they may be seen as evidence of new freedoms for gay couples, actually have the effect of reinforcing heterosexual ideologies of marriage. As she works through the process of planning and enacting the ceremony, she comes to feel that (again in Foucault's terms), this is 'askesis', an ethical practice of freedom, enabling her to pass into a new identity which is not fixed and changed, but which continues to be in process:

Ritual might, then, be a part of an anti-normalizing ethical way of life. It might be a practice of freedom (McWhorter 2004: 84).

For her, somewhat against her own expectations, the ritual performance of her ceremony with her partner proves to be transformative, enabling them to move into new identities and ways of relating that will continue to unfold:

> The process of creating the ceremony enabled me to arrive at the site and present myself, my happiness and conviction, to our friends and loved ones, but the ceremony itself produced new happiness and new conviction. It was not simply the final enactment of what we had planned; it exceeded its design in the transformative effects it had...Its primary purpose was not the fixing of our identities. It created something new and set in motion a joint, perhaps communal, creative process. And in doing so, it challenged fixed identities and enabled us to claim some power to re-create ourselves (McWhorter 2004: 91).

Performance in Women's Ritual Making

Many of the women I worked with speak of the importance of embodied symbols and symbolic action in their rituals, and of their sense of its transforming effect on their lives. They may begin by choosing symbols or symbolic actions to represent what they want to say, but they discover that the actual performing of them makes a difference to their consciousness and understanding.

Rebecca speaks of the difference between talking about something, and performing an action in ritual:

> Well for me it cements something, you know, it kind of makes it real...I have endless conversations but most of it I forget. I won't ever forget these rituals. Yes, so I think that doing something physically kind of cements it in the experience, makes it real and actually does ease the moving on, you know, makes it happen (Interview, Rebecca).

Nicola explicitly recognizes the performative dimension of her ritual: it is based upon a piece she has written earlier, and she is quite explicit about the difference between writing the piece and reading it in the company of others:

> even if I hadn't done the ritual, the writing of it was important and significant and it named a lot of things. But then it was the feeling I wanted to do more than that and did want it in some way enacted (Interview, Nicola).

For Jackie, it was the physical movement into another room to claim her identity that formed one of the most significant moments of the ritual. The movement for her not only mirrored or expressed, but actually enabled her and others to begin to create the new reality:

I think it did — it did create something that did not exist before in me —
but I think also for other people because it was that sort of shared
experience (Interview, Jackie).

Cora speaks of a number of different ritual actions she has
experienced, and sums up the sense of ritual as performative that is
conveyed less explicitly by many of the women:

You actually do something, you make a connection, you put your
energy into the earth or into a stone, a pot, a cauldron, we've done all
these different things. A piece of string, or a silver thread, that connects
you — you cut it and...that actually makes something happen. I'm
convinced of that, it makes something happen (Interview, Cora).

The women's rituals include all four of Driver's dimensions of
performance. In some ways, the theatrical element is the least
evident — there is no audience, only the participants, and the rituals
are not designed for the entertainment of spectators. Nevertheless,
there is often a deliberate setting of the scene, with detailed attention
to the use of colour and symbol in the creation of a centre-piece or
the lay-out of a room. The confessional element is strong, as the
rituals tell something of the woman's own experience of transition,
and relate to her sense of identity. Frequently there is a confessional
element for others too, as in Jane's ritual where members of the
group are invited to share their own experiences in relation to work,
the loss of identity, and creativity. The ethical dimension is seen in
the way many of the rituals look out to the wider world, and include
prayers of intercession, concern for others, and hopes for justice.
Finally, there is a clear and specific ritual element, in an intentional
relating of experience to faith and belief, whether this is Christian
theology and liturgy, or some form of Goddess spirituality.

It is possible therefore to see all the elements of performance in
these women's rituals. They are, however, much closer to the
ritualizing described by Grimes and Driver than the formal, set
ritual of Rappaport and Tambiah. It is precisely because there is no
set ritual for their situations that they create their own, using
imagery, symbolism and embodied action to relate to their own
bodily experience. Where these rituals differ from classic
performance theory, however, is that there is no 'misrecognition'
here. The women do not see ritual as a given, unchanging expression
of divine reality; although they may see God/Goddess at work
within the ritual process of sharing, their comments show that they

are also clearly conscious of their own agency and process in constructing the rituals.

Reclaiming Sacramental Theology

There is a long tradition in Christian thought that material realities and embodied actions can have transformative effects in human lives. In Roman Catholic tradition, there are seven sacraments as defined by Peter Lombard in 1150. According to Thomas Aquinas, they consist of the sign, the 'sacramentum' and the divine reality signified, the 'res', the thing itself (Kelly 1998). Although the sacrament must be an intentional ritual, since it is Christ who communicates with his people through the sign, there can be no question of its efficacy:

> It was rightly concluded that both the minister and the recipient of the sacrament must have the intention of participating, but the cause of the sacrament's effectiveness was the rite itself. From here derives the notion that a sacrament's effectiveness arises from 'the work worked', *'ex opere operato'* (Kelly 1998: 13).

The second Vatican Council stressed the experiential and pastoral nature of the sacraments, and their communal dimension, and affirmed the reality of the presence of Christ in the sacraments. As the sacraments marked important moments in the journey of faith and life, they could be seen as rites of passage, having the same performative effect as other rituals, although this is expressed in explicitly Christian terms:

> We can see, then, that on the whole sacraments take place at important human stages of life: birth, maturity, cementing relationships, important decisions of adulthood, illness. In this sense, the sacraments affirm our humanity and consecrate it to God. Indeed, they can transform our human reality, for the sacraments are a call to 'put on Christ', to be Christ to others (Kelly 1998: 23).

In contemporary Catholic theology there are changing attitudes to the sacraments. Joseph Martos stresses the reality of sacrament as a sign of grace and of living encounter with Christ, as symbolic actions celebrated within the church, the community of faith, and as symbols that relate to human life experiences. He too speaks of the transforming power of the sacraments, relating this to their power to construct and shape meaning in human life:

> The sacraments are the church's doors into a new realm of human meaning, a transforming meaning made available to all by the life, death, and resurrection of Christ (Martos 1981: 150).

Interestingly, he also talks of 'unofficial sacraments', practices which are not officially recognized as sacraments by the Catholic church, but which provide 'ways of entering into an experience of the sacred' (Martos 1981: 154). Amongst these he includes Pentecostal experiences of baptism in the Spirit and speaking in tongues, the marriage encounter movement, and retreats. These he describes as sacramental in a broader sense, although it seems from his use of the term almost any intense spiritual experience could be described as sacramental.

According to Louis-Marie Chauvet there are three models of sacramental theology to be found within Catholic understanding. The first he describes as 'objectivist'. Found in the catechism of 1947, it is based on the thinking of Thomas Aquinas, but is less flexible, stressing the concept of 'ex opere operato'. Theologically it emphasizes the sovereignty of God, and reinforces the power of the priest as the mediator of God's grace. A subjectivist view, held by some Catholics, but also found in Barth's thinking, he argues, places more emphasis on the subjective experience of the recipients of grace, and sees the sacrament as a means of conveying, rather than producing, God's grace:

> Whilst the objectivist model understood the sacrament as an instrument of *production* of grace, this model understands it as in instrument of *transmission* of grace, already given by God, into daily life (Chauvet 2001: xix).

The model found in Vatican II, he argues, is based on Thomas Aquinas, but seeks to restore flexibility and balance by placing the sacraments firmly within an understanding of the church as the primary sacrament, with baptism and Eucharist as signs of the church's identity.

Chauvet himself wants to argue for a more symbolic understanding of sacrament, claiming that a deeper understanding of the language of symbol and ritual leads to an interpretation of sacrament rooted and made concrete in the body. Whilst this is primarily true of the sacraments, the wider liturgy and celebration of the church is a symbolic speaking of the body to convey the word of God:

> The liturgy is the means by which this performance of the divine
> word is symbolically given to be seen and lived by. In the liturgy the
> word is made not only of words, but of materials, gestures, postures,
> objects...the word aims at becoming a gesture, at being inscribed on
> everyone's body (baptism) or placed inside everyone's body
> (eucharistic communion) (Chauvet 2001: 100–101).

This embodied nature of liturgy and sacrament is not accidental,
but is essential to an incarnational understanding of theology:

> The sacraments state that the word of God wants to enter our bodies,
> that is, our lives, and that for anyone in-dwelt by the Spirit the road of
> the God of Jesus Christ necessarily uses the human road (Chauvet
> 2001: 114).

Whilst a strongly developed sacramental theology is most often
associated with the Catholic tradition, a Protestant, Reformed, view
of the sacraments recognizes two rather than seven sacraments
(Baptism and Eucharist) as the two instituted by Christ himself.
David Peel argues that the Reformed tradition rejects any mechanical
view of the operation of sacraments, but also for the most part,
rejects any purely 'spiritual' view of the mediation of divine grace
in which physical and material realities play no part. The sacraments
are symbols, but they are symbols which 'participate in that to which
they point and grow out of the experiences of communities' (Peel
2002: 213). Peel sees the key features of a Protestant sacramental
theology as being the primacy of grace, of which sacraments are a
sign and seal, and of the Gospel. The symbolic actions (washing,
breaking, eating, pouring) are more important than the elements
(water, bread, wine) in that they gain their meaning and efficacy
from the work of Christ; and it is the action of Christ in the sacrament
that is transformative, rather than the action of the minister or
celebrant. In Reformed theology there is less emphasis on the
transforming power of sacrament; it is not entirely absent, but the
emphasis is on their nature as signs or symbols of what has already
happened in Christ. The sacraments are given to the church and to
embodied human beings as a material and tangible way of mediating
divine grace.

Tom Driver maintains that the celebration of the sacraments (in
particular the Eucharist) must be rooted in praxis, in the church's
struggle for justice. The sacraments both invite God's presence into
worship, and act as a means of bringing about God's justice within

the concrete, material world. They are not the mechanical action of God, nor the subjective experience of people, but a divine-human collaboration:

> Hence a Christian sacrament may be defined as *an action of God together with the people of God, ritually performed to celebrate freedom and to hasten the liberation of the whole world* (Driver 1998: 207).

They point towards justice and freedom from oppression; at the same time, as symbols, they must partake of that reality, and reflect it in the way in which they are enacted. For Driver, then, there is no fixed performance; the efficacy of the sacraments lies in both their rootedness in the ethical realm, and their ritual freedom and liminality:

> Because they are celebrations of the breaking of bondage, Christian sacraments have repeatedly to break open their own forms. They cannot always repeat themselves. They must find in particular situations, in quite immediate contexts, the means to laugh, cry, play, and searching truth-tell their way into the world-altering liberty of Christ's presence (1998: 203).

Debates about the validity and efficacy of the sacraments have pervaded the history of the church; but underlying both Catholic and Protestant theology is a wrestling with an understanding of the sacraments as performative action. Although there are developments in doctrine and differing understandings there is a common acknowledgement of the power of embodied action in conveying a sense of the sacred, or the divine. So David Power is able to talk of the transforming efficacy of liturgy and sacrament in relation to the faith of the community and the power of the word:

> If one were to ask whether this work develops a model for the interpretation of the liturgy, the answer would be that it offers a transformational model. In other words, the fundamental understanding of liturgy and sacrament is that when they are celebrated as acts of faith they transform human experience. This they do by bringing it to expression and thus relating it to the memory of Jesus Christ and his presence in the church through the Spirit (Power 1984: 3–4).

Bruce Morrill, too, talks of the power of the Eucharist to transform, and to lead to political action:

> narrative and ritual acts of remembrance precipitate moments of decision in their participants, decisions for attitude and action that

arise from the mystical knowledge of Christ experienced in commemorative performance (Morrill 2000: 163).

Others such as Macquarrie move beyond the particular Christian sacraments, to speak of a natural sacramental theology. Although we often speak of the two worlds of physical and spiritual, there is one world, created by God. We can interpret the whole universe as sacramental, so that the whole creation is seen as a vehicle for revelation and grace, which is then focused or embodied more specifically in the sacraments of the church:

> Perhaps the goal of all sacramentality and sacramental theology is to make the things of this world so transparent that in them and through them we know God's presence and activity in our very midst, and so experience his grace (Macquarrie 1997: 1).

Groups such as the Society of Friends (Quakers), following George Fox's concept of 'that of God in every man' take such an idea to its logical conclusion, and do not observe any sacraments. So, for example, there is no Eucharist, because every sharing of food and breaking of bread is sacramental and shows something of God.

A Feminist Sacramental Theology?

Sacramental theology has evoked considerable feminist critique. The sacraments have been seen as male-dominated, controlled and mediated by a patriarchal hierarchy. Whilst women may be recipients of the sacraments (apart from ordination) the refusal of ordination has meant that for the most part, women have been excluded from administering them. Although this has now changed in some traditions, there are others which continue to exclude women, and opposition and hostility to their participation lingers even in those traditions which accept the ministry of women.

However, sacraments are so central to the church's liturgy that some feminist theologians have attempted to reclaim them, and to rethink sacramental theology. Marjorie Proctor-Smith (1990) argues for a feminist critique and reinterpretation of the two sacraments of baptism and Eucharist. The Eucharist, which ideally should be a sacrament of unity, has instead all too often been the site of division and exclusion. The Eucharist can only be liberating for women, she argues, if it is celebrated by a community that is committed to or struggling for the emancipation of women. Women need to develop their own anamnesis, their own memory and recalling of women's bodies and struggles; moreover, the sacrament can only be efficacious if it discloses God's presence as sharing that struggle. Baptism too needs to be reclaimed. Although frequently imagery of gestation and birth is used in relation to baptism, Proctor-Smith argues that this often amounts to a patriarchal appropriation of women's experience. Rather, baptism needs to use symbols, language and imagery that are empowering for women, so that it can become a rite of liberation.

Sacramental and feminist theologies do share much common ground, however, and Susan Ross (2001) builds on this in developing a feminist sacramental theology. Both speak of the revelatory goodness of creation, both have a communal dimension, and both share an emphasis on the significance of the life and death of Jesus. In feminism these underlying sacramental principles need to be addressed through a critique of the church's attitude to sexuality and gender, and a reclaiming of the goodness and holiness of the female body as part of God's creation. A feminist critique needs to acknowledge the marginalization and invisibility of women in the liturgical community and reclaim their participation. A feminist sacramental theology needs to develop alternative understandings of atonement, salvation, and sacrifice. Therefore there are principles common to both, which feminist theologies can reclaim and use to develop a feminist sacramental theology. Such a theology must redefine the context of the sacraments and allow room for ambiguity, it must include a critique of body and gender, must give consideration to symbols and how they work, and must embody a concern for justice within the faith community and the wider world (Ross 2001).

The work of Ross argues for a broader and more ambiguous understanding of sacramentality, which is not dependent on clergy or patriarchal institution. The sacrament is no longer confined to the moment of ecclesial or liturgical celebration, but can be extended to all areas of life:

> This transformation involves an extension of the "sacramental moment" beyond the moment of actual canonical reception. It involves a far lessened reliance on clergy for an understanding of what sacramental validity means. It also means a greater continuity between ritual and everyday life (2001: 74–75).

The sacraments are also, in Ross' view, no longer confined to those rituals defined as such by the church. Other rituals, marking other transitions in women's lives, also have something of the sacramental about them in revealing and mediating the presence of Christ:

> This presence is not so much the symbol of the (absent) presence of God, a way of thinking that stresses the "otherness" of God, but rather the intentional assertion of God's presence here, in the bodies of women (Ross 2001: 167).

In this way Ross takes the underlying principles of sacramental theology and uses them to develop a way of understanding and interpreting women's liturgical participation that takes on board feminist critique and analysis.

Natalie Watson builds on Ross' work, but argues that Ross remains too individualistic in her interpretation of the sacraments, which need to be set in the context of the worshipping life of the church community. For Watson, a feminist interpretation of sacraments is central to her understanding of the liturgical life of the faith community. Sacraments are significant because they are the site of 'embodied interaction between the individual, the divine, and the community' (Watson 2002: 81). For her, sacramental theology is rooted in a celebration of the goodness of all bodies, female as well as male, and the whole of creation—it is therefore inextricably linked with a concern for ecology and the just sharing of resources. Like Ross, she wants to extend the notion of sacrament beyond the canonical sacraments of tradition, and to see the church in all its aspects as sacramental. The Christian story, and the performance of liturgy, must be one in which women's experience is included, and their story and agency acknowledged:

> Woman's assertion to be church and to always have been church is a sacramental reclaiming of the Christian story as the story of women, the struggle to write women into the Christian narrative, as performers of divine embodiment and speech (Watson 2002: 99).

Elizabeth Stuart argues that feminist theology has often lost the sense of transcendence and mystery associated with the sacramental. Thealogy and goddess religion capture something of a sense of mystery and magic, and postmodernism embraces a 're-enchantment' with the world that recognizes the sense of 'otherness'. Christian faith, she argues, in its sacramental understanding not only of the uniqueness of Christ but of the incorporation of the human into the divine, has the potential to overcome dualism whilst not losing that sense of God as other. In the sacramental system, the material and spiritual, the divine and the human, the temporal and the eternal meet:

> To be taken up into the divine life through the sacramental system, is also to be taken into authentic humanity, there is no dualism between the two although the Otherness of the divine is preserved by the mystery conveyed through the ritual preventing an easy and dangerous identification between the divine and the human (Stuart 2004: 232).

The Christian sacraments subvert all human constructions of class, gender, race and sexuality. In the light of the incorporation of the human into the divine they can be seen for what they are, as constructions, non-ultimate, secondary to the otherness of divine reality. In this sense, Christianity can be described as 'queer' — it unsettles, disturbs and renders void all human distinctions:

> Christianity has a divine mandate to be 'queer', to perform our socially constructed roles, our gender, our sexuality, our race, our class etc., in such a way as to point to their non-ultimacy. It is the sacramental energy of the body of Christ in which body is performed fundamentally different to the culture around that is poured out in the Eucharist and in the other sacraments (Stuart 2004: 234).

There is a tension here in that she is drawing on queer theory, with its emphasis on the constructed nature of gender and sexuality, whilst at the same time arguing for an understanding of the divine and of Christ as ultimate and 'other'. Christianity may be 'queer', but there is a givenness, a non-constructionist element to her sense of the reality of Christ which seems to underlie her insistence on the transcendent divine energy, mediated through the sacraments. Nevertheless, she makes a strong argument for reclaiming a sense of mystery and power associated with liturgy and ritual.

So, although there is a strand of feminist theology which recognizes and reclaims a sacramental view of liturgy and ritual, only one of the rituals, Nicola's, included a sacrament within the traditional definition. In her ritual, we find a conscious and intentional appropriation of Eucharist in relation to her own body and blood. Nicola herself comes from a sacramental tradition:

> So for me, in the tradition I come from, it's real — you know, real presence of Christ in the sacrament. And it is very real for me, but

again I'm not sure I was explicitly aware at the time but I was trying
to—I was trying to do something with Eucharist (Interview, Nicola).

Nicola is well aware of the feminist critique of Eucharist as a
patriarchal ritual, and shares some of the anger and frustration that
women have experienced at their exclusion from presidency in the
celebration of the sacrament. She consciously chooses the sharing
of bread and wine as the central symbol of her ritual (which she
holds in a room containing the reserved sacrament). The written
piece she used and subsequently published (Slee 2004b) intentionally
makes the connection between the canonical words of the Christian
Eucharist and her own body and blood and includes the feminist
anamnesis of which Proctor-Smith speaks, recalling the stories and
memories of her own body and those of other women. Again and
again she begins a stanza with the words 'This woman's body of
mine...' and ends it with the refrain 'This is my body, this is my
blood', so that the parallelism of the body of a woman with the
body and blood of Christ is reinforced in the language and the
poetry (Slee 2004b):

> Every time the Eucharist is celebrated it is about what's happening in
> our bodies and blood but that connection is so often not made
> (Interview, Nicola).

Nicola is not concerned about the validity of presidency at the
Eucharist—although an ordained priest is present, this is of
secondary importance. It is Nicola who takes the bread, and it is
the resonance with her own bodily experience that makes the ritual
a valid Eucharist. Her ritual is a subversion of the accepted forms
and conventions:

> Though there was a Church of England priest present she didn't
> consecrate the elements—I mean if anyone consecrated them I did but
> I didn't—I mean in a way that's ridiculous language to use cos I didn't—
> that just didn't arise. But I am absolutely clear that, you know, in terms
> of all the Eucharists I have ever received in my life, which must be
> thousands, that must be one of the most powerful. I have absolutely
> no doubt that it was a Eucharist in particular terms—that it was a valid
> Eucharist (Interview, Nicola).

Nicola has a broad understanding of sacrament which
corresponds in some ways to that developed by Ross—that all of
life is potentially sacramental. However, this is clearly interpreted
within a Christian framework—although many actions and words

may be performative in the broadest sense, it is their association with the life, death, and living presence of Christ that gives them their sacramental dimension:

> I mean, when I talk about things being sacramental it's about what they perform, what they proclaim...so I think I've probably got a wide sense of the sacramental. I think all poetry if it's good is performative language—it's sacramental in some sense. But there must also be something about...words or actions—ritual action—that in some way make Christ present—effect Christ's presence again. I mean, it's not that I don't believe Christ is present everywhere in time and space but the sacramental action and words—maybe it's just about they help us to realise in a very—in an embodied focused way that reality (Interview, Nicola).

The link with the Christian narrative or imagery may not always be explicit, and Nicola holds to a broad interpretation of Christ/ Christa which is consistent with her feminist theology:

> I suppose by that I don't mean there has to be an overt, specific link— or that Christ has always to be named or specifically acknowledged in sacramental actions or liturgies. I'd have a much broader notion of Christ/Christa than this, but for me there is still some kind of connection between the Christian narrative and symbolism (however implicit or understated) and feminist notions of sacrament (Email, Nicola).

Nevertheless, in her ritual we see a specific and intentional use of Christian symbolic embodied action, understood and interpreted in the framework of a feminist sacramental theology.

Other women use sacramental language, without directly naming their rituals as sacraments. Jackie speaks about the piece of card on which we made her name, and the action of doing so, as something sacred:

> It has that sense of sacredness...because of the way it was made and all the memories that evokes, it will always be precious and—I do want to use the word sacred, but it's not just the thing that's sacred, it's the context out of which it came (Interview Jackie).

She is reluctant to call her ritual a sacrament, remaining with the Protestant tradition of the two sacraments of baptism and Eucharist, but nevertheless sees the event as having a sacramental dimension to it in a way that resonates with the feminist sacramental theology of Susan Ross and Natalie Watson:

I can claim the sacramentality of it as I said, because it was a moment
in which heaven and earth, the eternal and the material, were coming
together, which is what happens in a sacrament. But I think I do still
want to hold to sacraments as being something different—I don't want
to extend them. But yes, blurring of boundaries and certainly
something which has the essence of sacrament—using the adjective
rather than the noun (Interview, Jackie).

In Louise's house-blessing, her action of sprinkling water as a
sign of blessing, draws on the Catholic tradition of 'asperges', which
she understands in a sacramental sense.

Cora, from outside the Christian tradition, does not use the word
sacramental, but, nonetheless, has an underlying conviction about
the potential for material objects to be vehicles of the sacred which
is very close to the feminist sacramental principles articulated
by Ross:

It's the way ordinary things can suddenly become imbued with
complete sacred significance—something as simple as a green
candle...sawdust or salt or a stone, yeah, it just needs that intention of
connecting to it, or allowing it to connect with us somehow, in its
essence, and it becomes something quite else, in another dimension
(Interview, Cora).

Others, whilst not talking so explicitly of sacramental or the
sacred, speak clearly about the performative power of symbolic,
embodied action. So for Alison, the action of her friends in taking
away the silver coins is performative—the doing of it accomplishes
the act; and for Jane, the visual image of her empty shells
transformed by the floating light marks a turning point. For Clare,
the action of the ritual in tying knots is in keeping with the tension
and knottedness of her experience:

I mean, tying the knots felt quite tense but I think that was what we
were dealing with and it needed to feel a little bit uncomfortable. And
I think actually doing something positive with it in terms of reweaving
was about moving on from that and releasing some of the energy
(Interview, Clare).

For Rebecca, the emotions and experiences she is dealing with in
ritual are felt and inscribed in her body:

They were very physical, all very visible...and I suppose I experience
things quite physically in my body so issues like holding in and
letting go are—it feels like they're in my physical structure almost
(Interview, Rebecca).

For these women, embodied symbolic action is performative—the rituals do not simply express emotion or experience, but in some way construct them. For some this is expressed directly in the theological terminology of sacrament; for others, it is less explicit, but reveals itself in an underlying assumption about the goodness and sacredness of women's bodies and actions.

Theories and Theo/alogies of the Body

Social theory has focused on developing an embodied sociology 'taking the embodiment of its practitioners as well as its subjects seriously through a commitment to the lived body and its being in the world, including the manner in which it both shapes and is shaped by society' (Williams and Bendelow 1998: 23). They chart the shift from thinking of the individual as a rational disembodied being through to ways in which the body is seen as the site on which differences in many areas are played out: childhood, sport, health and illness, gender, and social and political difference and inequality. In particular, feminist thought has focused on issues of social difference, and has used Foucault's thought to demonstrate how power and knowledge have been used in the construction of sex and gender. They draw too on anthropological work (particularly that of Mary Douglas) to show how ritual uses the body to symbolize and regulate social relations:

> Indeed, the body is a model which can stand for any bounded system and its boundaries can represent any boundaries which become threatened or endangered...Seen in these terms, the powers and dangers accredited to social structures are reproduced in small upon the human body (Williams and Bendelow 1998: 27).

But the body does much more than symbolize and express what is happening in the external world. As we have already seen from the concept of performativity in ritual, actions of and actions upon the body, shape, affect and construct the external world. What Williams and Bendelow in their conclusion claim for performance art could also be said of the performance of ritual:

> Performance art in particular, especially women's body art, enacts power and resistance on the site of the body itself as a mode of communicative praxis, thereby effacing the boundary between art and social theory. Here, the dilemmas of modernity and civilisation, power and ideology, emotions and rationality, pleasure and pain, life

and death, are vividly brought to life...In these and many other ways, art challenges the dominance of the spoken and written text, so prevalent in social theory today, providing powerful visual narratives and embodied statements of the human condition, past, present and future (1998: 211).

The concept of gender as a constructed performance is developed by Judith Butler. She examines the way in which feminist politics have been constructed on the basis of gender seen as a stable identity, and argues that feminism needs to go further in examining the way in which gender itself is not a stable, ontological reality but is constructed and performed in a world of shifting meaning and power:

> If a stable notion of gender no longer proves to be the foundational premise of feminist politics, perhaps a new sort of feminist politics is now desirable to contest the very reifications of gender and identity, one that will take the variable construction of identity as both a methodological and normative prerequisite, if not a political goal (Butler 1990: 5).

Butler argues that sex, gender and sexual desire are not ontological categories but constructions, repeated performances which are inscribed on the body and mistaken as essential reality:

> In other words, acts, gestures and desire produce the effect of an internal core or substance, but produce this *on the surface* of the body, through the play of signifying absences that suggest, but never reveal, the organizing principle of identity as a cause. Such acts, gestures, enactments, generally construed, are *performative* in the sense that the essence or identity that they otherwise purport to express are *fabrications* manufactured and sustained through corporeal signs and other discursive means. That the gendered body is performative suggests that it has no ontological status apart from the various acts which constitute its reality (Butler 1990: 136).

Like other ritual enactments, the repeated nature of these performances is crucial:

> As in other ritual social dramas, the action of gender requires a performance that is *repeated*. This repetition is at once a re-enactment and re-experiencing of a set of meanings already socially established; and it is the mundane and ritual form of their legitimation (Butler 1990: 140).

Any notion of a 'true' and primary gender identity thus breaks down; gender is seen as produced through dominant discourses and resistance to them. Performances such as impersonation, cross-dressing, drag, and the assuming of particular sexual roles and styles (such as butch and femme) parody any notion of a true essential gender and thus subvert it. This is not to claim that all parody is subversive — it can become domesticated and conventionalized in its turn. But depending on the context and reception of the performance, it can destabilize and subvert claims to an essential form of gender or sexual desire:

> And what kind of gender performance will enact and reveal the performativity of gender itself in a way that destabilizes the naturalized categories of identity and desire (1990: 139).

Butler's work allows for the possibilities of both construction of the subject through repeated bodily practices, but also agency, in which the self, so created, is able to resist and subvert the social construction of gender. McNay (2000), however, argues that the two possibilities are insufficiently integrated in Butler's work, partly because she works primarily with the symbolic, and does not place sufficient emphasis on the material, socio-economic practices which also constrain gender and sexuality. Thus, although Butler's view allows for the possibility of agency, she does not specify how the resistance to dominant gender and sexual relations can arise. Bodily performance needs to allow not only for the possibilities of gender as socially-constructed, but also as subversive performance.

Just as issues of the body, gender and sexuality have become central in social theory, so one of the main emphases in feminist theology from its earliest days has been embodiment. Starting from the recognition that much of Christian tradition has portrayed women's bodies and sexualities in a negative light, feminist liturgy and theology have sought to overcome the dualism which separates flesh and spirit, female and male, natural and cultural and to develop a holistic embodied view. Much of this is reflected in liturgy which celebrates women's bodies and uses symbols and activities from women's daily lives. Whilst this can lead to an over-idealized view of women's bodily existence, there is also liturgy and theology which addresses the harsh and painful realities of violence against women, abuse, and marginalized sexuality.

One of the key principles of feminist liturgy is that the female body is seen as a site of revelation — it has the potential for revealing divine attributes and activities. In the liturgies of Diann Neu, for example, this is worked out through the use of embodied action and gestures, the use of all the senses, and litanies of exorcism against the patriarchal powers which have defined women's bodies as unclean and impure (Neu 1993).

It is important to take the body seriously as a site of knowledge and power, but also to recognize its location in patriarchal society. Lisa Isherwood (2004) argues for women's theology that is situated in the body, in which women tell their bodily stories of marginalization and exclusion, stories that become the source of theology and challenge traditional notions of the Christ. Although this is a practice that breaks boundaries and can be transgressive of conventional norms, it is rooted in Christian understanding—in the bodily earthly, narrative of Jesus, in the stories of healings as political empowerment, and most of all in the incarnation, the Word made flesh. Through women's bodies the flesh needs to find words and a voice that has been silenced in male-dominated Christian theology:

> The flesh made word enables us to find a voice and to make our desires known (Isherwood 2004: 148).

Whilst much of traditional Christian theology is patriarchal and dualist, with a deep distrust of the body, feminist 'body theology' derives from assumptions at the heart of Christian faith. First, it is incarnational, asserting that the divine is present in human relations and in nature, and that this is most fully revealed in Jesus. Second, it sees sin and redemption as concrete realities in people's material and embodied lives, not as metaphysical qualities or spiritual states. Third, it assumes that women's experience is sited in the body which, they argue, includes mind and emotions—this is not a reworking of mind-body dualism or of the view that biology is destiny (Isherwood and Stuart 1998). Body theology, or a theology of embodiment, then, is not alien to Christian scripture or tradition, but a reclaiming of what is central to them:

> The Christian Scriptures naturally have embodiment at their heart. From the moment when Mary agrees to give birth to a special child, bodies become sites of revelation and redemptive action (Isherwood and Stuart 1998: 11).

However, thealogy, with its imagery of the divine as female, goes much further in resacralizing women's bodies. Seeing the divine as female (whether a female God or Goddess) means recognizing that women's bodily processes, often marginalized or considered unclean, are holy and revelatory. For many women, who have been taught to distrust, deny or fear their own bodies, this is liberating and empowering:

> The central claim of thealogy is that women image the divine in the embodied reality of their daily lives including the bodily changes and processes that patriarchal religion has found so difficult to deal with— menstruation, birth, sexual activity, menopause, ageing and death...Many women have found this identification between their own embodied reality and the divine extremely empowering and healing against a cultural background which still finds women's embodiment problematic in many respects (Isherwood and Stuart 1998: 79).

For Goddess-feminists, such as Melissa Raphael, the Goddess is not a personal, transcendent deity but a symbol of the sacredness of female, life-giving ways of living within, and relating to, the world. Goddess spirituality makes it possible for women to love and honour their bodies and their sexuality, and, with its insistence on the immanence of the Goddess, has an ecological dimension too. Her thealogy aims to:

> renegotiate the meaning of female sacrality—those qualities of femaleness that mediate the sacred—as a structure by which we can imagine how the divine is immanent in the world through female embodiment and in female ways of being and doing (Raphael 1996: 8).

However, Raphael's work shows a universalizing tendency, which, although she claims to reject the 'simplistic' essentialism often attributed to spiritual feminism, still seems to suggest an ontological and essentialist understanding of the sacred feminine. Kathleen McPhillips (1998), in an article describing a ritual she planned and enacted, acknowledges Raphael's rejection of patriarchal dualisms of spirit and body, but argues that she is in danger of falling into another dualism of sacred and profane, in which the female is always sacred (and therefore good); and the male, or patriarchal, is profane, and therefore bad.

Others move further from essentialism in giving a more constructionist account of the importance of thealogy in resacralizing the body. Ruth Mantin (2004) for example, claims that 'Goddess-talk' is more open to ideas of immanence, flow and change than Christian theology, which is still too constrained by the dominant male discourse. Thealogy sees a process in which the sacred is not given or revealed by a transcendent Other, but constructed and performed in our own imagings and refigurings of the divine:

> To determine the location of the sacred is a political act. I am, therefore,
> convinced of the need for feminist theo/alogies to travel further in
> recognising the socio-political implications of constructing our own
> post-metaphysical narratives of the sacred and in enacting performative
> sacrality (Mantin 2004: 222).

Liberation theologies, for all their emphasis on justice, have often
failed to engage with the oppression of women and the exclusion
of their sexuality. The stories of women's bodies need to be told—
stories that from the perspective of dominant patriarchal discourse
will be transgressive and indecent (Althaus-Reid 2004a). Women's
bodies, in their particularity and rootedness in concrete historical
conditions, can be the place of revelation and salvation:

> In other words, there is a space of redemption to be found in the
> interstices between the place of God and women's bodies: such space
> makes of women's bodies a place of salvation...we can read and be
> read by God in the midst of the concreticity of our history simply
> because God is inscribed in the passion and suffering of concrete
> women's bodies (2004b: 159).

In keeping with her rootedness in liberation theology, Althaus-
Reid moves beyond the individual body to stress passionately the
location of particular women's bodies in poverty, injustice and
economic oppression. It is from the bodies of poor, excluded and
oppressed women that we must do our theology and construct our
Christ. She uses the image of the Peruvian Coya women kneeling in
church with no underwear under their skirts, to demand a theology
and Christology which takes seriously women's bodies and their
social and economic location:

> The Coyas' sexuality, their children, their Christianity and even the
> baskets of produce which they sell in the market accompany them
> when praying to Christ. And that is a starting-point for a Christology
> done from women's bodies (2004a: 83).

The use of female divine imagery in women's liturgy and ritual
might seem to suggest an essentialism that is at odds with much
social theory on the construction of the body and gender. If women's
bodily experience is seen as an image of and vehicle for the divine,
then does this not suggest an essential, primary reality of gender
which can be identified with God/Goddess? Certainly some of the
language and imagery might seem to suggest this, but reading some
of the feminist theologians quoted above gives a different

perspective. There is a clear sense that traditional Christian theology with its dualisms and hierarchies is a male or patriarchal construction, which feminist theology challenges, not with a claim to the discovery of essential truth, but with deconstruction and reconstruction. So, for example, Isherwood, critiquing the slimming industry with its idealized and oppressive images of women's bodies, talks of the need for a 'fat Jesus' (Isherwood 2007). Mantin (2004) describes many Goddess-feminists as post-realists who recognize their Goddess-talk as a process of construction that makes sacred their bodily experiences. Stuart (2003) talks of baptism and Eucharist as 'parody' in much the same way that Butler uses the term—as a destablizing and 'queering' of conventional norms and categories of class, gender, race and sexuality. Althaus-Reid speaks of constructing not only gender, but of 'the construction of the Christ, the Messiah, a process that depends on the interrelationship between a man called Jesus and a community of women, men and children' (Althaus-Reid 2004a: 83). We could argue that whilst theological language shows an awareness of construction, liturgy and ritual is still working with a more naïve essentialism—but this is to re-establish the dichotomy between liturgy and theology which performance theory breaks down. The liturgy and ritual, the Christian or Goddess practice and habitus, gives shape to the theo/alogy; and both in turn are working with new (or reclaimed) constructions of body, gender and God/dess.

Discussions of the body, gender, and sexual difference have been dominated by the conflicts between essentialism and cultural determinism, and Paula Cooey (1994) argues that we need to move beyond the dualism which is implied by both. Religious symbolism with its imaginative use of the body and bodily experience and action, helps to provide a way of doing this. Religious rituals and practices recognize that symbolism can establish and sustain social and cultural cohesion; but can also therefore be turned round to counter existing hegemonies and establish new ways of seeing the world:

> religious and political movements, especially newly-emerging ones, cultivate experiences in response to the cultures they counter, experiences that alter consciousness through various practices...This drama of reciprocity, or in many cases battle for hegemony, is played out by means of ritual and discipline enacted upon and through the body as its site (Cooey 1994: 116).

Women's ritualizing is working consciously with bodily experiences and symbols to reconstruct theo/alogy. We can see this process at work in Nicola's ritual. Her text explicitly makes the connection between her woman's body and the body and blood of Christ. Her ritual is a parody of Eucharist in Elizabeth Stuart's sense — it is a repetition, but with the critical difference that subverts traditional notions and revisions the Eucharist as a making-sacred of women's bodily experience.

The women's rituals I have looked at, like all rituals, use embodied action. They are performative, not simply expressing belief, but shaping and constructing it. They draw on the resources of feminist theo/alogy — much of which has been shaped and honed through liturgy and ritual as much as through seminars and libraries — to claim the power of sacrament and symbol. They are not fixed and static in form, but creative and subversive, parodying patriarchal religion in a way that reveals and subverts its constructed nature. They celebrate the female body, its wisdom and power, its potential to reveal the divine, but at the same time recognize the force of construction and the possibility of reconstruction. But it is not only ritual and liturgy they are constructing — they are remaking theo/alogy, reconstructing an image of God/Goddess and in some cases of Christ in which they can find and name themselves:

> We have ample evidence that the work we do as theologians and thealogians is imaginative construction, particularly, though not exclusively, the construction of deity; thus we map the faces of our own values. Yet, we have only begun to map the theological and thealogical significance of bodies, either for imagination or for the imaginative construction of religious symbols (Cooey 1994: 128).

Women's ritual making is imaginative subversion, playing in the space between essentialism and determinism to create through bodily symbols and enactments a theo/alogy which speaks in and through and to the passages of their lives.

Chapter Nine

RE-IMAGING RITES: WHERE NEXT FOR WOMEN'S
RITUAL MAKING?

Grasping the Rainbow

The small church is decorated with flowers and cloths in bright colours. As members of the congregation enter, they are greeted at the door and given an order of service with a rainbow design on the cover and a piece of coloured ribbon. Soon the church is packed, and one of the three presiding ministers begins the service with words of welcome and introduction. She speaks of the joy of this day, but also of struggle and injustice. She welcomes the couple, and as music plays two women come up the aisle together, one of them almost dancing to the music and the other torn between laughter and tears. They stand at the front together, facing the congregation of family, friends, and colleagues; and make their promises to each other, using words they have written themselves. When they have made their promises and exchanged rings, the congregation tie together their pieces of ribbon and drape them round the couple as a sign of blessing. After an address using colours of the rainbow to symbolize aspects of the couple's experience, prayers of intercession, and a closing song and blessing, the couple make their way to the door of the church. They greet members of the congregation as they leave the building, before driving off in a classic Mercedes decorated with rainbow ribbons to an evening's party with food and drink, poetry, speeches, music, circle dancing and disco.

When I performed my ritual marking my resignation from the Baptist ministry, I never dreamt that thirteen years later I would be making a public commitment to my lesbian partner in front of a congregation of gay, straight and transgendered people. I had always imagined that such an occasion would be a private intimate ceremony, with a small circle of friends gathered in a home, followed by a bring-and-share meal — much like many of the rituals described in this book. Instead, we celebrated our love in the public space of a church building, with the blessing of the members, using a liturgy we had created for ourselves. We performed a ceremony that had many of the traditional features of a wedding — a church building and clergy, promises, the exchange of rings; but also with elements that spoke of a subversive, queer reclaiming — the rainbow symbol adopted by Gay Pride, words that spoke of injustice, struggle and resistance, and knotted rainbow ribbons for signs of blessing.

Women's ritual making has developed, for the most part, in small groups, creating sacred space and embodied action in domestic or private settings. It is part of a much broader picture in which women and men are reinventing and reconstructing liturgy and ritual for our changing times. But what of its future? If women's ritual making is to challenge the status quo, and offer resistance to patriarchal norms and values, how will it emerge and flourish? In a fragmented, pluralist, post-modern society, women's practice of constructing ritual has transforming potential for the liturgy of the church, and for feminist theology and spirituality in particular.

Speaking from the Margins

In this book I tell the stories of a number of women who create rituals and liturgies with their friends. They are, of course, not representative of all women! Some women will continue to be satisfied with established, traditional rituals; others may feel some dissatisfaction, but be unclear as to why, or what can be done; and some will continue to mark transitions in their lives by parties with friends or going down the pub. But for significant numbers of women, creating liturgy and performing ritual is liberating praxis, reclaiming agency and empowerment in their lives.

The women whose stories are told here are well-educated and articulate; many are in ministry, lay or ordained, and some are involved in theological education; some are published writers. Several of them are involved in creating liturgy or ritual for others, whether in a Christian or Goddess-spirituality framework. Whilst as white, professional, educated women in some senses they are far from being an oppressed group, in other ways they speak from the margins. Many of them work in church settings where women are still in a minority, and some feel further marginalized by working as lay people amongst clergy. Some are lesbian in a predominantly heterosexual society, and a largely homophobic church. For all of them, the particular experiences which have prompted their rituals are transitions which are usually invisible or marginalized in liturgy and ritual, if not in society as a whole. This study of their rituals grows out of what Haraway has called 'situated knowledge', and shows the partiality and particularity which I analyse in chapter three. The women in this study are speaking from a particular location on the margins, and I want to ask: what is that particularity saying? To pastoral liturgy, to practical theology, and to feminist theo/alogy and spirituality?

A Challenge to Pastoral Liturgy

I have argued for the need for new rituals, recognizing that existing rituals can become irrelevant, impersonal, or even oppressive. Many writers speak of the need for creativity and innovation in the ritualizing process, particularly Grimes, Driver, and Anderson and Foley. Driver has spoken of ritual boredom, and the need therefore to liberate our existing contemporary rituals. At the same time there is evidence of people's hunger for ritual and symbolic action. Flowers for Princess Diana, or at the road-side after fatal traffic accidents, candle-lit vigils for abducted and murdered schoolgirls Holly and Jessica, or silence for bomb victims speak of the need for a public and symbolic acknowledgement of grief. Organizations such as SANDS (Still-birth and Neo-Natal Death Society) have drawn attention to the need for ritual to mark the death of infants at birth or through miscarriage. Some years ago I visited the United States of America, and was moved by seeing the long line of people moving along the Vietnam Memorial in Washington. Registrars (and party-planners!) are creating new ceremonies to mark civil partnerships, and churches and congregations are having to face questions as to whether they will bless such unions. Questions of what ceremony can be used to welcome and name a child when baptism is considered inappropriate or undesirable are raised in both church and secular settings. Even in relation to the traditional rites of passage of birth, marriage and death there are questions and challenges to be faced, and the church no longer has a monopoly in seeking to provide the answers. For other passages or transitions, such as divorce, abortion, healing from abuse, or the kinds of transitions described here, there is little established ritual, although a growing wealth of resources upon which people can draw.

Women who create their own rituals therefore are making an implicit challenge to all those who have responsibility for creating liturgy, ritual or ceremony — whether this is Christian, more broadly spiritual, or a secular but public recognition. It is a challenge addressed specifically to the field of pastoral liturgy, to those responsible for writing or conducting liturgy which enables people to negotiate and interpret changes in their lives.

Women's ritual making grows out of women's needs to construct ritual for changes in their lives which are not normally acknowledged in the worshipping life of the church or faith community. This is part of a much wider process of creating liturgy which speaks to women's needs and experiences. Anderson and Foley (2001) talk of interweaving the divine and human stories, and different liturgical traditions put different emphases on these two elements; some focusing on the objective, revealed nature of Christian truth declared in word and symbol, others on liturgy which attempts to retell and interpret human experience in an authentic and meaningful way. Often, however, significant elements have been omitted from or marginalized in the human story, and need to be recovered. This is the challenge posed to pastoral liturgists: to learn from the expressed need of these women for their own rituals, to make their experience visible and enable them to claim some power of interpretation over their own lives. What has been true for women may well be true for other groups too, and declining congregations and the increasing eclecticism of postmodernism suggest that the church may be failing to listen to and speak for large numbers of people in contemporary Western culture. Mary Grey (1997), in *Beyond the Dark Night*, suggests that renewing and life-giving energy for the church may come from groups who are creative at the margins, and if pastoral liturgy is to be renewed, it needs to listen to those voices.

These women's rituals show a strong emphasis on symbol and symbolic action. Traditional rites of passage in church and society are celebrated with well-established symbolism — the water of baptism, or the exchange of rings at a wedding. For many, the familiarity and the associations of this symbolism carry their own power. But sometimes the symbolism has become weakened — contrast, for example, an Afro-Caribbean funeral with the participants filling in the grave whilst others sing, with the pushing of a button to close the curtains in the crematorium. For others, no longer nurtured in the traditions of the church, the meaning of the symbolism has been lost. For some rites of passage, there are scarcely any symbols — how do we symbolize puberty or adulthood? Symbols and rituals are no longer embodied, or in Grimes' phrase, 'inscribed in the bone' (2000: 7). The rituals studied here do not create new symbols for existing rituals, but they are creative, imaginative and contextual in their use of symbols and symbolic action. This poses a challenge to those responsible for rites of passage in our churches and congregations: there is an urgent need to expand the use of symbols beyond the traditional, and move beyond the devaluing of symbolic action to a recognition of its interpretive, constructive and performative character. It is vital, if liturgy is to come alive in all its creative power, that we find some way of honouring both the deeply personal nature of transition, but also the collective power to support and interpret the processes of change that confront people in their daily lives. There is a pastoral and liturgical challenge here, to create liturgy that is inclusive and meaningful.

Throughout my own active involvement in creating liturgy and ritual over the years, I have learned to be reflective about my own practice. I have developed an awareness of my own and others' process in creating ritual, with a recognition of my use of what Grimes (2000) calls 'plumber' and 'diviner' models. I have become even more convinced of the power of symbol and symbolic action, and as a Protestant, have gained an understanding of the sacramental as performative action. The strength of creative symbolic action must be reclaimed and woven into our pastoral and liturgical practice.

Speaking to Practical Theology

The discipline of practical theology has grown out of pastoral theology into a wide-ranging discipline with the focus on theological reflection on practice. Whether it is James Hopewell's (1987) focus on the story a congregation tells about itself, Don Browning's (1991) proposal for a fundamental practical theology, or Elaine Graham's (2002) concept of disclosive practice, the argument is that analysis of and reflection on pastoral practice reveals something of a faith community's beliefs and values. But within this growing discipline there has been relatively little attention paid to liturgical practice. There have been few studies that look at liturgy and ritual as a site for disclosure of belief. Most liturgical studies are historically and text based, although Susan White (2003) and Martin Stringer (2005) look at the history of Christian worship from a sociological perspective. Writing on practical theology focuses on congregational programmes and dynamics rather than acts of worship. When I was asked to contribute a section on 'The Worship and Action of the Local Church' to *Studying Local Congregations: A Handbook* (Cameron *et al* 2005) I realized how little was available on worship in the field of practical theology. In the rituals here, although women may come with particular theological convictions, the theology and ideas of God/dess take shape as they experiment with symbols and play with new images. There is no fixed canon with which they begin, and groups frequently operate with a wide range of beliefs. Liturgy and ritual here is not only disclosive, but constructive of theo/alogy and spirituality. Whether this is understood by the participants as a process of making conscious what has previously been unconscious, or the Spirit of God at work, or the channelling of divine energy within the universe, there is a clear understanding of a transformative power effective in the use of liturgy, ritual, and symbol. There is therefore a challenge to practical theologians to take seriously not only written liturgy and canonical texts, but the process of creating liturgy and ritual on the margins—which could include not only women's groups, but charismatic prayer and praise, alternative worship, or New Age rituals. Whilst much of this is often ignored or not taken seriously, the social and theological processes at work offer important insights into an interest in spirituality often found outside, or on the edges of, institutionalized religion. Practical theology needs to engage with the making of ritual as a constructed, creative process which is interpreted as transformative and liberating by its participants. Making ritual is a way of doing theology.

Dialogue with Feminist Theo/alogy and Spirituality

In chapter two I argued that women's ritual making has its origin and roots in what has been described in various ways, as the women's liturgical movement, or the feminist spirituality movement. It is therefore important that the particular voices of women's ritual making speak back to their roots not only with acknowledgement, but with questions and challenges. Much of the early growth of feminist theology and spirituality was through grassroots groups and original, 'home-grown' liturgies, with written texts and scholarships only beginning to emerge at a later stage. Until relatively recently, there has been little critical scholarship analysing such liturgies, and it is important that that is carried out, so that academic scholarship and the liturgical life of women's groups can be integrated and nourish one another. Feminist liturgy is a rich and fruitful resource for images of God, and new models of God/ human relationship. The symbols, images, and metaphors found in such liturgy, however, should not be accepted uncritically; but need the analysis of scholarship to show their historical or cultural roots, to evaluate their impact on Christian tradition, and to bring them into dialogue with diverse forms of faith and spirituality.

It is also important that Christian and Goddess feminists can engage in what Grimes and Northup call 'ritual criticism'. This book has shown the rich variety of symbolism and symbolic action in women's ritual making, but has also highlighted the possibility of an eclectic co-opting of symbols from other cultures without thought of possible exploitation. I have shown the power of ritual in helping women tell and interpret their stories of change in their lives, but also the potential for ritual to contain change and maintain the status quo. I have argued that although women's ritual making originates in the desire to include experiences often invisible, its need for safety and the boundary of a safe space can sometimes work to exclude others. By consenting to interviews and being part of my research, the women here engaged in the process of reflecting on their rituals; but critical reflexivity needs to become an essential element in the practice of creating or constructing ritual. Creative ritual making and academic scholarship need to be recognized, not as hierarchically structured activities, one taking priority over the other, but as complementary voices in an ongoing dialogue which is stimulating and life-giving for both.

Women's Ritual Making as Transformative Practice

Throughout this book I have laid stress on women's ritual making as a conscious, interpretive practice adopted by women, in contrast to the fixity and repetition of established social rites. It is a practice which enables women to exercise agency and shape their own identity, in dialogue with, and often in resistance to, conventions within church and society. It enables them to express and interpret emotions and experiences, constructing a story which gives them a framework in which to make sense of major changes in their lives. It both arises from, and strengthens, communal bonds, taking what is private and personal, and giving it shape and voice in a wider political arena. It gives embodied form to symbolic action, and makes sacred the material and physical realities of women's lives.

I have stressed women's agency in shaping their identity, building supportive community, and engaging in performative action; however, I have also acknowledged that ritual making can be seen as a safe outlet for the desire for change which allows it to be tamed. The women themselves, however, claim that for them the process of making ritual has been transformative. For women's ritual making to continue to be transformative in a wider arena it is important that there is an ongoing dialogue, in which the practice and critique of ritual continue to challenge feminist theo/alogians to maintain a radical edge, not allowing spirituality to become a privatized ghetto, but a living construction of belief which makes a difference in bringing justice to the world.

Where Now for Women's Ritual Making?

There is a sense in which women's ritual making is itself in a transitional or liminal phase. It has grown up in response to traditional ritual, but has not yet become 'ritual' in the formal sense of repetitive, fixed action; it is still 'emerging ritual' (Mitchell 1995) or 'ritualizing' (Grimes 1993, Northup 1997). In that there is both strength and weakness — a strength in its innovative, creative power, but a weakness in that its creativity and vitality could become dissipated — hived off into small groups that may contain the energy for change in a safe and eventually taming way.

Women's ritual making is on a threshold. It is possible that mainstream, established ritual will learn from the symbolism and content of women's ritual making, whilst ignoring or side-lining the process. So we will see some attempts at including women's experience (at least the less threatening elements of it), some attempts at inclusive language and new images of God, and a greater freedom in using symbols. There are already indications of this happening as churches and congregations seek to adapt their worship to a postmodern age. No doubt in some places the insights of women's ritual making will be absorbed at the cost of becoming tamed and domesticated; patriarchy has not yet lost its power of co-option!

But it is vital that women's ritual making does not become too much part of the status quo, but continues as a strategic practice of resistance. The patterns and processes by which women create ritual must retain their freedom to experiment and play with new possibilities. The making of ritual increasingly needs to be seen as a creative, collaborative process, a strategy for change which nonetheless sees the power of some element of repetition and familiarity in giving a sense of continuity.

Women have discovered the power of making ritual. It offers them a means of resistance, empowerment and liberation; and has the potential to offer the same to other marginalized groups, as they too grasp the rainbow of promise. However we re-imagine the future, women's ritual making is a creative, rich place of playing in the margins, which offers prophetic challenge and hope to theo/alogy and spirituality in a fragmented, postmodern church and world.

APPENDIX ONE: SUMMARY OF THE RITUALS

Name	Occasion	Brief description
Alison	Redundancy	A ritual held in Alison's home; friends took away 30 silver coins, signs of betrayal, and replaced them by lighting 30 candles to symbolize resources for hope and justice.
Andrea	Blessing of new home	Participants met outside, then walked around the house, with appropriate words and gifts in each room, finishing with words of commitment.
Carol	10 years in ministry and leaving a pastorate	I planned the ritual in my home; we created a mosaic to celebrate the gifts and achievements of Carol's ministry, and all lit candles for hopes for the future.
Clare	Ending of thesis	Clare invited people who had supported her to her home for a ritual; participants tied knots in ribbons to symbolize struggle or difficulty, then wove them into a dreamcatcher as a symbol of celebration.
Cora	Birthday Menopause	Cora planned a time of space and solitude outdoors around her home, visiting stone circles and gateways a croning ritual in a sweat lodge which Cora had participated in a year earlier.
Jackie	Renaming after divorce	Ritual held in Jackie's home; Jackie burnt and threw away some objects and papers related to her previous marriage, sealing others in a box for children. All participants shared in making her name on card, moving into another room and declaring her

new name. Prayers for the future were accompanied by pouring water over glass beads and lighting candles.

Jane	Redundancy	Jane planned a group ritual in her home around themes of work and redundancy. Participants placed shells in water to symbolize loss of identity, and added glass beads and fish for positive aspects of work. Jane lit a floating candle in the bowl as a sign of transformation, and participants lit small candles for hope for the future.
Louise	Blessing new extension to house	Participants moved around the house using bunches of herbs to sprinkle water as a sign of blessing, and finished by using water to bless one another.
Nicola	Preparation for a hysterectomy	Nicola invited friends to the small chapel in the community where she was living. They shared bread and wine in Eucharist, and blessed one another with scented water.
Rebecca	Redundancy	Four separate rituals over a period of three months, using leaves to symbolize different aspects of letting go.
Runa	Renaming after childhood abuse	Runa invited friends to her home, and the exchanged symbolic gifts reflecting different aspects of her personality and relationship.
Sue	60th birthday and retirement	Sue invited friends to her home and garden for an evening of poems, readings and circle dancing. They lit candles for celebration and thanksgiving.

BIBLIOGRAPHY

Althaus-Reid, Marcella, *From Feminist Theology to Indecent Theology: Readings on Poverty, Sexual Identity and God* (London: SCM Press, 2004a).

_____ 'Pussy, Queen of Pirates: Acker, Isherwood and the Debate on the Body in Feminist Theology' in *Embodying Feminist Liberation Theologies: A Special Edition of Feminist Theology* 12.2 (2004b): 157–67.

Anderson, Herbert and Edward Foley, *Mighty Stories, Dangerous Rituals: Weaving Together the Human and the Divine* (San Francisco, CA: Jossey-Bass, 2001).

Anderson, Sherry Ruth and Patricia Hopkins, *The Feminine Face of God: The Unfolding of the Sacred in Women* (New York: Bantam, 1992).

Antze, Paul and Michael Lambek, *Tense Past: Cultural Essays in Trauma and Memory* (New York: Routledge, 1996).

Arendt, Hannah, *The Human Condition* (Chicago, IL: University of Chicago Press, 2nd edn, 1998).

Austin J.L., *How to do Things with Words* (Oxford: Oxford University Press, 2nd edn, 1976).

Baxter, Elizabeth, 'Beloved Community: A Glimpse into the Life of Holy Rood House' in Jonathan Baxter (ed.), *Wounds that Heal: Theology, Imagination and Health* (London: SPCK, 2007).

Bell, Catherine, *Ritual Theory, Ritual Practice* (New York: Oxford University Press, 1992).

Bell, Diane, 'Women's Business is Hard Work: Central Australian Aboriginal Women's Love Rituals' in Ronald L. Grimes (ed.), *Readings in Ritual Studies* (Upper Saddle River, NJ: Prentice Hall, 1996).

Benhabib, Seyla, *Situating the Self: Gender, Community and Postmodernism in Contemporary Ethics* (Cambridge: Polity Press, 1992).

Bennett Moore, Zoe, *Introducing Feminist Perspectives on Pastoral Theology* (Sheffield: Sheffield Academic Press, 2002).

Berger, Teresa, *Women's Ways of Worship: Gender Analysis and Liturgical History* (Collegeville, MN: The Liturgical Press, 1999).

Berger, Teresa, 'Prayers and Practices of Women: Lex Orandi Reconfigured' in Susan K. Roll, Annette Esser and Brigitte Enzner-Probst (eds.), *Women, Ritual and Liturgy*, Yearbook of the European Society of Women in Theological Research 9 (2001): 63–77.

Bewley, Anne R., 'Re-membering Spirituality: Use of Sacred Ritual in Psychotherapy' in Judith Ochshorn and Ellen Cole (eds), *Women's Spirituality, Women's Lives* (Women and Therapy Vol. 16, Nos 2/3:201–13, New York: Haworth Press, 1995).

Birch, Maxine, 'Re/constructing Research Narratives: Self and Sociological Identity in Alternative Settings' in Jane Ribbens and Rosalind Edwards (eds), *Feminist Dilemmas* in *Qualitative Research: Public Knowledge and Private Lives* (London: Sage Publications, 1998).

Bons-Storm, Riet, *The Incredible Woman: Listening to Women's Silences in Pastoral Care and Counseling* (Nashville, TN: Abingdon Press, 1996).

Brown, Gavin, 'Theorizing Ritual as Performance: Explorations of Ritual Intederminacy' in *Journal of Ritual Studies* 17.1 (2003): 3–18.

Browning, Don S., *A Fundamental and Practical Theology: Descriptive and Strategic Proposals* (Minneapolis, MN: Fortress Press, 1991).

Buckland, Stephen, 'Ritual, Bodies and Cultural Memory' in Louis-Marie Chauvet and Francois Kabasele Lumbala (eds), *Liturgy and the Body*, Concilium (1995/3) London: SCM Press and Maryknoll: Orbis 1993: 49–56.

Budapest, Z., *The Holy Book of Women's Mysteries Part I* (Los Angeles, CA: Susan B. Anthony Coven Number One 1979).

_____ *The Holy Book of Women's Mysteries Part II* (Los Angeles: Susan B. Anthony Coven Number One 1980).

Burgess, Ruth (ed.), *Bare Feet and Buttercups: Resources for Ordinary Time* (Glasgow: Wild Goose Publications 2008).

Butler, Judith, *Gender Trouble: Feminism and the Subversion of Identity* (NY: Routledge, 1990).

Bynum, Caroline Walker, 'Women's Stories, Women's Symbols: A Critique of Victor Turner's Theory of Liminality' in *Fragmentation and Redemption: Essays on Gender and the Human Body in Medieval Religion* (New York: Zone Books, 1992).

Cady, Linell Elizabeth, 'Identity, Feminist Theory, and Theology' in *Horizons in* Rebecca S. Chopp and Sheila Greeve Davaney (eds), *Feminist Theology: Identity, Tradition and Norms* (Minneapolis, MN: Fortress Press, 1997).

Cameron, Helen, Philip Richter, Douglas Davies and Frances Ward (eds), *Studying Local Churches: A Handbook* (London: SCM Press, 2005).

Caplan Paula J., *Lifting a Ton of Feathers: A Woman's Guide to Surviving in the Academic World* (Toronto: University of Toronto Press, 1994).

Caron C., *To Make and Make Again: Feminist Ritual Thealogy* (New York: Crossroads, 1993).

Cavarero, Adriana, *Relating Narratives: Storytelling and Selfhood* (London: Routledge, 2000).

Chauvet, Louis-Marie, *The Sacraments: The Word of God at the Mercy of the Body* (Collegeville, MN: The Liturgical Press, 2001).

Chopp, Rebecca S., *Saving Work: Feminist Practices of Theological Education* (Louisville, KY: Westminster/John Knox Press, 1995).

Clifford, James and George E. Marcus (eds), *Writing Culture: The Poetics and Politics of Ethnography* (Berkeley, CA: University of California Press, 1986).

Clifford, James, 'On Ethnographic Authority' in Yvonna S. Lincoln and Norman K. Denzin (eds), *Turning Points in Qualitative Research: Tying Knots in a Handkerchief* (Walnut Creek, CA: Altamira Press, Rowman and Littlefield, 2003).

Coffey, Amanda, *The Ethnographic Self: Fieldwork and the Representation of Identity* (London: Sage Publications, 1999).

Collins, Mary, 'Principles of Feminist Liturgy' in Marjorie Procter-Smith and Janet Walton (eds), *Women at Worship: Interpretations of North American Diversity* (Louisville, KY: Westminster/John Knox Press, 1993).

Conn, Joann Wolski, 'Women's Spirituality: Restriction and Reconstruction' in Joann Woski Conn (ed.), *Women's Spirituality: Resources for Christian Development* (New York: Paulist Press, 1986).

Conquergood, Dwight, 'Rethinking Ethnography: Towards a Critical Cultural Politics' in Yvonna S. Lincoln and Norman K. Denzin (eds), *Turning Points in Qualitative Research: Tying Knots in a Handkerchief* (Walnut Creek, CA: Altamira Press, Rowman and Littlefield, 2003).

Cooey Paula M., *Religious Imagination and the Body: A Feminist Analysis* (New York: Oxford University Press, 1994).

Cooper-White, Pamela, 'The Ritual Reason Why: Explorations of the Unconscious through Enactment and Ritual in Pastoral Psychotherapy' in *Journal of Supervision and Training in Ministry* 19 (1998–99): 68–75.

Crossley, Michele L., *Introducing Narrative Psychology: Self, Trauma, and the Construction of Meaning* (Burlington, PA: Open University Press, 2000).

Crossley, Nick, 'Ritual, Body Technique, and (Inter)subjectivity' in Kevin Schilbrack (ed.), *Thinking Through Rituals: Philosophical Perspectives* (New York: Routledge, 2004).

Daggers, Jenny, *The British Christian Women's Movement: A Rehabilitation of Eve* (Aldershot: Ashgate, 2002).

Daly, Mary, *Beyond God the Father: Towards a Philosophy of Women's Liberation* (London: The Women's Press, 1986).

DeMarinis, Valerie M., *Critical Caring: A Feminist Model for Pastoral Psychology* (Louisville, KY: Westminster/John Knox Press, 1993).

Derway, Cindy S., *The First Six: Interviews with the Founding Members of the Women's Liturgy Group of New York City* (New York City: Women's Liturgy Group, 2001).

DeVault, Marjorie L., *Liberating Method: Feminist and Social Research* (Philadelphia, PA: Temple University Press, 1999).

Donaldson, Laura E., 'On Medicine Women and White Shame-ans: New Age Native Americanism and Commodity Fetishism as Pop Culture Feminism' in Elizabeth A. Castelli (ed.), with Rosamond C. Rodman, *Women, Gender, Religion: A Reader* (New York: Palgrave, 2001).

Driver, Tom F., *Liberating Rites: Understanding the Transformative Power of Ritual* (Boulder, CO: Westview Press, Harper Collins, 1998).

Duncan, Geoffrey (ed.), *Dare to Dream: A Prayer and Worship Anthology from Around the World* (London: HarperCollins, 1995).

Durber, Susan, *Preaching Like a Woman* (London: SPCK, 2007).

Durkheim, Emile, *The Elementary Forms of the Religious Life* (London: George Allen & Unwin Ltd, 2nd edn, 1976 [1915]).

Edwards, Rosalind and Jane Ribbens, 'Living on the Edges: Public Knowledge, Private Lives' in Jane Ribbens and Rosalind Edwards (eds), *Feminist Dilemmas in Qualitative Research: Public Knowledge and Private Lives* (London: Sage Publications, 1998).

Eller, Cynthia, *Living in the Lap of the Goddess: The Feminist Spirituality Movement in America* (New York: Crossroads, 1993).

Felman, Shoshana and Dori Laub, *Testimony: Crises of Witnessing in Literature, Psychoanalysis and History* (New York: Routledge, 1992).

Finch, Janet, 'It's Great to Have Someone to Talk to': Ethics and Politics of Interviewing Women' in *Martyn Hammersley (ed.), Social Research: Philosophy, Politics and Practice* (London: Sage Publications, 1993).

Forrester, Duncan B., *Truthful Action: Explorations in Practical Theology* (Edinburgh: T & T Clark, 2000).

Frank, Arthur W., *The Wounded Storyteller: Body, Illness and Ethics* (Chicago, IL: University of Chicago Press, 1995).

Fulkerson, Mary McClintock, *Changing the Subject: Women's Discourse and Feminist Theology* (Minneapolis, MN: Fortress Press, 1994).

_____ 'Contesting the Gendered Subject: A Feminist Account of the Imago Dei' in Rebecca S. Chopp and Sheila Greeve Davaney (eds), *Horizons in Feminist Theology: Identity, Tradition and Norms* (Minneapolis, MN: Fortress Press, 1997).

Galloway, Kathy, 'Exodus Experience' in *Talking to the Bones* (London: SPCK, 1996).

Gaskin, Jean, 'Blessing on a new home' in Hannah Ward and Jennifer Wild (eds), *Human Rites: Worship Resources for an Age of Change* (London: Mowbray, 1995).

Gateley, Edwina, 'The Sharing' in Hannah Ward, Jennifer Wild and Janet Morley (eds), *Celebrating Women: The New Edition* (London: SPCK, 1995).

Geertz, Clifford, *The Interpretation of Cultures: Selected Essays* (New York: Basic Books, 1973).

Gerson, Kathleen and Ruth Horowitz, 'Observation and Interviewing: Options and Choices in Qualitative Methods' in Tim May (ed.), *Qualitative Research in Action* (London: Sage Publications, 2002).

Giblin, Paul, 'Ritual and Family Therapy: Contributions to Pastoral Supervision' in *Journal of Supervision and Training in Ministry* 19 (1998–99): 94–105.

Gjerding, Iben and Katherine Kinnamom (eds), *No Longer Strangers: A Resource for Women and Worship* (Geneva: World Council of Churches, 1983).

Goldman, Carol, 'Creating Sacred Emotional Space' in Elizabeth Dodson Gray (ed.), *Sacred Dimensions of Women's Experience* (Wellsley, MA: Roundtable Press, 1988).

Graham, Elaine, *Transforming Practice: Pastoral Theology in an Age of Uncertainty* (Eugene, OR: Wipf and Stock, 2nd edn, 2002).

Graham, Elaine, Heather Walton and Frances Ward, *Theological Reflection: Methods* (London: SCM Press, 2005).

Grainger, Roger, *The Ritual Image: The Phenomenology of Liturgical Experience* (London: Avon books, 1994).

Grania, Janice (ed.), *Images: Women in Transition* (Nashville, TN: The Upper Room, 1976).

Gray, Ann, 'I want to tell you a story: the narrative of Video Playtime' in Beverley Skeggs (ed.), *Feminist Cultural Theory: Process and Production* (Manchester: Manchester University Press, 1995).

Gray, Elizabeth Dodson (ed.), *Sacred Dimensions of Women's Experience* (Wellsley, MA: Roundtable Press, 1988).

Greider, Kathleen J., Gloria A. Johnson and Kristen Leslie, 'Three Decades of Women Writing for Our Lives' in Bonnie J. Miller-McLemore and Brita L. Gill-Austern (eds), *Feminist and Womanist Pastoral Theology* (Nashville, TN: Abingdon Press, 1999).

Grey, Mary C., *Beyond the Dark Night: A Way Forward for the Church?* (London: Cassell, 1997).

Griffith James L. and Melissa Elliott Griffith, *Encountering the Sacred in Psychotherapy: How to Talk with People about their Spiritual Lives* (New York: The Guilford Press, 2002).

Grimes, Ronald L., *Reading, Writing and Ritualizing: Ritual in Fictive, Liturgical and Public Places* (Washington DC: The Pastoral Press, 1993).

_____ 'Ritual Criticism and Infelicitous Performances' in Ronald L. Grimes (ed.), *Readings in Ritual Studies* (Upper Saddle River, NJ: Prentice-Hall, 1996).

_____ *Deeply Into The Bone: Reinventing Rites of Passage* (Berkeley, CA: University of California Press, 2000).

Hammersley, Martyn and Paul Atkinson, *Ethnography: Principles in Practice* (London: Routledge, 2nd edn, 1995).

Haraway, Donna J., *Simians, Cyborgs and Women: The Reinvention of Nature* (Free Association Books, 1991).

Hauerwas, Stanley and William H. Willimon, *Resident Aliens: Life in the Christian Colony* (Nashville, TN: Abingdon Press, 1989).

Hinchman, Lewis P. and Sandra K. Hinchman, *Memory, Identity and Community: The Idea of Narrative in the Human Sciences* (New York: State University of New York Press, 2001).

Hollywood, Amy, 'Practice, Belief, and Feminist Philosophy of Religion' in Kevin Schilbrack (ed.), *Thinking Through Rituals: Philosophical Perceptions* (New York: Routledge, 2004).

Hopewell, James F., *Congregation: Stories and Structures* (Philadelphia, PA: Fortress Press, 1987).

Imber-Black, Evan, 'Ritual Themes in Families and Family Therapy' in Evan Imber-Black, Janine Roberts, and Richard A. Whiting (eds), *Rituals in Families and Family Therapy* (New York: W. W. Norton and Company, 1988).

Isasi-Diaz, Ada Maria, 'Mujerista Liturgies and the Struggle for Liberation' in Louis-Marie Chauvet and Francois Kabasele Lumbala (eds), *Liturgy and the Body*, Concilium 3 (1995): 104–11 (London: SCM and Maryknoll: Orbis Books, 1995).

Isherwood, Lisa, 'The Embodiment of Feminist Liberation Theology: The Spiralling of Incarnation' in *Embodying Feminist Liberation Theologies: A Special Edition of Feminist Theology* 12.2 (Jan 2004): 140–56.

_____ *The Fat Jesus: Feminist Explorations in Boundaries and Transgressions* (London: Darton Longman and Todd, 2007).

Isherwood, Lisa and Elizabeth Stuart, *Introducing Body Theology* (Sheffield: Sheffield Academic Press, 1998).

Jackson, Michael, *The Politics of Storytelling: Violence, Transgression and Intersubjectivity* (Copenhagen: Museum Tusculanum Press, 2002).

Jackson, Stevi, 'Telling Stories: Memory, Narrative and Experience in Feminist Research and Theory' in Karen Henwood, Christine Griffin and Ann Phoenix (eds), *Standpoints and Differences: Essays in the Practice of Feminist Psychology* (London: Sage Publications, 1998).

Kelly, Liam, *Sacraments Revisited: What Do They Mean Today?* (London: Darton Longman & Todd, 1998).

Kertzer, David, *Ritual, Politics and Power* (New Haven, CT: Yale University Press, 1988).

King, Ursula and Tina Beattie (eds), *Gender, Religion and Diversity: Cross-cultural Perspectives* (London: Continuum, 2005).

Kirmayer, Laurence J., 'Landscapes of Memory: Trauma, Narrative and Disassociation' in Paul Antze and Michael Lambek, *Tense Past: Cultural Essays in Trauma and Memory* (New York: Routledge, 1996).

LaCapra, Dominick, *Writing History, Writing Trauma* (Baltimore, WA: The John Hopkins University Press, 2001).

Laird, Joan, 'Women and Ritual in Family Therapy' in Evan Imber-Black, Janine Roberts and Richard A. Whiting (eds), *Rituals in Families and Family Therapy* (New York and London: W.W. Norton and Company, 1988).

Langellier, Kristin M., 'Personal Narrative, Performance, Performativity: Two or Three Things I Know for Sure' in Yvonna S. Lincoln and Norman K. Denzin (eds), *Turning Points in Qualitative Research: Tying Knots in a Handkerchief* (Walnut Creek, CA: Altamira Press, Rowman and Littlefield, 2003).

Lara, Maria Pia, *Moral Textures: Feminist Narratives in the Public Sphere* (Cambridge: Polity Press, 1998).

Larson-Miller, Lizette, 'Remembering Who We Are: Women and Ritual' in *Where Now? Women's Spirituality after the Ecumenical Decade*, The Way supplement No 3 (1998): 66–79.

Lewin, Ann, 'Not the last word' in *Candles and Kingfishers* (Winchester: Optimum Litho, 1993).

Lincoln, Yvonna S. and Egon G. Guba, *Naturalistic Inquiry* (Newbury Park: Sage 1985).

Lunn, Pam, 'Do Women Need the GODDESS? Some Phenomenological and Sociological Reflections' in Feminist Theology 4 (September 1993): 17–38.

———— 'This is My Body' in Heather Walton and Susan Durber (eds), *Silence in Heaven: A Book of Women's Preaching* (London: SCM, 1994).

Lyall, David, *The Integrity of Pastoral Care* (London: SPCK, 2001).

McCarthy Brown, Karen, 'Roundtable Discussion: On Feminist Methodology' in *Journal of Feminist Studies in Religion* 1.2 (1985): 76–79.

McDade, Carolyn and Lucile Schuck Longview, 'Coming Home Like Rivers to the Sea: A Women's Ritual' in Elizabeth Dodson Gray (ed.), *Sacred Dimensions of Women's Experience* (Wellsley, MA: Roundtable Press, 1988).

MacIntyre, Alasdair, 'The Virtues, The Unity of a Human Life and the Concept of a Tradition' in Stanley Hauerwas and L. Gregory Jones (eds), *Why Narrative? Readings in Narrative Theology* (Grand Rapids, MI: William B. Eerdmans, 1989).

McNay, Lois, *Gender and Agency: Reconfiguring the Subject in Feminist and Social Theory* (Cambridge: Polity Press in association with Blackwell, 2000).

McPhillips, Kathleen, 'Rituals, Bodies and Thealogy: Some Questions' in *Feminist Theology* 18 (1998): 9–27.

Macquarrie, John, *A Guide to the Sacraments* (London: SCM Press Press, 1997).

McWhorter, Ladelle, 'Rites of Passing: Foucault, Power, and Same-sex Commitment Ceremonies' in Kevin Schilbrack (ed.), *Thinking Through Rituals: Philosophical Perspectives* (New York: Routledge, 2004).

Madison, D. Soyini, *Critical Ethnography: Method, Ethics, and Performance* (Thousand Oaks, CA: Sage Publications, 2005).

Mantin, Ruth, 'Thealogical Reflections on Embodiment' in *Embodying Feminist Liberation Theologies: A Special edition of Feminist Theology* 12.2 (Jan 2004): 212–27.

Martos, Joseph, *Doors to the Sacred: A Historical Introduction to Sacraments in the Christian Church* (London: SCM Press Press, 1981).

Metz, Johann Baptist, 'A Short Apology of Narrative' in Stanley Hauerwas and L. Gregory Jones (eds), *Why Narrative? Readings in Narrative Theology* (Grand Rapids, MI: William B. Eerdmans, 1989).

Mies, Maria, 'Towards a Methodology for Feminist Research' in Martyn Hammersley (ed.), *Social Research: Philosophy, Politics and Practice* (London: Sage Publications, 1993).

Mitchell, Nathan, 'Emerging Rituals in Contemporary Culture' in Louis-Marie Chauvet and Francois Kabasele Lumbala (eds), *Liturgy and the Body*, Concilium 1995/3: 121–29 (London: SCM and Maryknoll, 1995).

Morley, Janet, *All Desires Known* (London: SPCK 1992, 2nd edn, [1988]).

Morrill, Bruce T., *Anamnesis as Dangerous Memory: Political and Liturgical Theology in Dialogue* (Collegeville, MN: The Liturgical Press, 2000).

Morton, Nelle, *The Journey is Home* (Boston, MA: Beacon Press, 1985).

Neu, Diann L., 'Women Revisioning Religious Rituals' in Lesley A. Northup (ed.), *Women and Religious Ritual* (Washington DC: The Pastoral Press, 1993a).

_____ 'Women-Church Transforming Liturgy' in Marjorie Procter-Smith and Janet Walton (eds), *Women at Worship: Interpretations of North American Diversity* (Louisville, KY: Westminster/John Knox Press, 1993b).

_____ 'Women's Empowerment Through Feminist Rituals' in Judith Ochshorn and Ellen Cole (eds), *Women's Spirituality, Women's Lives, Women and Therapy* 16 Nos 2/3: 185–99 (New York: Haworth Press, 1995).

_____ *Women's Rites: Feminist Liturgies for Life's Journey* (Cleveland, OH: The Pilgrim Press, 2003).

Neuger, Christie Cozad, 'Women and Relationality' in Bonnie J. Miller-McLemore and Brita L. Gill-Austern (eds), *Feminist and Womanist Pastoral Theology* (Nashville, TN: Abingdon Press, 1999).

_____ 'Narratives of Harm: Setting the Developmental Context for Intimate Violence' in Jeanne Stevenson-Moessner (ed.), *In Her Own Time: Women and Developmental Issues in Pastoral Care* (Minneapolis, MN: Fortress Press, 2000).

Northup, Lesley A., (ed.), *Women and Religious Ritual* (Washington DC: The Pastoral Press, 1993).

_____ 'Expanding the X-axis: Women, Religious Ritual and Culture' in Lesley A. Northup (ed.), *Women and Religious Ritual* (Washington DC: The Pastoral Press, 1993).

_____ *Ritualizing Women* (Cleveland, OH: The Pilgrim Press, 1997).

Oakley, Ann, 'Interviewing Women: A Contradiction in Terms' in Helen Roberts (ed.), *Doing Feminist Research* (London: Routledge and Kegan Paul 1990 [1981]).

Ochs, Elinor and Lisa Capps, *Living Narrative: Creating Lives in Everyday Storytelling* (Cambridge, MA: Harvard University Press, 2001).

Parks, Sharon, 'The Meaning of Eating and the Home as Ritual Space' in Elizabeth Gray (ed.), *Sacred Dimensions of Women's Experience* (Wellesley, MA: Roundtable Press, 1988).

Peel, David, *Reforming Theology: Explorations in the Theological Traditions of the United Reformed Church* (London: The United Reformed Church, 2002).

Plummer, Ken, *Telling Sexual Stories: Power, Change and Social Worlds* (London: Routledge, 1995).

Power, David, *Unsearchable Riches: The Symbolic Nature of Liturgy* (New York: Pueblo Publishing Company, 1984).

Procter-Smith, Marjorie, *In Her Own Rite: Constructing Feminist Liturgical Tradition* (Nashville, TN: Abingdon Press, 1990).

_____ *Praying With Our Eyes Open: Engendering Feminist Liturgical Prayer* (Nashville, TN: Abingdon Press, 1995).

_____ 'Feminist Ritual Strategies: The Ekklesia Gynaikon at Work' in Fernando F. Segovia (ed.), *Toward a New Heaven and a New Earth: Essays in Honor of Elisabeth Schüssler Fiorenza* (Maryknoll, NY: Orbis Books, 2003).

Ramazanoğlu, Caroline, and Janet Holland, *Feminist Methodology: Challenges and Choices* (London: Sage Publications, 2002).

Ramshaw, Elaine, *Ritual and Pastoral Care* (Philadelphia, PA: Fortress Press, 1987).

Raphael, Melissa, *Thealogy and Embodiment: The Post-Patriarchal Reconstruction of Female Sacrality* (Sheffield: Sheffield Academic Press, 1996).

Rappaport, Roy A., *Ecology, Meaning and Religion* (Berkeley, CA: North Atlantic Books, 1979).

Reinharz, Shulamit, *Feminist Methods in Social Research* (New York: Oxford University Press, 1992).

Ricoeur, Paul, 'The Model of the Text: Meaningful Action Considered as Text' in *Social Research* 38 (Autumn 1971): 529–62.

_____ *Time and Narrative Vol. 3* (Chicago, IL: University of Chicago Press, 1990).

_____ 'Life: A Story in Search of a Narrator' in Mario J. Valdes (ed.), *A Ricoeur Reader: Reflection and Imagination* (New York: Harvester Wheatsheaf, 1991).

_____ *Oneself as Another* (Chicago, IL: The University of Chicago Press, 1994).

_____ *Figuring the Sacred: Religion, Narrative and Imagination* (Minneapolis, MN: Fortress Press, 1995).

Roberts, Helen, 'Women and their Doctors: Power and Powerlessness in the Research Process' in Helen Roberts (ed.), *Doing Feminist Research* (London: Routledge and Kegan Paul, 1990).

Roberts, Janine, 'Setting the Frame: Definition, Function and Typology of Rituals' in Evan Imber-Black, Janine Roberts and Richard A. Whiting (eds), *Rituals in Families and Family Therapy* (New York and London: W.W. Norton and Company, 1988).

Roberts, Wendy Hunter, 'In Her Name: Towards a Feminist Thealogy of Pagan Ritual' in Marjorie Procter-Smith and Janet Walton (eds), *Women at Worship: Interpretations of North American Diversity* (Louisville, KY: Westminster/John Knox Press, 1993).

Roll, Susan, 'Traditional Elements in New Women's Liturgies' in *Questions Liturgiques: Studies in Liturgy* 72 (1991/1): 43–59.

_____ 'Liturgy in Company of Women: The ESWTR Conference' in *Questions Liturgiques: Studies in Liturgy* 74 (1993): 231–34.

_____ 'Women's Liturgy: Dancing at the Margins' in *Doctrine and Life* 44 (September 1994) No. 7: 387–96.

_____ *Blessing the Apple: A Rite of Transformation,* panel presentation to Sacramental and Liturgical Theology Group, Ottawa Conference: Catholic Theological Society of America, 1998.

Ross, Susan A., *Extravagant Affections: A Feminist Sacramental Theology* (York: Continuum, 2001).

Ruether, Rosemary Radford, *Women-church: Theology and Practice of Feminist Liturgical Communities* (San Francisco, CA: Harper and Row, 1985).

St. Hilda Community, *Women Included: A Book of Services and Prayers* (London: SPCK, 1991).

Savage, Mary C., 'Can Ethnographic Narrative Be a Neighborly Act?' in Yvonna S. Lincoln and Norman K. Denzin (eds), *Turning Points in Qualitative Research: Tying Knots in a Handkerchief* (Walnut Creek, CA: Altamira Press, Rowman and Littlefield, 2003).

Say, Elizabeth A., *Evidence in Her Own Behalf: Women's Narrative as Theological Voice* (Savage, MD: Rowman and Littlefield, 1990).

Scarry, Elaine, *The Body in Pain: The Making and Unmaking of the World* (New York: Oxford University Press, 1985).

Schüssler Fiorenza, Elisabeth, *In Memory of Her: A Feminist Theological Reconstruction of Christian Origins* (London: SCM Press, 1983).

_____ *Bread Not Stone: The Challenge of Feminist Biblical Interpretation* (Boston, MA: Beacon Press, 1985).

_____ *But She Said: Feminist Practices of Biblical Interpretation* (Boston, MA: Beacon Press, 1992).

Silva, Silvia Regina de Lima, 'In the Movement of Wisdom: Wisdom Rituals and Liturgies as Spiritual Resources in the Struggle for Justice' in Maria Pilar Aquino and Elisabeth Schüssler Fiorenza (eds), *In the Power of Wisdom: Feminist Spiritualities of Struggle*, Concilium 5 (2000): 120–28 (London: SCM Press, 2000).

Simpson, J., 'Pakeha Whahapapa: Welcoming a New Academic in a Ritual of Room Blessing' in *Journal of Ritual Studies* 13. 1 (1999): 53–62.

Skeggs, Beverley (ed.), *Feminist Cultural Theory: Process and Production* (Manchester: Manchester University Press, 1995).

Skeggs, Beverley, 'Techniques for Telling the Reflexive Self' in Tim May (ed.), *Qualitative Research in Action* (London: Sage Publications, 2002).

Slee, Nicola, *Faith and Feminism: An Introduction to Christian Feminist Theology* (London: Darton Longman and Todd, 2003).

_____ *Women's Faith Development: Patterns and Processes* (Aldershot: Ashgate, 2004a).

_____ *Praying Like A Woman* (London: SPCK, 2004b).

Smith, Theodore M., 'Pastoral and Ritual Response to Perinatal Death: A Narrative of a Departmental Policy Change' in *Journal of Supervision and Training in Ministry* 19 (1998–99): 25–35.

Stanley, Liz and Sue Wise, *Breaking Out Again: Feminist Ontology and Epistemology* (London: Routledge, 2nd edn, 1993).

Starhawk, *The Spiral Dance: A Rebirth of the Ancient Religion of the Great Goddess* (San Francisco, CA: Harper and Row, 1979).

_____ *Dreaming the Dark: Magic, Sex and Politics* (Boston, MA: Beacon Press, 1982).

Stone, Merlin, *The Paradise Papers: The Suppression of Women's Rites* (London: Virago, 1979).

Stringer, Martin D., *A Sociological History of Christian Worship* (Cambridge: Cambridge University Press, 2005).

Stuart, Elizabeth, *Gay and Lesbian Theologies: Repetitions and Critical Difference* (Aldershot: Ashgate, 2003).

Stuart, Elizabeth, 'Exploding Mystery: Feminist Theology and the Sacramental' in *Embodying Feminist Liberation Theologies: A Special Edition of Feminist Theology* 12.2 (Jan 2004): 228–36.

Swidler, Arlene (ed.), *Sistercelebrations: Nine Worship Experiences* (Philadelphia, PA: Fortress Press, 1974).

Swinton, John and Mowat, Harriet, *Practical Theology and Qualitative Research* (London: SCM Press, 2006).

Tambiah, Stanley J., *Culture, Thought and Social Action: An Anthropological Perspective* (Cambridge, MA: Harvard University Press, 1985).

Tisdale, Leonora Tubbs, *Preaching as Local Theology and Folk Art* (Minneapolis, MN: Augsburg Fortress, 1997).

Turner, Victor, *The Ritual Process: Structure and Anti-Structure* (London: Routledge and Kegan Paul, 1969).

_____ *Dramas, Fields and Metaphors: Symbolic Action in Human Society* (Ithaca, NY: Cornell University Press, 1974).

Van Gennep, Arnold, *The Rites of Passage* (Chicago, IL: The University of Chicago Press, 1960 [1908]).

Visweswaran, Kamala, *Fictions of Feminist Ethnography* (Minneapolis, MN: University of Minnesota Press, 1994).

Walkerdine, Valerie, Helen Lucey and Jane Melody, 'Subjectivity and Qualitative Method' in Tim May (ed.), *Qualitative Research in Action* (London: Sage Publications, 2002).

Walton, Heather, 'Speaking in Signs: Narrative and Trauma in Pastoral Theology' in *Scottish Journal of Health Care Chaplaincy* 5.2 (2002): 2–5.

Walton, Janet R., *Feminist Liturgy: A Matter of Justice* (Collegeville, MN: The Liturgical Press, 2000).

Ward, Hannah and Jennifer Wild (eds), *Human Rites: Worship Resources for an Age of Change* (London: Mowbray, 1995).

Ward, Hannah, Jennifer Wild and Janet Morley (eds), *Celebrating Women: The New Edition* (London: SPCK, 1995 [1986]).

Watson, Natalie K., *Introducing Feminist Ecclesiology* (London: Sheffield Academic Press, 2002).

White, Susan J., *A History of Women in Christian Worship* (London: SPCK, 2003).

Williams, Simon J. and Gillian Bendelow, *The Lived Body: Sociological Themes, Embodied Lives* (London: Routledge, 1998).

Willimon, William H., *Worship as Pastoral Care* (Nashville, TN: Abingdon, 1979).

Winter, Miriam Therese, Adair Lummis and Allison Stokes, *Defecting in Place: Women Claiming Responsibility for Their Own Spiritual Lives* (New York: Crossroad, 1994).

Wootton, Janet H., *Introducing a Practical Feminist Theology of Worship* (Sheffield: Sheffield Academic Press, 2000).

Young, Iris Marion, *Justice and the Politics of Difference* (Princeton, NJ: Princeton University Press, 1990).

_____ 'House and Home: Feminist Variations on a Theme' in Marion Young (ed.), *Intersecting Voices: Dilemmas of Gender, Political Philosophy, and Policy* (Princeton, NJ: Princeton University Press, 1997).

Zuesse, Evan M., 'Ritual' in Mircea Eliade (ed.), *The Encyclopaedia of Religion Vol. 12* (New York: Simon and Schuster MacMillan, 1993).

Subject Index

Index of Authors

Lightning Source UK Ltd.
Milton Keynes UK
31 October 2009

145685UK00001B/4/P